# THE ULTIMATE
# INSTANT POT
## — COOKBOOK —
# 1001

Days Easy and Quick Instant Pot Pressure Cooker Recipes
for Your Whole Family on a Budget

D1717077

**VINCENT C. JAMES**

**© Copyright 2020 – By Tracy Peterson All rights reserved.**

This book is copyright protected. It is only for personal use. You cannot amend, distribute, sell, use, quote or paraphrase any part of the content within this book, without the consent of the author or publisher.

Under no circumstances will any blame or legal responsibility be held against the publisher, or author, for any damages, reparation, or monetary loss due to the information contained within this book, either directly or indirectly.

**Disclaimer Notice:**

Please note the information contained within this document is for educational and entertainment purposes only. All effort has been executed to present accurate, up to date, reliable, complete information. No warranties of any kind are declared or implied. Readers acknowledge that the author is not engaged in the rendering of legal, financial, medical or professional advice. The content within this book has been derived from various sources. Please consult a licensed professional before attempting any techniques outlined in this book.

By reading this document, the reader agrees that under no circumstances is the author responsible for any losses, direct or indirect, that are incurred as a result of the use of the information contained within this document, including, but not limited to, errors, omissions, or inaccuracies.

# Table of Content

## Chapter 7 Fish and Seafood .....65

## Chapter 8 Poultry .........................76

## Chapter 9 Pork ........................89

## Chapter 10 Beef ......................99

## Chapter 11 Lamb...................... 113

## Chapter 12 Vegetarian and Vegan ........................................ 120

## Chapter 13 Soups, Stews, and Chilis ........................................ 134

## Chapter 14 Appetizers and Snacks .....................................151

## Chapter 15 Desserts .................163

# Introduction

The Instant Pot entered the market in 2006, and since then, I knew we needed to have one. In my household of five, we love our Instant Pot. With two busy, working adults and three very energetic and picky children, the Instant Pot is capable of creating meals that we all love.

Life gets very busy, but that does not mean you have to sacrifice flavorful and delicious food in the process. An Instant Pot can save the day, cooking your food while you work, sleep, and live your life. With minimal effort, you can make several one-pot meals to satisfy all appetites. Because you can create so many different recipes in your Instant Pot, you will be sure to find ingredients that the whole family will love. When placed together in the Instant Pot, the natural flavors are drawn out. Capable of so much more than a slow cooker, the Instant Pot steams, warms, cooks, pressurizes, and sautés your food to perfection.

The interface is very easy to use, no matter the brand. Equipped with various presets, you simply plug the device in and select your settings. There are so many things you can do with your Instant Pot. To experience its full benefits, you can create the following dishes to enjoy:

- Slow-cooked meals
- Pressure cooked meals
- Homemade yogurt
- Steamed rice
- Other steamed foods
- Sautéed foods
- Warmed foods

With such versatility, you won't require another appliance to finish off your meal. The Instant Pot saves you time and money. Instead of cooking over a traditional stovetop, you can engage in your normal routine while your food is still being cooked. It is unbelievably easy and convenient.

Since there are many different models on the market, you might find some Instant Pots that are capable of cooking eggs, baking cakes, and sterilizing items. If your Instant Pot is big enough, you can even insert cake pans and cupcake pans directly into the pot, baking your cakes to perfection. You can also use aluminum foil if you want to separate your ingredients, creating a different space for each one.

I am proud to say that my family enjoys a home-cooked dinner each night, and most of the time, the Instant Pot is my shining trophy. I just have to plan ahead what I want to make, get the ingredients together, and the Instant Pot does the rest. We used to be one of those families that got take-out a lot. This was tasty at first, but it became redundant and expensive. My kids actually began to ask me to cook for them more, and I couldn't say no. I knew I had to find a way to balance my busy work schedule, never-ending chores, and cooking for my family.

In this cookbook, I have compiled all of my best tips and tricks for using an Instant Pot. It doesn't matter how many people you're feeding or how busy you are—the Instant Pot will still work for your lifestyle. All of the recipes I included in this book were personally selected by myself or members of my family. These are our favorite Instant Pot creations, all compiled in an easy-to-read way so you can make them in your home.

# Chapter 1 The Complete Instant Pot Basics

There are about 20 different models to choose from. The difference is mostly in the size of the pot. The three-quart pot is suitable for a small family of two to three people. A larger model can hold up to eight quarts, which is great for families of six or more. If you are looking for something in the middle, go for a five-quart or six-quart model. Some models come with smart technology features, such as Wi-Fi capability that allows you to control your Instant Pot from an app on your phone. It just depends on if these features are going to be useful for your lifestyle.

**To get a better idea of the different models out there, consider these comparisons to find the one that is just right for your family:**

**Instant Pot Ultra:** This is a 10-in-1 model with eight quarts of space and 16 different modes. It replaces your standard pressure cooker, slow cooker, rice maker, steamer, warmer, egg maker, and more.

**Instant Pot Max:** This is a six-quart pot with nine different functions. It is known as the best cooker for canning. It comes with a large touch screen that allows you to control the time, temperature, pressure level, and delay start.

**Instant Pot Duo Mini:** A smaller take, this three-quart pot is great for smaller portions. Whether you are cooking for yourself or your small family, you can use this pot to slow cook, steam cook, sauté, and warm. It comes with 14 one-touch presets to save you time while cooking.

**Instant Pot Smart Wi-Fi (Instant Pot equipped with Wi-Fi capabilities):** If you are looking for something high-tech, this is the Instant Pot for you. This pot can be controlled from an app on your phone. It is great for cooking on the go, when you are unable to stay in the kitchen while your meal is being prepared. This six-quart pot gives you the freedom you crave while delivering wonderful meals to your table.

*As you plan for this new lifestyle, I hope that my tips and recipes help inspire you along the way! Tailor them to fit your needs and your family's needs. Anything in this book can be altered to become more suitable to your liking. Remember that the Instant Pot is meant to make your life easier, not more stressful. Enjoy it and try to imagine what you ever used to do before you had one—it's hard to think!*

## Benefits of Using Instant Pot

- Less time spent cooking traditionally over the stove

- The ability to cook your food while you are at work

- Easily managing large portions of food to feed the entire family

- Time to spend with your family while your meal cooks

- A device that can cook food in many different ways

## Preparation Before Getting Start

When you first get your Instant Pot, you probably won't be able to wait even an hour before you start crafting your first meal. After you unwrap it from its packaging, make sure to wash the accessories, inner pot, and lid in warm soapy water. Then, set up your inner pot, simply by placing it into the Instant Pot. Make sure that you practice opening and closing the lid. You will need to master sealing the lid securely to keep all of the pressure and steam inside to cook your food. There are markings on the top that will help you with this part.

Another very important part of the setup is to ensure that your silicone seal is properly installed. This ring provides a lock-tight seal for your Instant Pot. If it is not placed correctly, your pot isn't going to cook effectively. Do not use force when checking this seal—it will potentially damage it. If you plan on using your pot to cook both sweet and savory foods, it is recommended to have a backup ring handy because scents will be absorbed.

You already know about the pressure release valve, but you can refresh your memory by identifying where it is located and that it is unobstructed. If you plan on using the trivet, don't forget to place it inside of your pot before you begin cooking. Your pot also comes with two small plastic cups that often get overlooked, or even discarded. These are your condensation collectors, and they can be set up to collect moisture while you are using your pot. To install, just find the slot on the back of your pot and slide the cup right in.

The final step is to prep your ingredients, and then you will be ready to get started! Using your Instant Pot is supposed to be an efficient and positive experience. There is no reason for you to stress too much over the preparation. As long as you make sure that all parts are in working order, you should be good to get started on your cooking endeavors.

# The Panel Settings

When you are ready to cook your food, you might feel stumped at which settings to use. The more familiar you become with your Instant Pot, the easier this process gets. In the beginning, it is smart to learn about the five most common buttons. From there, you should be able to use your best judgment when cooking anything. After some time, you will also likely become more confident and work on figuring out alternative settings depending on what you are cooking.

1. **Manual:** Use this button to select your desired pressure cooking time. The maximum amount of time that you can select is four hours. On newer models, this button might be called the "Pressure Cook" button.

2. **+ & -:** The plus and minus buttons are meant to let you increase or decrease the cooking time. Even if you set your Instant Pot up to cook for an hour, if you feel that your food needs more time, you can easily add it by using the plus button.

3. **Adjust:** You can use this button to change your pot from its normal setting to a "more" setting or a "less "setting.

4. **Sauté:** This one is self-explanatory. You can use it to sauté, brown, and simmer with the lid of the pot open. Here, the adjust button comes in handy if you want to move from the default sauté setting to the more setting or the less setting to increase or decrease the temperature.

5. **Keep Warm/Cancel:** You can press this button to cancel any action or to turn off your Instant Pot. If you press this button first, it will enter a warming mode that will keep your food warm for up to 10 hours.

Your Instant Pot will also come with buttons that are one-click options that are pre-set with various times and temperatures that you can use for specific meals. The following are some that you will likely have on your pot:

| Bean/Chili: | Meat/Stew: |
|---|---|
| **Normal setting:** high pressure for 30 minutes; | **Normal setting:** high pressure for 35 minutes; |
| **More setting:** high pressure for 40 minutes; | **More setting:** high pressure for 45 minutes; |
| **Less setting:** high pressure for 25 minutes | **Less setting:** high pressure for 20 minutes |

**Multigrain:**

**Normal setting:** high pressure for 40 minutes;

**More setting:** warm water soaking for 45 minutes, then high pressure for 60 minutes;

**Less setting:** high pressure for 20 minutes

**Porridge:**

**Normal setting:** high pressure for 20 minutes;

**More setting:** high pressure for 30 minutes;

**Less setting:** high pressure for 15 minutes

**Poultry:**

**Normal setting:** high pressure for 15 minutes;

**More setting:** high pressure for 30 minutes;

**Less setting:** high pressure for five minutes

**Soup:**

**Normal setting:** high pressure for 30 minutes;

**More setting:** high pressure for 40 minutes;

**Less setting:** high pressure for 20 minutes

**In newer models, you might have the following additional presets:**

**Egg:**

**Normal setting:** high pressure for four minutes;

**More setting:** high pressure for five minutes;

**Less setting:** high pressure for three minutes

**Cake:**

**Normal setting:** high pressure for 40 minutes;

**More setting:** high pressure for 50 minutes;

**Less setting:** high pressure for 25 minutes

## Methods of Pressure Release

Your Instant Pot has the ability to release steam in two different ways. It is important to become familiar with both, as they each serve a different purpose. The first method is the natural release method. To do this, no action needs to be taken on your end. Your Instant Pot has a valve that will naturally release the steam by itself over time. The float valve will then drop to indicate that no more steam is inside the pot. The second method, the quick-release method, involves turning the steam release handle. Self-explanatory, this vents your seal and quickly depressurizes your Instant Pot.

There is a third alternative you can choose, and it involves a combination of the two methods. The timed pressure release occurs when you allow the pot to naturally release over 10-15 minutes and then you flip the switch to quick-release the steam to release any remaining pressure. This can benefit you if you feel that your food still needs a little bit more time. It is a great way to cook, without having to wait for too much longer.

# Instant Pot Pantry List

You are now ready to get started with the cooking process! As you prepare to enjoy all of the benefits of your Instant Pot, keep these tips and tricks in mind. It is a wonderfully simple appliance to use once you get the hang of it. You will appreciate its convenience and ease as you experiment with different recipes and cuisines. When stocking your pantry, consider the following staple items to keep on hand. They will benefit you in many dishes, allowing you to create wonderful and flavorful meals.

## Broth Concentrates/Bone Broth/ Bouillon Cubes

One of the main uses of these ingredients is to create flavorful soups, broths, and sauces. Any great soup or stew needs to have a flavorful base. The ingredients you add to it become secondary. You can keep a variety of these products in your pantry, as they do not expire very quickly if they are unopened. Keep in mind that you can also use them to flavor foods that are not liquid-based, such as rice, pasta, potatoes, and meats.

## Curry Paste

Using curry paste while you cook is sure to give any food a burst of flavor. You can add it to soups for a quick boost of seasoning in your meal. Its most common use, however, is in curries and stews. You don't have to stick to these traditional uses, though. Add it to noodles, salad dressings, and seafood—it makes a nice flavorful addition to nearly any meal.

## Dried Fruits and Vegetables

Because your Instant Pot relies on steam to cook your food, using dried fruits and vegetables is a smart decision. You can keep them in stock in your pantry without worrying about them going bad. The steam heats them perfectly, providing you with tender ingredients that add a flavorful addition to your meals. Sometimes, using fresh fruits and veggies is less favorable because they might get soggy or mushy while cooking in the steam.

## Grains and Beans

Not only do they taste great, but grains and beans are great for you. When you are making anything that needs a little bit more nutritional value, adding some grains or beans will prove to be beneficial. There are countless varieties of each one, so you can choose some of your favorites to always keep stocked up in your pantry. Grains and beans are so great because they do not just belong to one type of cuisine. They are universal ingredients.

## Tomato Paste

Generally used to thicken and enrich tomato sauces, tomato paste can also be used to flavor other semi-liquid meals, such as stews and soups. Because the flavor is not very strong, tomato paste is suitable for many different dishes. It is meant to elevate the flavors of your meal, even if you are not creating an Italian classic. You will see that tomato paste will become a staple item as you work with your Instant Pot more.

## Worcestershire Sauce

This is a very flavorful sauce that is unknowingly used in many of your favorite meals. It is added to Caesar salad dressing, cocktail sauce, and many barbeque sauces. Keeping it handy will give you the option to add a necessary boost of flavor to your dishes. It doesn't take much because it is so potent, so you shouldn't have to purchase a new bottle very frequently.

## Cornstarch

A thickening agent, cornstarch is a very useful ingredient when you are using an Instant Pot to cook. Whether you are making a soup, gravy, custard, or other semi-liquid meal, you can always add cornstarch for extra thickness. It is sometimes preferred over flour because it creates a flavorless and translucent option for your meals. Many Instant Pot recipes will call for cornstarch, so it is best to always keep some in your pantry just in case.

## Cream Cheese

Cream cheese makes a nice addition to many dishes. It provides a creamy and delicious flavor that gives comfort food its feeling. You can even add it to your scrambled eggs, polenta, and mac and cheese. There are no rules when it comes to how you'd like to use cream cheese. Anything that needs to be a little more flavorful and creamier will benefit from its addition to the recipe.

## Garlic

Not only is garlic very flavorful, but it is also healthy for your heart. Almost any recipe that you make can benefit from the addition of one or two cloves of garlic. When you let it cook for a prolonged period of time, the flavors come out boldly. Adding garlic to your dishes will give them a nice touch and add to their wonderful flavors. It even brings out the natural flavors of the other ingredients you use.

## Lemons and Limes

Two zesty fruits, and they both make great additions to your dishes. Whether you use slices of lemons and limes to compliment your meals, or you extract their juices or zest, both of them come in handy while cooking savory and sweet foods. For a quick way to add flavor to your Instant Pot creation, make sure that you always have some in your house.

## Cleaning Up

After you make any meal, you will want to ensure that you clean your Instant Pot correctly. This will make it last longer and keep you safe from any germs or bacteria that might build up. This does not have to be a complex process. With the following steps, you can make sure you are doing everything properly.

- **Clean the Exterior Housing Rim with a Cloth:** A microfiber cloth works great for this. Use one to wipe off any residue that might have stained the pot's exterior during cooking.

- **Clean the Rim with a Brush:** To get the actual underside of the rim clean, you might have to switch to a brush. This will allow you to reach those more difficult nooks and crannies.

- **Wash the Inner Pot:** The inner pot is dishwasher-safe, which makes it super easy to clean! If you don't have a dishwasher, you can hand wash it with some warm, soapy water and a sponge.

- **Remove Stains from the Inner Pot:** If you notice a rainbow-tinged stain appear at the bottom of your inner pot, this is normal. This discoloration happens fairly easily, but it is just as easy to remove. You can try white vinegar to clean this up, or a Magic Eraser cleaning sponge.

- **Wash the Lid:** During normal use, your lid will likely only require a quick rinse under some water. If there are excessive food stains, you can wash it by hand with warm, soapy water and a sponge. Putting the Instant Pot lid in the dishwasher is not recommended.

- **Wash the Seal Ring:** The silicone seal is dishwasher-safe. Simply pop it out of your Instant Pot and run it through the wash. Alternatively, you can also wash it by hand. This is one of the main ways to prevent any bacteria from collecting in your Instant Pot.

## Tools and Accessories

The great part about your Instant Pot is that it can be used with accessories. These items are not essential, but they can make your cooking experience even better!

### Mini Mitts

These silicone mitts cover your fingers to protect you from getting burned. You can use them while removing your lid, the trivet, or your inner pot.

### Sautéing Spatula

This is a solid spatula that is often angled for the easy stirring of your vegetables, or other ingredients, that are being sautéed. They come in wooden or silicone varieties.

### Extra Inner Pot

It is always good to have an extra inner pot available. If your original pot is dirty or is housing your leftovers, you won't even have to transfer the food to continue to cook with your backup inner pot.

### Tempered Glass Lid

This lid is ideal if you plan on slow cooking your food or using the sauté feature. It makes it very easy for you to serve your food, and it is also easy to clean.

### Immersion Blender

After you finish cooking in your Instant Pot, you can use an immersion blender to blend your recipe until smooth. This works great for soups and sauces, creating a very nice texture.

### Fat Separator

A fat separator resembles a pitcher with a long spout. It works by straining your liquid. Because fat rises to the top and the accessory resembles a funnel, you can re-pour your liquid and the fat will be reserved in the fat separator.

### Kitchen Tongs

Useful for many recipes, kitchen tongs can help you reach and rotate your food in the Instant Pot. You can also use the tongs to safely remove the food once it is finished. It provides you with a mess-free and safe way to handle all solid ingredients.

### Extra Sealing Rings

As mentioned, it is a good idea to store some extra silicone sealing rings. Whether your other one becomes worn or smelly, it is a simple solution to replace your rings frequently.

### Flexible Turner

A turner is like a spatula with no cutouts. It gives you a flat and flexible surface to easily turn over your ingredients while you are cooking.

### Kitchen Thermometer

When you are cooking large pieces of meat, it can be difficult to tell when they are fully cooked without cutting into them. A meat thermometer will help you by ensuring that the meat has reached its proper temperature.

### Wire Metal Steam Rack

This is an insert that allows you to steam your food above the surface of the water. It has handles on each side for easy removal. This steam rack is also known as the trivet.

### Tall Steam Rack

As it sounds, this rack is taller. By raising your food to a higher distance from the water, it will steam more slowly.

## FAQs about Using Instant Pot

**"I have a six-quart pot. Can I cook six quarts of food in it?"**

Interestingly, the maximum amount of food you can cook in a six-quart pot is four quarts. You must account for room for the water at the bottom of the pot. As well, some foods expand after they have been cooked, such as grains and rice.

**"Why is my pot taking so long to come to pressure?"**

Ensure that your valve has not been mistakenly turned to its "open" position. If you notice that there is no pressure building up, then it is probably escaping somehow. Make sure the lid is sealed properly.

**"How do I adjust the cooking time and pressure setting?"**

You can use the + and - buttons to adjust your cooking time. If you are using a preset button, this will set the appropriate time automatically. To adjust your pressure setting, select the Manual button.

**"Is it okay to fill my pot above the max line, to the brim?"**

No, if you fill your Instant Pot too much, this can clog its venting knob. It is best to keep your levels to the fill line to avoid any accidental overflow or clogs. Your food also won't be able to cook properly if the pot is too full.

**"Can I cook frozen meat directly in the Instant Pot?"**

Yes, you can safely cook frozen meat in your Instant Pot. Unlike a traditional pressure cooker, the Instant Pot cooks your food quickly, preventing it from staying at a dangerous temperature for too long.

**"My Instant Pot won't seal. What's the matter?"**

Make sure to check that you have the silicone seal ring installed correctly. If it is not properly in place, your pot will not want to close or seal properly. This will also prevent pressure and steam from building inside.

**"Why can't I open my Instant Pot?"**

It is probably in its locked position. Take a look at the indicators. Remember, you must turn your pot's lid clockwise to open and unlock the pot. The indicator should read "Open."

**"Can I cook in the Instant Pot without the stainless steel pot liner?"**

It is not recommended, as you can break or damage your pot. If you accidentally pour something into your pot without the liner in place, unplug the pot as soon as you notice. Dry it off as much as you can, and let it air dry until all the moisture is gone.

**"How do I know when the natural pressure release is complete?"**

Pay attention to your float valve. When the natural pressure release is complete, your float valve will drop, and your lid will unlock and open.

**"What does releasing the pressure for X amount of time do in a recipe?"**

The timing of your pressure release matters for different recipes because your food is still cooking when it is pressurized. This slow method of cooking makes your food more soft or tender, depending on what you are making.

**"My Instant Pot releases steam when it comes to pressure. Is this normal?"**

Yes, this is normal. You might even hear a hissing noise while this is happening. As long as your pot is completely sealed and you have enough liquid in the pot, you can allow it to steam and hiss while it cooks. The steam should be coming from the float valve or steam release area. If you notice that it is coming out of the sides of your pot, your seal ring is probably installed incorrectly.

### Instant Pot White or Brown Rice

**Prep time: 2 minutes | Cook time: 3 or 25 minutes | Serves 4**

1 cup white or brown rice (do not use instant or ready rice)

1 cup water or broth of your choice

1. Put the rice in a fine-mesh strainer and rinse it under cold running water for 1 minute, shaking it around until the water coming through goes from cloudy to clear.
2. Place the rice and pour water into the Instant Pot and stir well.
3. Secure the lid. Select the Manual mode and set the cooking time for 3 minutes at High Pressure for white rice, 25 minutes for brown rice.
4. Once cooking is complete, do a natural pressure release for 10 minutes, then release any remaining pressure. Carefully remove the lid.
5. Fluff the rice with a fork and serve warm.

### Baked Potato

**Prep time: 1 minute | Cook time: 15 minutes | Serves 4 to 6**

1 cup water
4 to 6 medium Russet or Idaho potatoes, rinsed,

scrubbed, with skins pierced all over with a fork

1. Put a trivet in the Instant Pot and pour in the water, then place the pierced potatoes on the trivet.
2. Lock the lid. Press the Manual button on the Instant Pot and set the cooking time for 15 minutes at High Pressure.
3. When the timer beeps, perform a natural pressure release for 10 minutes, then release any remaining pressure. Carefully remove the lid.
4. Using tongs, remove the potatoes from the pot to a plate. Cool for 5 minutes before serving.

### Coconut Milk Custard

**Prep time:5 minutes | Cook time: 30 minutes | Serves 4**

3 eggs
1 cup coconut milk
$^1/_3$ cup Swerve
1 teaspoon vanilla

extract
Cooking spray
2 cups water

1. Spritz a baking dish with cooking spray. Set aside.
2. Beat together the eggs, coconut milk, Swerve, and vanilla and in a large mixing bowl until well incorporated.
3. Transfer the egg mixture to the prepared baking dish and cover with foil.
4. Add the water and trivet to the Instant Pot, then place the baking dish on top of the trivet.
5. Secure the lid. Select the Manual mode and set the cooking time for 30 minutes at High Pressure.
6. Once cooking is complete, do a natural pressure release for 10 minutes, then release any remaining pressure. Carefully open the lid.
7. Allow to cool for 5 to 10 minutes before removing and serving.

### Hard-Boiled Eggs

**Prep time: 1 minute | Cook time: 5 minutes | Serves 6**

8 to 10 large eggs        1 cup water

1. Add the water and trivet to the Instant Pot, then place the eggs on top of the trivet.
2. Lock the lid. Select the Manual mode and set the cooking time for 5 minutes at High Pressure.
3. When the timer beeps, perform a natural pressure release for 5 minutes, then release any remaining pressure. Carefully remove the lid.
4. Transfer the eggs to a bowl of ice water to cool for at least 1 minute. Once cooled, peel and serve immediately.

## Creamy Alfredo

**Prep time: 5 minutes | Cook time: 6 minutes | Serves 4**

| | |
|---|---|
| ½ pound (227 g) dry linguine noodles, break in half | ¾ cup shredded Parmesan cheese |
| 1½ cups vegetable broth | 1 teaspoon minced garlic |
| 1½ cups heavy cream | Salt and pepper, to taste |

1. Combine all the ingredients in the Instant Pot.
2. Secure the lid. Select the Manual mode and set the cooking time for 6 minutes at High Pressure.
3. Once cooking is complete, do a quick pressure release. Carefully open the lid.
4. Cool for 5 minutes before serving.

## Fish Stock

**Prep time: 5 minutes | Cook time: 50 minutes| Serves 10**

| | |
|---|---|
| 1 tablespoon olive oil | 1 cup roughly chopped carrots |
| 2 salmon heads, cut into quarters, rinsed, and patted dry | 2 lemongrass stalks, roughly chopped |
| 2 cloves garlic, sliced | 8 cups water |
| 1 cup roughly chopped celery | Handful fresh thyme, including stems |

1. Press the Sauté button on the Instant Pot and heat the oil.
2. Add the salmon to the Instant Pot and lightly sear the fish on both sides, about 4 minutes.
3. Add the remaining ingredients to the Instant Pot and stir to combine.
4. Secure the lid. Select the Soup mode and set the cooking time for 45 minutes at High Pressure.
5. Once cooking is complete, do a natural pressure release for 15 minutes, then release any remaining pressure. Remove the lid.
6. Over a large bowl, carefully strain the stock through a fine-mesh strainer.
7. Serve immediately or refrigerate until ready to use.

## Pork Broth

**Prep time: 5 minutes | Cook time: 1 hour | Serves 8**

| | |
|---|---|
| 3 pounds (1.4 kg) pork bones | 1 bay leaf |
| 3 large carrots, cut into large chunks | 1 tablespoon apple cider vinegar |
| 3 large stalks celery, cut into large chunks | 8 cups water |
| 2 cloves garlic, sliced | 1 teaspoon whole peppercorns |
| | Salt, to taste |

1. Place all the ingredients into the Instant Pot and stir to incorporate.
2. Secure the lid. Select the Manual mode and set the cooking time for 1 hour at High Pressure.
3. When the timer beeps, perform a natural pressure release for 10 minutes, then release any remaining pressure. Carefully remove the lid.
4. Allow the broth to cool for 10 to 15 minutes. Strain the broth through a fine-mesh strainer and discard all the solids.
5. Serve immediately or store in a sealed container in the refrigerator for 4 to 5 days or in the freezer for up to 6 months.

## Chicken Stock

**Prep time: 5 minutes | Cook time: 1 hour | Makes 4 cups**

| | |
|---|---|
| 2 pounds (907 g) chicken bones and parts | smashed (optional) |
| 1 large garlic clove, | ¼ teaspoon kosher salt (optional) |
| | 8 cups water |

1. Place the chicken bones and parts and the garlic (if desired) into the Instant Pot. Sprinkle with the salt, if desired.
2. Add the water to the Instant Pot, making sure the chicken is fully submerged.
3. Lock the lid. Select the Manual mode and cook for 1 hour at High Pressure.
4. Once cooking is complete, do a natural pressure release for 15 minutes, then release any remaining pressure. Remove the lid.
5. Carefully pour the stock through a fine-mesh strainer into a large bowl.
6. Serve immediately or refrigerate in an airtight container for up to 4 days.

## Beef Stock

**Prep time: 10 minutes | Cook time: 1 hour 30 minutes | Makes 4 cups**

| | |
|---|---|
| 1 tablespoon oil | ¼ teaspoon kosher |
| 2 pounds (907 g) | salt (optional) |
| meaty beef bones | 8 cups water |

1. Press the Sauté button on the Instant Pot and heat the oil until shimmering.
2. Working in batches, arrange the beef bones in a single layer and sear each side for 6 to 8 minutes. Season with salt (if desired).
3. Add the water to the Instant Pot, making sure the bones are fully submerged.
4. Lock the lid. Select the Manual mode and set the cooking time for 75 minutes at High Pressure.
5. Once cooking is complete, do a natural pressure release for 15 minutes, then release any remaining pressure. Remove the lid.
6. Carefully pour the stock through a fine-mesh strainer into a large bowl.
7. Serve immediately or store in an airtight container in the refrigerator for up to 4 days or in the freezer for 6 to 12 months.

## Vegetable Stock

**Prep time: 5 minutes | Cook time: 30 minutes| Serves 8**

| | |
|---|---|
| 8 cups water | garlic |
| 4 celery stalks, cut | 2 bay leaves |
| into chunks | 2 green onions, |
| 4 carrots, cut into | sliced |
| chunks | 10 whole black |
| 4 thyme sprigs | peppercorns |
| 6 parsley sprigs | 1½ teaspoons salt |
| 2 teaspoons chopped | |

1. Except for the salt, add all the ingredients to the Instant Pot.
2. Secure the lid. Select the Soup mode and set the cooking time for 30 minutes at High Pressure.
3. Once cooking is complete, do a natural pressure release for 15 minutes, then release any remaining pressure. Remove the lid.
4. Sprinkle with the salt and whisk well.
5. Over a large bowl, carefully strain the stock through a fine-mesh strainer.
6. Serve immediately or store in an airtight container in the refrigerator for 4 to 5 days or in the freezer for up to 3 months.

## Tabasco Sauce

**Prep time: 5 minutes | Cook time: 1 hour | Makes 2 cups**

| | |
|---|---|
| 18 ounces (510 g) | chopped |
| fresh hot peppers | 1¾ cups apple cider |
| or any kind, stems | 3 teaspoons smoked |
| removed and | or plain salt |

1. Combine all the ingredients in the Instant Pot.
2. Lock the lid. Press the Manual button on the Instant Pot and set the cooking time for 1 hour at High Pressure.
3. Once cooking is complete, do a natural pressure release for 15 minutes, then release any remaining pressure. Carefully open the lid.
4. Purée the mixture with an immersion blender until smooth.
5. Serve immediately or refrigerate until ready to use.

## Berry Sauce

**Prep time: 5 minutes | Cook time: 5 minutes | Serves 6**

| | |
|---|---|
| 1 pound (454 g) | Juice from 1 orange |
| cranberries (fresh or | 1 teaspoon grated |
| frozen) | lemon zest |
| 10 strawberries, | 1 teaspoon grated |
| chopped | orange zest |
| 1 apple, cored and | 1 cup sugar |
| chopped | ¼ cup water |
| Juice from 1 lemon | 1 cinnamon stick |

1. Combine all the ingredients in the Instant Pot.
2. Secure the lid. Select the Manual mode and set the cooking time for 5 minutes at High Pressure.
3. Once cooking is complete, do a natural pressure release for 10 minutes, then release any remaining pressure. Carefully open the lid.
4. Serve immediately or refrigerate until ready to use.

## Seafood Stock

**Prep time: 5 minutes | Cook time: 30 minutes | Serves 8**

8 cups water
Shells and heads from ½ pound (227 g) prawns
3 cloves garlic, sliced
4 carrots, cut into

chunks
4 onions, quartered
2 bay leaves
1 teaspoon whole black peppercorns

1. Place all the ingredients into the Instant Pot.
2. Secure the lid. Select the Manual mode and set the cooking time for 30 minutes at High Pressure.
3. Once cooking is complete, do a natural pressure release for 15 minutes, then release any remaining pressure. Remove the lid.
4. Over a large bowl, carefully strain the stock through a fine-mesh strainer.
5. Serve immediately or store in an airtight container in the refrigerator for 3 days or in the freezer for up to 3 months.

## Tomato Basil Sauce

**Prep time: 5 minutes | Cook time: 16 minutes | Serves 4**

1 tablespoon olive oil
3 cloves garlic, minced
2½ pounds (1.1 kg) Roma tomatoes,

diced
½ cup chopped basil
¼ cup vegetable broth
Salt, to taste

1. Set your Instant Pot to Sauté and heat the olive oil.
2. Add the minced garlic and sauté for 1 minute until fragrant. Stir in the tomatoes, basil, and vegetable broth.
3. Lock the lid. Press the Manual button on the Instant Pot and cook for 10 minutes at High Pressure.
4. Once cooking is complete, do a quick pressure release. Carefully open the lid.
5. Set your Instant Pot to Sauté again and cook for another 5 minutes.
6. Blend the mixture with an immersion blender until smooth.
7. Season with salt to taste. Serve chilled or at room temperature.

## Caramel Sauce

**Prep time: 5 minutes | Cook time: 15 minutes | Serves 4**

1 cup sugar
$1/3$ cup water
3 tablespoons coconut oil

$1/3$ cup condensed coconut milk
1 teaspoon vanilla extract

1. Press the Sauté button on the Instant Pot and add the sugar and water. Stir well.
2. Sauté the mixture for 12 minutes, stirring occasionally.
3. Add the coconut oil, coconut milk, and vanilla and keep whisking until smooth.
4. Let the sauce stand for 10 minutes. Serve warm or refrigerate until chilled.

## Marinara Sauce

**Prep time: 5 minutes | Cook time: 13 minutes | Makes 4 cups**

2 tablespoons oil
1 medium onion, grated
3 garlic cloves, roughly chopped
1 (28-ounce / 794-g) can or carton whole or crushed tomatoes
1 teaspoon kosher

salt, plus more as needed
Freshly ground black pepper, to taste
½ teaspoon dried oregano or 2 oregano sprigs
Pinch granulated or raw sugar (optional)

1. Press the Sauté button on the Instant Pot and heat the oil until it shimmers.
2. Add the grated onion and sauté for 2 minutes until tender. Add the garlic and sauté for 1 minute.
3. Fold in the tomatoes, salt, oregano, and pepper and stir well.
4. Secure the lid. Select the Manual mode and set the cooking time for 10 minutes at High Pressure.
5. Once cooking is complete, do a quick pressure release. Carefully open the lid.
6. Taste and adjust the seasoning, if needed. Add the sugar to balance the acidity of the tomatoes, if desired.
7. Store in an airtight container in the refrigerator for up to 4 days or freeze for up to 6 months.

## Mushroom and Corn Stock

**Prep time: 10 minutes | Cook time: 15 minutes | Serves 8**

4 large mushrooms, diced
2 cobs of corns
1 small onion, unpeeled and halved
1 celery stalk, chopped into thirds
1 teaspoon dried bay leaf
1 teaspoon grated

ginger
1 sprig fresh parsley
1 teaspoon kosher salt
½ teaspoon ground turmeric
½ teaspoon whole black peppercorns
8 cups water

1. Place all the ingredients into the Instant Pot and stir well.
2. Lock the lid. Press the Manual button on the Instant Pot and set the cooking time for 15 minutes at High Pressure.
3. Once cooking is complete, do a natural pressure release for 10 minutes, then release any remaining pressure. Carefully open the lid.
4. Strain the stock through a fine-mesh strainer and discard all the solids.
5. Serve immediately or refrigerate in an airtight container for 3 to 4 days.

## Chili Sauce

**Prep time: 5 minutes | Cook time: 8 minutes | Serves 4**

4 medium-sized Ancho chili peppers, stems and seeds removed
2 teaspoons kosher salt
1½ teaspoons sugar
½ teaspoon ground dried oregano

½ teaspoon ground cumin
1½ cups water
2 cloves garlic, crushed
2 tablespoons heavy cream
2 tablespoons apple cider vinegar

1. On your cutting board, chop the peppers into small pieces.
2. Place the pepper pieces into the Instant Pot along with the salt, sugar, oregano, and cumin. Pour in the water and stir to combine.
3. Lock the lid. Press the Manual button on the Instant Pot and set the cooking time for 8 minutes at High Pressure.

4. Once cooking is complete, do a natural pressure release for 10 minutes, then release any remaining pressure. Carefully open the lid.
5. Transfer the mixture to a food processor. Add the garlic, heavy cream, and apple cider vinegar. Process until smooth and creamy.
6. Serve chilled or at room temperature.

## Bone Broth

**Prep time: 5 minutes | Cook time: 2 hours | Serves 8**

8 cups water
4 pounds (1.8 kg) beef bones
5 cloves garlic, smashed
2 carrots, peeled and sliced in half
2 ribs celery, sliced in half
1 medium yellow onion, with skin-on, quartered

10 whole black peppercorns
1 tablespoon apple cider vinegar
1 teaspoon poultry seasoning
1 teaspoon kosher salt
2 sprigs rosemary
2 sprigs thyme
2 bay leaves

1. Add all the ingredients to the Instant Pot and stir to combine.
2. Lock the lid. Press the Manual button on the Instant Pot and set the cooking time for 2 hours at High Pressure.
3. When the timer beeps, perform a natural pressure release for 30 minutes, then release any remaining pressure. Carefully remove the lid.
4. Let the broth cool for 15 minutes. Strain the broth through a fine-mesh strainer and discard all the solids.
5. Serve immediately or store in a sealed container in the refrigerator for 1 week or in the freezer for up to 3 months.

## Mushroom Broth

**Prep time: 5 minutes | Cook time: 15 minutes | Serves 8**

4 ounces (113 g) dried mushrooms, soaked and rinsed
½ cup celery, chopped
½ cup carrots, chopped
4 cloves garlic, crushed
4 bay leaves
1 onion, quartered
8 cups water
Salt and ground black pepper, to taste.

1. Add all the ingredients except the salt and pepper to the Instant Pot and stir well.
2. Lock the lid. Press the Manual button on the Instant Pot and set the cooking time for 15 minutes at High Pressure.
3. Once cooking is complete, do a quick pressure release. Open the lid.
4. Add the salt and pepper to taste.
5. Over a large bowl, carefully strain the stock through a fine-mesh strainer. Discard all the solids.
6. Serve immediately or store in a sealed container in the refrigerator for 4 to 5 days or in the freezer for up to 6 months.

## Creamy Cauliflower Sauce

**Prep time: 5 minutes | Cook time: 3 minutes | Serves 4**

12 ounces (340 g) cauliflower florets
½ cup water
¼ teaspoon pepper
¼ teaspoon garlic salt
2 tablespoons almond milk

1. Except for the almond milk, combine all the ingredients in the Instant Pot.
2. Secure the lid. Select the Manual mode and set the cooking time for 3 minutes at High Pressure.
3. Once cooking is complete, do a quick pressure release. Remove the lid.
4. Purée the mixture with an immersion blender until smooth.
5. Pour in the almond milk and whisk to combine.
6. Serve chilled or at room temperature.

## Tomato Salsa

**Prep time: 10 minutes | Cook time: 30 minutes | Serves 6**

6 cups fresh tomatoes, diced, peeled, and deseeded
1½ (6-ounce / 170-g) cans tomato paste
1½ green bell peppers, diced
1 cup jalapeño peppers, deseeded and chopped
¼ cup vinegar
2 yellow onions, diced
½ tablespoon kosher salt
1½ tablespoons sugar
1 tablespoon cayenne pepper
1 tablespoon garlic powder

1. Place all the ingredients into the Instant Pot and stir to incorporate.
2. Secure the lid. Select the Manual mode and set the cooking time for 30 minutes at High Pressure.
3. Once cooking is complete, do a natural pressure release for 10 minutes, then release any remaining pressure. Carefully open the lid.
4. Serve immediately or refrigerate in an airtight container for up to 5 days.

## BBQ Sauce

**Prep time: 5 minutes | Cook time: 5 minutes | Serves 6**

8 ounces (227 g) Heinz ketchup
4 ounces (113 g) water
2 ounces (57 g) apple cider vinegar
½ ounce (14 g) lemon juice
½ ounce (14 g) light corn syrup
½ ounce (14 g) Worcestershire sauce
2½ tablespoons white sugar
2½ tablespoons brown sugar
½ tablespoon jerk rub
¼ tablespoon onion powder
¼ tablespoon dry mustard powder
¼ tablespoon freshly ground black pepper

1. Combine all the ingredients in the Instant Pot.
2. Lock the lid. Press the Manual button on the Instant Pot and set the cooking time for 5 minutes at High Pressure.
3. Once cooking is complete, do a natural pressure release for 10 minutes, then release any remaining pressure. Carefully open the lid.
4. Serve chilled or at room temperature.

## Chicken and Mushroom Stock

**Prep time: 5 minutes | Cook time: 1 hour | Serves 8**

2½ pounds (1.1 kg) chicken, bones only
1 cup diced cremini mushrooms
1 small onion, unpeeled and halved
1 leek, finely chopped
1 teaspoon dried bay leaf
1 teaspoon kosher salt
½ teaspoon white pepper
½ teaspoon whole black peppercorns
8 cups water

1. Place all the ingredients into the Instant Pot and stir well.
2. Lock the lid. Select the Manual mode and set the cooking time for 1 hour at High Pressure.
3. Once cooking is complete, do a natural pressure release for 10 minutes, then release any remaining pressure. Carefully open the lid.
4. Strain the stock through a fine-mesh strainer and discard all the solids. Remove the layer of fat that forms on the top, if desired.
5. Serve immediately or store in an airtight container in the refrigerator for 3 to 4 days or in the freezer for up to 6 months.

## Almond Oatmeal with Cherries

**Prep time: 10 minutes | Cook time: 5 minutes | Serves 6**

4 cups vanilla almond milk, plus additional as needed
1 cup steel-cut oats
$1/3$ cup packed brown sugar
1 cup dried cherries
½ teaspoon ground cinnamon
½ teaspoon salt

1. Combine all ingredients in the Instant Pot.
2. Secure the lid. Select the Manual mode and set the cooking time for 5 minutes at High Pressure.
3. Once cooking is complete, do a natural pressure release for 10 minutes, then release any remaining pressure. Carefully open the lid.
4. Allow the oatmeal to sit for 10 minutes. Serve with additional almond milk, if desired.

## Cinnamon Raisin Oatmeal

**Prep time: 10 minutes | Cook time: 5 minutes | Serves 6**

3 cups vanilla almond milk
¾ cup steel-cut oats
3 tablespoons brown sugar
¾ cup raisins
4½ teaspoons butter
½ teaspoon salt
¾ teaspoon ground cinnamon
1 large apple, peeled and chopped
¼ cup chopped pecans

1. Combine all the ingredients except the apple and pecans in the Instant Pot.
2. Secure the lid. Select the Manual mode and set the cooking time for 5 minutes at High Pressure.
3. Once cooking is complete, do a natural pressure release for 10 minutes, then release any remaining pressure. Carefully open the lid.
4. Scatter with the chopped apple and stir well. Allow the oatmeal to sit for 1o minutes. Ladle into bowls and sprinkle the pecans on top. Serve immediately.

## Applesauce Oatmeal

**Prep time: 10 minutes | Cook time: 5 minutes | Serves 8**

6 cups water
1½ cups steel-cut oats
1½ cups unsweetened applesauce
¼ cup maple syrup, plus more for topping
½ teaspoon ground nutmeg
1½ teaspoons ground cinnamon
⅛ teaspoon salt
1 large apple, chopped

1. Except for the apple, combine all the ingredients in the Instant Pot.
2. Lock the lid. Select the Manual mode and set the cooking time for 5 minutes at High Pressure.
3. Once cooking is complete, do a natural pressure release for 10 minutes, then release any remaining pressure. Carefully open the lid.
4. Add the chopped apple and stir well. Allow the oatmeal to sit for 10 minutes. Ladle into bowls and top with a drizzle of maple syrup, if desired. Serve warm.

## Pumpkin Oatmeal

**Prep time: 5 minutes | Cook time: 10 minutes | Serves 6**

3 cups water
1½ cups 2% milk
1¼ cups steel-cut oats
3 tablespoons brown sugar
1½ teaspoons pumpkin pie spice
1 teaspoon ground cinnamon
¾ teaspoon salt
1 (15-ounce / 425-g) can solid-pack pumpkin

1. Place all the ingredients except the pumpkin into the Instant Pot and stir to incorporate.
2. Secure the lid. Select the Manual mode and set the cooking time for 10 minutes at High Pressure.
3. Once cooking is complete, do a natural pressure release for 10 minutes, then release any remaining pressure. Carefully open the lid.
4. Add the pumpkin and stir well. Allow the oatmeal to sit for 5 to 10 minutes to thicken. Serve immediately.

## Carrot and Pineapple Oatmeal

**Prep time: 10 minutes | Cook time: 10 minutes | Serves 8**

4½ cups water
2 cups shredded carrots
1 cup steel-cut oats
1 (20-ounce / 567-g) can crushed pineapple, undrained
1 cup raisins
2 teaspoons ground cinnamon
1 teaspoon pumpkin pie spice
Cooking spray
Brown sugar (optional)

1. Spritz the bottom of the Instant Pot with cooking spray. Place the water, carrots, oats, raisins, pineapple, cinnamon, and pumpkin pie spice into the Instant Pot and stir to combine.
2. Secure the lid. Select the Manual mode and set the cooking time for 10 minutes at High Pressure.
3. Once cooking is complete, do a natural pressure release for 10 minutes, then release any remaining pressure. Carefully open the lid.
4. Let the oatmeal stand for 5 to 10 minutes. Sprinkle with the brown sugar, if desired. Serve warm.

## Chocolate Chip and Pumpkin Balls

**Prep time: 5 minutes | Cook time: 5 minutes | Serves 5 to 6**

2 tablespoons salted grass-fed butter, softened
2 cups sugar-free chocolate chips
½ cup organic pumpkin purée, or more to taste
¾ cup raw coconut butter
⅓ cup Swerve, or more to taste
2 teaspoons shredded coconut (optional)
⅛ teaspoon ground cinnamon

1. Press the Sauté button on the Instant Pot and melt the butter.
2. Fold in the chocolate chips, pumpkin purée, coconut butter, Swerve, coconut (if desired), and cinnamon and stir until melted. Transfer the mixture to a silicone mini-muffin mold and freeze until firm.
3. Serve chilled.

## Chocolate Butter Fat Bombs with Pecans

**Prep time: 5 minutes | Cook time: 5 minutes | Serves 5 to 6**

2 tablespoons salted grass-fed butter, softened
1 cup raw coconut butter

1 cup sugar-free chocolate chips
½ cup chopped pecans, or more to taste

1. Press the Sauté button on the Instant Pot and melt the butter.
2. Fold in the coconut butter, chocolate chips, and pecans and stir until the mixture is smooth.
3. Transfer the mixture to a silicone mini-muffin mold and freeze until firm.
4. Remove from the muffin mold and serve chilled.

## Maple Steel-Cut Oatmeal

**Prep time: 5 minutes | Cook time: 14 minutes | Serves 2**

½ cup steel-cut oats
1½ cups water
¼ cup maple syrup, plus additional as needed
2 tablespoons packed brown sugar

¼ teaspoon ground cinnamon
Pinch kosher salt, plus additional as needed
1 tablespoon unsalted butter

1. Press the Sauté button on the Instant Pot. Add the steel-cut oats and toast for about 2 minutes, stirring occasionally.
2. Add the water, ¼ cup of maple syrup, brown sugar, cinnamon, and pinch salt to the Instant Pot and stir well.
3. Lock the lid. Select the Manual mode and set the cooking time for 12 minutes at High Pressure.
4. Once cooking is complete, do a natural pressure release for 10 minutes, then release any remaining pressure. Carefully open the lid.
5. Stir the oatmeal and taste, adding additional maple syrup or salt as needed.
6. Let the oatmeal sit for 10 minutes. When ready, add the butter and stir well. Ladle into bowls and serve immediately.

## Cranberry Compote with Raisins

**Prep time: 5 minutes | Cook time: 3 minutes | Makes 2½ cups**

1 (12-ounce / 340-g) package fresh or 3 cups frozen cranberries
¼ cup thawed orange juice concentrate
2/3 cup packed brown sugar

2 tablespoons raspberry vinegar
½ cup golden raisins
½ cup chopped dried apricots
½ cup chopped walnuts, toasted

1. Combine the cranberries, orange juice concentrate, brown sugar, and vinegar in the Instant Pot.
2. Secure the lid. Select the Manual mode and set the cooking time for 3 minutes at High Pressure.
3. Once cooking is complete, do a natural pressure release for 5 minutes, then release any remaining pressure. Carefully open the lid.
4. Stir in the raisins, apricots, and walnuts and serve warm.

## Cinnamon Apple Butter

**Prep time: 15 minutes | Cook time: 3 minutes | Makes 5 cups**

4 pounds (1.8 kg) large apples, cored and quartered
¾ to 1 cup sugar
¼ cup water
3 teaspoons ground cinnamon
¼ teaspoon ground

cloves
¼ teaspoon ground allspice
¼ teaspoon ground nutmeg
¼ cup creamy peanut butter

1. Combine all the ingredients except the butter in the Instant Pot.
2. Secure the lid. Select the Manual mode and set the cooking time for 3 minutes at High Pressure.
3. Once cooking is complete, do a natural pressure release for 5 minutes, then release any remaining pressure. Carefully open the lid.
4. Blend the mixture with an immersion blender. Add the peanut butter and whisk until smooth.
5. Let the mixture cool to room temperature. Serve immediately.

## Hawaiian Breakfast Hash

**Prep time: 20 minutes | Cook time: 20 minutes | Serves 6**

4 bacon strips, chopped
1 tablespoon canola or coconut oil
2 large sweet potatoes, peeled and cut into ½-inch pieces
1 cup water

2 cups cubed fresh pineapple
½ teaspoon salt
¼ teaspoon paprika
¼ teaspoon chili powder
¼ teaspoon pepper
⅛ teaspoon ground cinnamon

1. Press the Sauté button on the Instant Pot and add the bacon. Cook for about 7 minutes, stirring occasionally, or until crisp.
2. Remove the bacon with a slotted spoon and drain on paper towels. Set aside.
3. In the Instant Pot, heat the oil until it shimmers.
4. Working in batches, add the sweet potatoes to the pot and brown each side for 3 to 4 minutes. Transfer the sweet potatoes to a large bowl and set aside.
5. Pour the water into the pot and cook for 1 minute, stirring to loosen browned bits from pan.
6. Place a steamer basket in the Instant Pot. Add the pineapple, salt, paprika, chili powder, pepper, and cinnamon to the large bowl of sweet potatoes and toss well, then transfer the mixture to the steamer basket.
7. Secure the lid. Select the Steam mode and set the cooking time for 2 minutes at High Pressure.
8. Once cooking is complete, do a quick pressure release. Carefully open the lid.
9. Top with the bacon and serve on a plate.

## Vanilla Applesauce

**Prep time: 10 minutes | Cook time: 3 minutes | Makes 5 cups**

7 medium apples (about 3 pounds / 1.4 kg), peeled and cored
½ cup water

½ cup sugar
1 tablespoon lemon juice
¼ teaspoon vanilla extract

1. Slice each apple into 8 wedges on your cutting board, then slice each wedge crosswise in half.
2. Add the apples to the Instant Pot along with the remaining ingredients. Stir well.
3. Secure the lid. Select the Manual mode and set the cooking time for 3 minutes at High Pressure.
4. Once cooking is complete, do a natural pressure release for 10 minutes, then release any remaining pressure. Carefully open the lid.
5. Blend the mixture with an immersion blender until your desired consistency is achieved.
6. Serve warm.

## Rhubarb Compote With Yogurt and Almonds

**Prep time: 10 minutes | Cook time: 3 minutes | Serves 6**

**Compote:**
2 cups finely chopped fresh rhubarb

¼ cup sugar
⅓ cup water

**For Serving:**
3 cups reduced-fat plain Greek yogurt
2 tablespoons honey

¾ cup sliced almonds, toasted

1. Combine the rhubarb, sugar, and water in the Instant Pot.
2. Secure the lid. Select the Manual mode and set the cooking time for 3 minutes at High Pressure.
3. Once cooking is complete, do a natural pressure release for 10 minutes, then release any remaining pressure. Carefully open the lid.
4. Transfer the mixture to a bowl and let rest for a few minutes until cooled slightly. Place in the refrigerator until chilled.
5. When ready, whisk the yogurt and honey in a small bowl until well combined. Spoon into serving dishes and top each dish evenly with the compote. Scatter with the almonds and serve immediately.

## Eggs In Purgatory

**Prep time: 15 minutes | Cook time: 24 minutes | Serves 4**

2 (14½-ounce / 411-g) cans fire-roasted diced tomatoes, undrained
½ cup water
1 medium onion, chopped
2 garlic cloves, minced
2 tablespoons canola oil
2 teaspoons smoked paprika
½ teaspoon crushed

red pepper flakes
½ teaspoon sugar
¼ cup tomato paste
4 large eggs
¼ cup shredded Monterey Jack cheese
2 tablespoons minced fresh parsley
1 (18-ounce / 510-g) tube polenta, sliced and warmed (optional)

1. Place the tomatoes, water, onion, garlic, oil, paprika, red pepper flakes, and sugar into the Instant Pot and stir to combine.
2. Secure the lid. Select the Manual mode and set the cooking time for 4 minutes at High Pressure.
3. Once cooking is complete, do a quick pressure release. Carefully open the lid.
4. Set the Instant Pot to Sauté and stir in the tomato paste. Let it simmer for about 10 minutes, stirring occasionally, or until the mixture is slightly thickened.
5. With the back of a spoon, make 4 wells in the sauce and crack an egg into each. Scatter with the shredded cheese.
6. Cover (do not lock the lid) and allow to simmer for 8 to 10 minutes, or until the egg whites are completely set.
7. Sprinkle the parsley on top and serve with the polenta slices, if desired.

## Broccoli Egg Cups

**Prep time: 10 minutes | Cook time: 6 minutes | Serves 4**

7 large eggs, divided
1½ cups half-and-half
3 tablespoons shredded Swiss cheese
1 teaspoon minced fresh basil
2 teaspoons minced

fresh parsley
¼ teaspoon salt
⅛ teaspoon cayenne pepper
Cooking spray
1½ cups frozen broccoli florets, thawed
1 cup water

1. Spritz four ramekins with cooking spray and set aside.
2. Beat together three eggs with the half-and-half, cheese, basil, parsley, salt, and cayenne pepper in a large bowl until well incorporated.
3. Pour the egg mixture evenly into the greased ramekins. Divide the broccoli florets among the ramekins and top each with one remaining egg.
4. Add the water and trivet to the Instant Pot, then place the ramekins on top of the trivet. Cover them loosely with foil.
5. Lock the lid. Select the Steam mode and set the cooking time for 6 minutes at High Pressure.
6. Once cooking is complete, do a quick pressure release. Carefully open the lid.
7. Allow to cool for 5 minutes before removing and serving.

## Hot Chocolate Breakfast Bowl

**Prep time: 5 minutes | Cook time: 0 minutes | Serves 4**

2 cups filtered water
2 cups full-fat coconut milk
1 cup dried unsweetened coconut
1 cup sugar-free chocolate chips
1 cup macadamia nuts
⅓ cup Swerve, or

more to taste
¼ cup blanched almond flour
2 tablespoons unsweetened cocoa powder
½ teaspoon kosher salt
½ teaspoon ground cinnamon

1. Press the Sauté button on your Instant Pot. Add the filtered water and the coconut milk.
2. Add the remaining ingredients and stir until well mixed.
3. Secure the lid. Press the Manual button on the Instant Pot and set the cooking time for 0 minutes on High Pressure.
4. Once the timer goes off; do a quick pressure release. Carefully open the lid.
5. Divide the cereal among four serving bowls and serve warm.

## Cheesy Arugula Frittata

**Prep time: 5 minutes | Cook time: 5 minutes | Serves 2**

3 eggs, beaten
¼ cup loosely packed arugula
¼ red onion, chopped
¼ cup feta cheese crumbles
¼ teaspoon garlic powder
Kosher salt, to taste
Freshly ground black pepper, to taste
1 cup water

1. Stir together the eggs, arugula, onion, feta cheese crumbles, garlic powder, salt, and pepper in a medium bowl. Pour the egg mixture into a greased round cake pan and cover with foil.
2. Add the water and trivet to the Instant Pot, then place the cake pan on top of the trivet.
3. Lock the lid. Select the Manual mode and set the cooking time for 5 minutes at High Pressure.
4. Once cooking is complete, do a natural pressure release for 10 minutes, then release any remaining pressure. Carefully open the lid.
5. Let the frittata rest for 5 minutes in the pan before cutting and serving.

## Parmesan Asparagus Frittata with Leek

**Prep time: 10 minutes | Cook time: 10 minutes | Serves 4**

6 eggs
¼ teaspoon fine sea salt
Freshly ground black pepper, to taste
8 ounces (227 g) asparagus spears, woody stems removed and cut into 1-inch pieces
1 cup thinly sliced
leeks
¼ cup grated Parmesan cheese
1 cup water
Chopped green onions, for garnish (optional)
Fresh flat-leaf parsley, for garnish (optional)

1. Whisk together the eggs, salt, and black pepper in a large mixing bowl until frothy.
2. Add the asparagus pieces, leeks, and cheese and stir to combine. Pour the mixture into a greased round cake pan.
3. Add the water and trivet to the Instant Pot, then place the pan on top of the trivet.
4. Lock the lid. Select the Manual mode and set the cooking time for 10 minutes at High Pressure.
5. Once cooking is complete, do a natural pressure release for 10 minutes, then release any remaining pressure. Carefully open the lid.
6. Allow the frittata to cool for 5 minutes. Garnish with the green onions and parsley, if desired. Cut the frittata into wedges and serve warm.

## Egg Bites with Cheese

**Prep time: 5 minutes | Cook time: 10 minutes | Serves 2 to 4**

1 cup filtered water
6 eggs
½ cup shredded full-fat Cheddar cheese
½ cup bell peppers, finely chopped
½ cup spinach, finely chopped
½ teaspoon dried cilantro
½ teaspoon kosher salt
½ teaspoon freshly ground black pepper
Cooking spray

1. Place the trivet in the bottom of your Instant Pot and add the water.
2. Mix together the eggs, cheese, bell peppers, spinach, cilantro, salt, and pepper in a large bowl. Stir well.
3. Spritz a silicone egg mold with cooking spray and ladle the mixture into the impressions in the mold.
4. Put the mold on the trivet with a sling and wrap loosely in aluminum foil.
5. Secure the lid and select Press the Manual button on the Instant Pot and set the cooking time for 10 minutes at High Pressure.
6. When the timer beeps, use a quick pressure release. Carefully open the lid.
7. Remove the egg mold from the pot. Remove the foil and allow to cool for 5 minutes.
8. Scoop the egg bites out of the mold with a spoon and transfer to a serving dish. Serve.

## Herbed Spinach and Cheese Strata

**Prep time: 5 minutes | Cook time: 40 minutes | Serves 4**

1 cup filtered water
6 eggs
1 cup chopped spinach
1 cup shredded full-fat Cheddar cheese
¼ small onion, thinly sliced
½ tablespoon salted grass-fed butter, softened
½ teaspoon Dijon mustard
½ teaspoon kosher salt
½ teaspoon freshly ground black pepper
½ teaspoon cayenne pepper
½ teaspoon paprika
½ teaspoon dried sage
½ teaspoon dried cilantro
½ teaspoon dried parsley

1. Pour the water into the the Instant Pot, then place the trivet.
2. Whisk together the eggs, spinach, cheese, onion, butter, mustard, salt, black pepper, cayenne pepper, paprika, sage, cilantro, and parsley in a large bowl until well incorporated. Pour the egg mixture into a greased baking dish. Cover the dish loosely with aluminum foil. Put the dish on top of the trivet.
3. Secure the lid. Select the Manual mode and set the cooking time for 40 minutes at High Pressure.
4. Once cooking is complete, do a natural pressure release for 10 minutes, then release any remaining pressure. Carefully open the lid.
5. Let the strata rest for 5 minutes and serve warm.

## Spinach and Bacon Quiche

**Prep time: 5 minutes | Cook time: 35 minutes | Serves 3**

1 cup filtered water
5 eggs, lightly beaten
½ cup spinach, chopped
½ cup full-fat coconut milk
½ cup shredded full-fat Cheddar cheese
2 slices no-sugar-added bacon, cooked
and finely chopped
½ teaspoon dried parsley
½ teaspoon dried basil
½ teaspoon freshly ground black pepper
¼ teaspoon kosher salt

1. Pour the water into the the Instant Pot, then place the trivet.
2. Stir together the remaining ingredients in a baking dish. Cover the dish loosely with aluminum foil. Place the dish on top of the trivet.
3. Secure the lid. Select the Manual mode and set the cooking time for 35 minutes at High Pressure.
4. Once cooking is complete, do a natural pressure release for 10 minutes, then release any remaining pressure. Carefully open the lid.
5. Serve warm.

## Vanilla Blueberry French Toast

**Prep time: 15 minutes | Cook time: 20 minutes | Serves 4**

$1^1/_3$ cups 2% milk
3 tablespoons sugar
2 large eggs
1 teaspoon vanilla extract
1 teaspoon ground cinnamon
¼ teaspoon salt
Cooking spray
6 cups cubed French bread, about 6 ounces (170 g), divided
¾ cup fresh or frozen blueberries, divided
1 cup water
Maple syrup, for serving

1. Stir together the milk, sugar, eggs, vanilla, cinnamon, and salt. Spray a baking dish with cooking spray and place 3 cups of bread cubes in the dish. Place half the milk mixture and half the blueberries on top. Repeat layers.
2. Add the water to your Instant Pot and put the trivet in the bottom of the pot. Wrap the baking dish in aluminum foil. Create a foil sling and carefully lower the baking dish into the Instant Pot.
3. Secure the lid. Press the Manual button on the Instant Pot and set the cooking time for 20 minutes on High Pressure.
4. Once cooking is complete, use a natural pressure release for 10 minutes and then release any remaining pressure. Carefully remove the baking dish using the foil sling. Let sit for 10 minutes.
5. Serve with the syrup.

## Cheesy Breakfast Potato Casserole

**Prep time: 20 minutes | Cook time: 35 minutes | Serves 6**

6 large eggs
½ cup 2% milk
½ teaspoon salt
¼ teaspoon pepper
4 cups frozen shredded hash brown potatoes, thawed
2 cups shredded Cheddar cheese
1 cup cubed fully cooked ham
½ medium onion, chopped
1 cup water

1. In a medium bowl, beat together the eggs with the milk, salt, and pepper until combined. In another bowl, thoroughly combine the potatoes, cheese, ham, and onion, then transfer to a greased baking dish. Pour the egg mixture over top. Cover the dish with foil.
2. Pour the water into the Instant Pot and insert a trivet. Place the baking dish on top of the trivet.
3. Secure the lid. Select the Manual mode and set the cooking time for 35 minutes at High Pressure.
4. Once cooking is complete, do a natural pressure release for 10 minutes, then release any remaining pressure. Carefully open the lid.
5. Allow the casserole cool for 5 to 10 minutes before serving.

## Paprika Cauliflower Hash

**Prep time: 5 minutes | Cook time: 10 minutes | Serves 4**

2 tablespoons grass-fed butter, softened
1 pound (454 g) cauliflower, chopped into small pieces
½ teaspoon garlic
½ teaspoon fresh paprika
½ teaspoon kosher salt
½ teaspoon freshly ground black pepper

1. Press the Sauté button on the Instant Pot and melt the butter.
2. Place the cauliflower into the Instant Pot, along with the garlic, paprika, salt, and pepper. Keep stirring until the cauliflower hash is completely cooked.
3. Divide the cauliflower hash among fours bowls and serve.

## Western Omelet

**Prep time: 5 minutes | Cook time: 20 minutes | Serves 2**

2 tablespoons avocado oil
¼ cup red bell pepper, finely chopped
¼ cup green bell pepper, finely chopped
¼ cup onion, chopped
6 eggs
½ cup shredded full-fat Cheddar cheese
2 slices no-sugar-added bacon, cooked
and finely cut (optional)
½ teaspoon dried parsley
½ teaspoon dried basil
½ teaspoon kosher salt
½ teaspoon crushed red pepper
½ teaspoon freshly ground black pepper
Cooking spray
1 cup filtered water

1. Press the Sauté button on your Instant Pot. Add and heat the oil. Add the bell pepper and onion and sauté for 4 minutes.
2. Mix together the eggs, cheese, bacon (if desired), parsley, basil, salt, and pepper in a medium bowl and stir well.
3. Spray a glass dish with cooking spray and pour in the mixture. Fold in the sautéed bell pepper and onion, scraping the bits from the pot, and mix well.
4. Add 1 cup of filtered water to the inner pot of the Instant Pot and then place the trivet in the bottom of the pot. Carefully lower the dish into the Instant Pot with a sling.
5. Secure the lid. Press the Manual button on the Instant Pot and set the cooking time for 20 minutes at High Pressure.
6. When the timer beeps, use a natural pressure release for about 10 minutes and then release any remaining pressure. Carefully open the lid.
7. Remove the dish and serve.

## Maple Buckwheat Groat Bowls

**Prep time: 5 minutes | Cook time: 1 minute | Serves 6**

2 cups buckwheat groats, soaked for at least 20 minutes, drained, and rinsed
3 cups water
¼ cup pure maple syrup
1 teaspoon ground cinnamon
¼ teaspoon fine sea salt
1 teaspoon vanilla extract
Chopped or sliced fresh fruit, for serving (optional)

1. In the Instant Pot, combine the buckwheat groats, water, maple syrup, cinnamon, salt, and vanilla.
2. Lock the lid. Select the Manual mode and set the cooking time for 1 minute at High Pressure.
3. Once cooking is complete, do a natural pressure release for 10 minutes, then release any remaining pressure. Carefully open the lid and stir well.
4. Serve chilled or warm with the fresh fruits, if desired.

## Creamy Cauliflower Breakfast Bowl

**Prep time: 5 minutes | Cook time: 5 minutes | Serves 2**

½ cup full-fat coconut milk
1/3 cup riced cauliflower
¼ cup Swerve, or more to taste
2 tablespoons grass-fed butter
½ cup heavy whipping cream
½ cup chopped pecans

1. Mix together all the ingredients except the heavy whipping cream and pecans in the Instant Pot and stir to combine.
2. Secure the lid. Select the Manual mode and set the cooking time for 5 minutes at High Pressure.
3. Once cooking is complete, do a natural pressure release for 10 minutes, then release any remaining pressure. Carefully open the lid.
4. Stir in the heavy whipping cream and pecans and serve.

## Chicken Breakfast Platter

**Prep time: 5 minutes | Cook time: 10 minutes | Serves 4**

2 tablespoons avocado oil
1 pound (454 g) ground chicken
½ cup shredded full fat Cheddar cheese (optional)
½ cup filtered water
1 jalapeño pepper, finely chopped
1 teaspoon hot sauce
1 teaspoon lime juice
½ teaspoon kosher salt
½ teaspoon freshly ground black pepper
1 cup mashed avocado
¾ cup low-sugar salsa

1. Press the Sauté button on the Instant Pot and melt the avocado oil.
2. Add the ground chicken, cheese (if desired), water, jalapeño, hot sauce, lime juice, salt, and black pepper to the Instant Pot and stir to incorporate.
3. Secure the lid. Select the Manual mode and set the cooking time for 10 minutes at High Pressure.
4. Once cooking is complete, do a quick pressure release. Carefully open the lid.
5. Serve topped with the mashed avocado and salsa.

## Canja (Chicken Congee)

**Prep time: 5 minutes | Cook time: 5 minutes | Serves 4**

1 pound (454 g) chicken breasts, cooked and shredded
4 cups grass-fed bone broth
1 cup chopped cauliflower
2 tablespoons grass-fed butter, softened
¼ small onion, thinly sliced
½ teaspoon garlic
½ teaspoon dried parsley
2 bay leaves

1. Combine all the ingredients in the Instant Pot.
2. Secure the lid. Select the Manual mode and set the cooking time for 5 minutes at High Pressure.
3. Once cooking is complete, do a quick pressure release. Carefully open the lid.
4. Ladle into bowls and serve warm.

## Spicy Beef Breakfast Bowl

**Prep time: 5 minutes | Cook time: 10 minutes | Serves 4**

2 tablespoons avocado oil
1 pound (454 g) ground grass-fed beef
½ teaspoon dried cilantro
½ teaspoon ground turmeric

½ teaspoon crushed red pepper
½ teaspoon kosher salt
½ teaspoon cayenne pepper
½ teaspoon freshly ground black pepper
½ cup filtered water

1. Press the Sauté button on the Instant Pot and melt the avocado oil.
2. Put the ground beef in the Instant Pot, breaking it up gently. Stir in the cilantro, turmeric, red pepper, salt, cayenne pepper, and black pepper.
3. Pour in the water. Secure the lid. Select the Manual mode and set the cooking time for 10 minutes at High Pressure.
4. Once cooking is complete, do a natural pressure release for 10 minutes, then release any remaining pressure. Carefully open the lid.
5. Allow to cool for 5 minutes before serving.

## Breakfast Quinoa Salad

**Prep time: 15 minutes | Cook time: 1 minute | Serves 4**

2 cups quinoa, rinsed well
2 cups vegetable or chicken broth
Salad:
1 (15-ounce / 425-g) can chickpeas, drained and rinsed
1 cucumber, diced
1 cup chopped flat-leaf parsley
¼ cup extra-virgin olive oil

1 red onion, diced
1 red bell pepper, diced
3 cloves garlic, minced
Juice of 2 lemons
2 tablespoons red wine vinegar
Salt and pepper, to taste
1 to 2 cups crumbled feta cheese (optional)

1. Place the quinoa and broth into the Instant Pot and stir to incorporate.
2. Lock the lid. Select the Manual mode and set the cooking time for 1 minute at High Pressure.

3. Once cooking is complete, do a natural pressure release for 10 minutes, then release any remaining pressure. Carefully open the lid.
4. Fluff the quinoa with a fork and allow to cool for 5 to 10 minutes.
5. Remove the quinoa from the pot to a large bowl and toss together with all the salad ingredients until combined. Serve immediately.

## Stuffed Apples with Coconut Muesli

**Prep time: 10 minutes | Cook time: 3 minutes | Serves 2**

$1/3$ cup water
2 large unpeeled organic apples, cored and tops removed
Filling:
½ cup coconut muesli

2 tablespoons butter, cubed
½ teaspoon ground cinnamon
2 teaspoons packed brown sugar

1. Pour the water into the Instant Pot and set aside.
2. Mix together all the ingredients for the filling in a bowl, mashing gently with a fork until incorporated.
3. Stuff each apple evenly with the muesli mixture, then arrange them in the Instant Pot.
4. Lock the lid. Select the Manual mode and set the cooking time for 3 minutes at Low Pressure, depending on how large the apples are.
5. Once cooking is complete, do a natural pressure release for 10 minutes, then release any remaining pressure. Carefully open the lid.
6. Let the apples cool for 5 minutes and serve.

## Cheesy Chicken and Spinach Breakfast

**Prep time: 5 minutes | Cook time: 10 minutes | Serves 4**

2 tablespoons coconut oil
1 pound (454 g) ground chicken
1 cup shredded full-fat Cheddar cheese
2 tablespoons sugar-free or low-sugar salsa
½ cup chopped spinach
1 teaspoon curry powder

½ teaspoon dried basil
½ teaspoon dried parsley
½ teaspoon dried cilantro
1 tablespoon hot sauce
½ teaspoon kosher salt
½ teaspoon freshly ground black pepper
1 cup filtered water

1. Press the Sauté button on the Instant Pot and heat the coconut oil.
2. Fold in the ground chicken, cheese, salsa, spinach, curry powder, basil, parsley, cilantro, hot sauce, salt, and pepper and stir thoroughly.
3. Pour in the water. Secure the lid. Select the Manual mode and set the cooking time for 10 minutes at High Pressure.
4. Once cooking is complete, do a quick pressure release. Carefully open the lid.
5. Serve warm.

## Avocado and Bacon Breakfast Burger

**Prep time: 5 minutes | Cook time: 10 minutes | Serves 2**

2 tablespoons coconut oil
2 eggs, lightly beaten
3 slices no-sugar-added bacon
½ cup shredded full-fat Cheddar cheese
½ teaspoon kosher salt

½ teaspoon freshly ground black pepper
1 cup shredded lettuce
1 avocado, halved and pitted
2 tablespoons sesame seeds

1. Press the Sauté button on the Instant Pot and melt the coconut oil.
2. Fold in the beaten eggs, bacon, cheese, salt, and pepper and stir thoroughly and continuously.
3. When cooked, remove the egg mixture from the pot to a bowl.
4. Assemble the burger: Place an avocado half on a clean work surface and top with the egg mixture and shredded lettuce, and finish with the other half of the avocado. Scatter the sesame seeds on top and serve immediately.

## Pumpkin and Pecan Porridge

**Prep time: 5 minutes | Cook time: 10 minutes | Serves 2 to 4**

¼ cup unsweetened coconut flakes
2 cups filtered water
2 cups full-fat coconut milk
1 cup organic pumpkin purée
1 cup pecans, chopped

¼ cup organic coconut flour
½ teaspoon ground cinnamon
½ teaspoon ginger, finely grated
Swerve, to taste (optional)

1. Press the Sauté button on your Instant Pot and toast the coconut flakes, stirring occasionally. Pour in the filtered water and milk.
2. Secure the lid. Press the Manual button on the Instant Pot and set the cooking time for 0 minutes on High Pressure.
3. Once cooking is complete, use a natural pressure release for about 10 minutes and then release any remaining pressure. Carefully remove the lid.
4. Fold in the pumpkin, pecans, flour, cinnamon, ginger, and Swerve (if desired). Let stand for 2 to 4 minutes until desired consistency, stirring occasionally.
5. Ladle the porridge into bowls and serve warm.

## Protein-Packed Scrambled Eggs

**Prep time: 5 minutes | Cook time: 20 minutes | Serves 2**

4 eggs
2 tablespoons coconut oil, plus more for greasing the pot
1 cup filtered water
4 slices no-sugar-added bacon, cooked and finely cut
1 cup spinach, chopped
½ cup shredded full-fat Cheddar cheese
¼ cup full-fat
coconut milk
½ teaspoon chili powder
½ teaspoon dried parsley
½ teaspoon dried basil
½ teaspoon ground cumin
½ teaspoon kosher salt
½ teaspoon freshly ground black pepper

1. Grease the inner pot of your Instant Pot. Add all the ingredients. and stir until well mixed.
2. Add the filtered water to the pot.
3. Secure the lid. Press the Manual button on your Instant Pot and set the cooking time for 20 minutes at High Pressure.
4. Once cooking is complete, use a natural pressure release for about 10 minutes and then release any remaining pressure. Carefully remove the lid.
5. Transfer to a serving dish and serve.

## Shakshuka with Kale

**Prep time: 10 minutes | Cook time: 5 minutes | Serves 4**

1 tablespoon extra-virgin olive oil
2 cloves garlic, minced
½ yellow onion, chopped
Fine sea salt, to taste
2½ cups marinara
sauce
1 cup chopped kale, stems removed
¼ cup water
4 eggs
Freshly ground black pepper, to taste

1. Press the Sauté button on your Instant Pot. Add and heat the olive oil.
2. Add the garlic, onion, and a pinch of salt and sauté for about 5 minutes until soft. Add the marinara sauce, kale, and water and stir well with a wooden spoon, scraping the bits from the pot.
3. Create four small wells evenly spaced in the marinara sauce with the spoon and then crack an egg into each well. Sprinkle the eggs with salt and pepper.
4. Lock the lid. Press the Manual button on your Instant Pot and set the cooking time for 0 minutes on High Pressure.
5. Once cooking is complete, use a quick pressure release. Carefully open the lid.
6. Scoop the eggs, sauce, and cooked vegetables into a small serving dish with a slotted spoon. Serve immediately.

## Corn on the Cob

**Prep time: 5 minutes | Cook time: 5 minutes | Serves 4**

1 cup water      4 ears corn
¼ teaspoon salt

1. Add the water and salt to the Instant Pot. Put the trivet in the bottom of the pot.
2. Lay the ears of corn on the trivet.
3. Lock the lid.
4. Set the Instant Pot to Manual and set the cooking time for 5 minutes on High Pressure.
5. Once cooking is complete, perform a quick pressure release. Carefully open the lid.
6. Transfer the corn to a plate and serve.

## Creamy Crabby Corn

**Prep time: 5 minutes | Cook time: 1 minute | Serves 4 to 6**

1 cup water | Parmesan cheese
30 ounces (850 g) frozen corn | ½ cup heavy cream or half-and-half
½ pound (227 g) lump crabmeat | 1½ teaspoons granulated sugar
4 ounces (113 g) cream cheese, cut into chunky cubes | 1 teaspoon black pepper
½ cup grated | 3 tablespoons salted butter

1. Add the water to your Instant Pot and insert a steamer basket. Arrange the corn in the basket.
2. Lock the lid. Press the Manual button on your Instant Pot and set the cooking time for 1 minute at High Pressure.
3. When the timer goes off, use a quick pressure release. Carefully open the lid.
4. Drain the corn and dump back into the pot.
5. Add the remaining ingredients and stir until the cream cheese has melted completely.
6. Serve immediately.

## Cheesy Buffalo Wing Potatoes

**Prep time: 15 minutes | Cook time: 5 minutes | Serves 6**

1 cup water | sauce
2 pounds (907 g) Yukon Gold potatoes, cut into 1-inch cubes | ½ cup shredded Cheddar cheese
½ small red onion, chopped | Optional Toppings: Sliced green onions
1 small sweet yellow pepper, chopped | Sour cream
¼ cup Buffalo wing | Crumbled cooked bacon

1. Add the water to your Instant Pot and insert a steamer basket.
2. Place the potatoes, onion and yellow pepper in the basket. Secure the lid.
3. Select the Manual mode and set the cooking time for 3 minutes on High Pressure. Once cooking is complete, perform a quick pressure release. Remove the vegetables to a bowl.
4. Drain the cooking liquid and discard.
5. Drizzle the vegetables with the Buffalo wing sauce and stir until coated. Scatter the cheese on top and let stand covered for 1 to 2 minutes, or until the cheese has melted.
6. Top with toppings of your choice and serve immediately.

## Curry-Flavored Cauliflower

**Prep time: 5 minutes | Cook time: 13 minutes | Serves 4**

2 tablespoons olive oil | ½ teaspoon curry powder
1 medium head cauliflower, cut into florets | ⅛ teaspoon salt
 | ⅛ teaspoon black pepper

1. Press the Sauté button on your Instant Pot. Add the oil and let heat for 1 minute.
2. Add the remaining ingredients and stir well. Lock the lid and sauté for 12 minutes, or until the florets are crisp-tender.
3. Transfer to a plate and serve hot.

## Garlicky Mashed Potatoes

**Prep time: 10 minutes | Cook time: 8 minutes | Serves 4**

| | |
|---|---|
| 2½ pounds (1.1 kg) russet potatoes, peeled | ¾ cup whole milk, warm |
| ½ teaspoon salt | 2 tablespoons butter |
| 1 cup chicken broth | cloves garlic, minced |

1. Add the potatoes, salt, and broth to the Instant Pot. Lock the lid.
2. Press the Manual button on the Instant Pot and cook for 8 minutes on High Pressure.
3. Once cooking is complete, use a quick pressure release and then carefully open the lid.
4. Drain the broth and discard.
5. Mash the potatoes in the pot with a potato masher. Mix in the warm milk and stir well.
6. Stir in the butter until melted. Add garlic and stir again.
7. Transfer to a plate and serve warm.

## Mashed Sweet Potatoes with Ginger

**Prep time: 10 minutes | Cook time: 10 minutes | Serves 6**

| | |
|---|---|
| 2½ pounds (1.1 kg) sweet potatoes, peeled and diced large | fresh ginger |
| | 1 tablespoon butter |
| | 1 tablespoon pure maple syrup |
| 2 cups water | ½ teaspoon sea salt |
| 1 tablespoon minced | ¼ cup milk |

1. Add the potatoes and water to your Instant Pot. Secure the lid.
2. Select the Manual mode and set the cooking time for 10 minutes at High Pressure.
3. Once the timer goes off, use a natural pressure release for 10 minutes and then release any remaining pressure. Carefully open the lid.
4. Drain the water and add the remaining ingredients to the potatoes. Blend until desired consistency with an immersion blender.
5. Transfer to a serving plate and serve warm.

## Creamy Mashed Cauliflower

**Prep time: 5 minutes | Cook time: 4 minutes | Serves 4 to 6**

| | |
|---|---|
| 1 cup chicken or vegetable broth | ½ cup milk, heavy cream, or half-and-half |
| 1 head cauliflower, stalk and green leaves removed, cut into large chunks | Seasoned salt and black pepper, to taste |
| 2 tablespoons (¼ stick) salted butter | Chopped chives, for garnish |

1. Place the trivet in the bottom of your Instant Pot, add in the broth, and layer the cauliflower on top.
2. Lock the lid and press the Manual button your Instant Pot and set the cooking time for 4 minutes on High Pressure. When the timer beeps, perform a quick pressure release.
3. Transfer the cauliflower to a food processor. Add in about $1/3$ of the broth from the pot and purée until smooth.
4. Fold in the butter, milk, seasoned salt, and pepper. Purée again until totally creamy.
5. Transfer to a plate and serve garnished with chives.

## Maple-Glazed Carrots

**Prep time: 10 minutes | Cook time: 5 minutes | Serves 6**

| | |
|---|---|
| 1 pound (454 g) carrots, peeled and diced large | 1 tablespoon ghee |
| | 1 tablespoon minced fresh dill |
| 1 tablespoon pure maple syrup | 1 cup water |
| | ½ teaspoon sea salt |

1. Place all the ingredients in the Instant Pot. Secure the lid.
2. Select the Manual mode and set the cooking time for 5 minutes on High Pressure.
3. Once cooking is complete, perform a natural pressure release for 10 minutes and then release any remaining pressure. Carefully open the lid.
4. Transfer to a serving dish and serve immediately.

## Carrots with Honey Glaze

**Prep time: 10 minutes | Cook time: 16 minutes | Serves 4**

⅓ cup olive oil
1 pound (454 g) carrots, cut into ½-inch slices
1 teaspoon cumin

½ teaspoon salt
¼ teaspoon black pepper
¼ cup honey

1. Press the Sauté button on your Instant Pot. Add the oil and let heat for 1 minute.
2. Add the carrots, cumin, salt, and pepper. Lock the lid and sauté for 10 minutes.
3. Stir in the honey and secure the lid. Sauté for another 5 minutes, or until the carrots are evenly glazed.
4. Transfer to a serving dish and serve hot.

## Citrus Bacon Brussels Sprouts

**Prep time: 5 minutes | Cook time: 7 to 9 minutes | Serves 4**

1 tablespoon avocado oil
2 slices bacon, diced
½ cup water
½ cup freshly squeezed orange

juice
1 pound (454 g) Brussels sprouts, trimmed and halved
2 teaspoons orange zest

1. Press the Sauté button on your Instant Pot. Add the avocado oil and let heat for 1 minute.
2. Add the bacon. Sauté for 3 to 5 minutes, or until the bacon is almost crisp and the fat is rendered. Pour in the water and orange juice and deglaze the Instant Pot by scraping the bits from the pot.
3. Fold in the Brussels sprouts. Secure the lid.
4. Press the Manual button on your Instant Pot and set the cooking time for 3 minutes at High Pressure.
5. Once the timer goes off, use a quick pressure release and then release any remaining pressure. Carefully open the lid.
6. Remove the Brussels sprouts from the Instant Pot to a serving dish with a slotted spoon.
7. Serve warm garnished with the orange zest.

## Spiced Orange Carrots

**Prep time: 5 minutes | Cook time: 4 to 5 minutes | Serves 6**

2 pounds (907 g) medium carrots or baby carrots, cut into ¾-inch pieces
½ cup orange juice
½ cup packed brown sugar
2 tablespoons butter

¾ teaspoon ground cinnamon
¼ teaspoon ground nutmeg
½ teaspoon salt
¼ cup cold water
1 tablespoon cornstarch

1. Mix together all the ingredients except the water and cornstarch in your Instant Pot.
2. Secure the lid. Press the Manual button on your Instant Pot and cook for 3 minutes on Low Pressure.
3. When the timer goes off, use a quick pressure release. Carefully remove the lid.
4. Press the sauté button on your Instant Pot and bring the liquid to a boil. Fold in the water and cornstarch and stir until smooth.
5. Continue to cook for 1 to 2 minutes and stir until the sauce is thickened.
6. Transfer to a serving dish and serve immediately.

## Steamed Broccoli with Lemon

**Prep time: 5 minutes | Cook time: 0 minutes | Serves 4**

1 cup water
1 medium head broccoli, chopped
2 teaspoons ghee

1 teaspoon lemon juice
½ teaspoon sea salt

1. Add the water to the Instant Pot. Place a steamer basket and layer the broccoli on top. Secure the lid.
2. Select the Steam mode and set the cooking time for 0 minutes on High Pressure.
3. When the timer goes off, do a quick pressure release. Carefully open the lid.
4. Remove the broccoli from the steamer basket to a serving dish. Mix in the ghee, lemon juice, and salt and toss to combine.
5. Serve warm.

## Broccoli with Garlic

**Prep time: 5 minutes | Cook time: 9 minutes | Serves 4**

3 tablespoons olive oil
2 medium heads broccoli, cut into florets
½ teaspoon salt
½ teaspoon black pepper
4 cloves garlic, minced

1. Press the Sauté button on your Instant Pot. Add the oil and let heat for 1 minute.
2. Add the broccoli and sprinkle with the salt and pepper. Secure the lid and sauté for 4 minutes.
3. Stir in the garlic and lock the lid. Sauté for another 4 minutes.
4. Transfer to a serving bowl and serve hot.

## Garlic Mashed Root Vegetables

**Prep time: 15 minutes | Cook time: 5 minutes | Serves 4**

2 medium parsnips, peeled and diced
2 medium turnips, peeled and diced
3 cloves garlic, peeled and halved
1 large Yukon gold potato, peeled and diced
1 medium shallot, peeled and quartered
½ cup chicken broth, plus more as needed
1 cup water
2 tablespoons ghee
¼ cup unsweetened almond milk
½ teaspoon sea salt
½ teaspoon ground black pepper

1. Place the parsnips, turnips, garlic, potato, shallot, broth, and water in the Instant Pot. Secure the lid.
2. Select the Manual mode and set the cooking time for 5 minutes on High Pressure.
3. Once the timer goes off, use a natural pressure release for 10 minutes and then release any remaining pressure. Carefully open the lid.
4. Remove the vegetables from the pot to a medium bowl.
5. Stir in the ghee, milk, salt, and pepper. Blitz the mixture with an immersion blender until smooth. Add more broth, 1 tablespoon at a time, from the Instant Pot if a thinner consistency is desired.
6. Transfer to a serving plate and serve warm.

## Instant Pot Black-Eyed Peas With Ham

**Prep time: 10 minutes | Cook time: 18 minutes | Serves 10**

4 cups water
1 package (16-ounce / 454-g) dried black-eyed peas, rinsed
1 cup cubed fully cooked ham
3 garlic cloves, minced
1 medium onion, finely chopped
2 teaspoons seasoned salt
1 teaspoon pepper
Thinly sliced green onions, for garnish (optional)

1. Combine all the ingredients except the green onions in the Instant Pot.
2. Lock the lid. Select the Manual mode and set the cooking time for 18 minutes at High Pressure.
3. Once cooking is complete, do a natural pressure release for 10 minutes, then release any remaining pressure. Carefully open the lid.
4. Serve garnished with the sliced green onions, if desired.

## Sriracha Collard Greens

**Prep time: 10 minutes | Cook time: 10 minutes | Serves 6**

2 pounds (907 g) collard greens, washed, spines removed, and chopped
1 cup chicken broth
1 small onion, peeled and diced
¼ cup apple cider vinegar
1 slice bacon
1 teaspoon sriracha
½ teaspoon sea salt
¼ teaspoon ground black pepper

1. Combine all the ingredients in Instant Pot.
2. Secure the lid. Select the Manual mode and set the cooking time for 10 minutes at High Pressure.
3. Once cooking is complete, do a natural pressure release for 10 minutes, then release any remaining pressure. Carefully open the lid.
4. Discard the bacon and transfer the collard greens to a bowl. Serve immediately.

## Healthy Strawberry Applesauce

**Prep time: 10 minutes | Cook time: 5 minutes | Serves 6**

4 cups frozen strawberries
6 cups roughly chopped Gala apples
½ cup water
½ cup granulated sugar
¼ teaspoon salt

1. Place the strawberries and apples in your Instant Pot.
2. Mix in the water, sugar, and salt and stir well. Lock the lid.
3. Press the Manual button on your Instant Pot and cook for 5 minutes at High Pressure.
4. Once cooking is complete, perform a natural pressure release for 15 minutes and then release any remaining pressure. Carefully open the lid.
5. Blend the mixture with an immersion blender until smooth.
6. Place in the refrigerator for 2 hours.
7. Serve chilled.

## Bacon and Red Cabbage with Apple

**Prep time: 10 minutes | Cook time: 18 minutes | Serves 4**

1 tablespoon olive oil
1 small onion, peeled and diced
3 slices bacon, diced
5 cups chopped red cabbage
1 small apple, peeled, cored, and diced
½ cup apple cider vinegar
1 cup chicken broth
½ teaspoon sea salt
¼ cup crumbled goat cheese

1. Set your Instant Pot to Sauté and heat the oil.
2. Add the onion and sauté until translucent, 3 to 5 minutes. Add the bacon and sauté for 3 minutes more, stirring occasionally, or until the bacon begins to crisp. Stir in the cabbage, apple, chicken broth, and vinegar.
3. Secure the lid. Select the Manual mode and set the cooking time for 10 minutes at High Pressure.
4. Once cooking is complete, do a quick pressure release. Carefully open the lid.
5. Remove from the Instant Pot to a plate and season with salt. Sprinkle the goat cheese on top for garnish before serving.

## Cheesy Zucchini and Corn Casserole

**Prep time: 15 minutes | Cook time: 1 hour 5 minutes | Serves 6**

1½ cups water
Cooking spray
2 teaspoons baking powder
¾ cup cornmeal
1½ cups all-purpose flour
1 teaspoon salt
¼ teaspoon black pepper
1 cup whole milk
¼ cup vegetable oil
2 large eggs, beaten
4 cups shredded zucchini
1½ cups Monterey Jack cheese

1. Add the water to your Instant Pot and put the trivet in the bottom of the pot. Spritz a cake pan with cooking spray and set aside.
2. Stir together the baking powder, cornmeal, flour, salt, and pepper in a large bowl.
3. Create a well inside the dry mixture and pour in the milk, oil, and egg. Stir well to combine.
4. Fold in the zucchini and stir until well mixed. Then stir in the cheese.
5. Pour the casserole batter into the prepared cake pan. Place a paper towel on top and wrap top of the pan in aluminum foil. Create a foil sling and carefully lower the cake pan into your Instant Pot.
6. Lock the lid.
7. Press the Manual button on your Instant Pot and set the cooking time for 65 minutes on High Pressure.
8. When the timer goes off, do a quick pressure release. Carefully open the lid.
9. Remove the cake pan from your Instant Pot using the foil sling and serve hot.

## Crunchy Green Beans with Shallots

**Prep time: 5 minutes | Cook time: 6 minutes | Serves 4**

¾ teaspoon salt, divided
1 cup water
1 pound (454 g) green beans, trimmed

2 tablespoons olive oil
1 medium shallot, peeled and minced
½ teaspoon black pepper

1. Add ½ teaspoon of salt and the water to the Instant Pot and insert a steamer basket. Place green beans on top of the basket. Lock the lid.
2. Press the Steam button on the Instant Pot and set the cooking time for 0 minutes on High Pressure.
3. When the timer goes off, do a quick pressure release and then carefully open the lid. Remove the green beans and drain the cooking liquid.
4. Select the Sauté mode and add the oil to the pot.
5. Add the green beans and shallot and sauté for 6 minutes, or until the green beans are crisp-tender.
6. Sprinkle with the remaining ¼ teaspoon of salt and pepper.
7. Transfer to a serving plate and serve.

## Balsamic Brussels Sprouts

**Prep time: 5 minutes | Cook time: 5 minutes | Serves 4 to 6**

2 tablespoons (¼ stick) salted butter
2 shallots, diced
2 to 3 pounds (907 g to 1.4 kg) Brussels sprouts, stems trimmed and halved
¼ cup maple syrup

$1/3$ cup balsamic vinegar
10 to 20 almonds, crushed
1 cup dried cranberries
Balsamic glaze, for topping (optional)

1. Set your Instant Pot to Sauté and melt the butter.
2. Add the shallots and sauté until slightly softened, about 3 minutes.
3. Add the Brussels sprouts, maple syrup, vinegar, almonds, and cranberries and stir until the Brussels sprouts are fully coated in the sauce.

4. Lock the lid. Select the Manual mode and set the cooking time for 1 minute at High Pressure.
5. Once cooking is complete, do a quick pressure release. Carefully open the lid.
6. Transfer the Brussels sprouts to a platter, along with their sauce. Serve with a drizzle of balsamic glaze, if desired.

## Zucchini-Parmesan Cheese Fritters

**Prep time: 15 minutes | Cook time: 24 minutes | Serves 4**

4 cups shredded zucchini
1 teaspoon salt
$1/3$ cup shredded Parmesan cheese
$1/3$ cup all-purpose flour
1 large egg, beaten

2 cloves garlic, minced
½ teaspoon black pepper
6 tablespoons olive oil, plus more as needed

1. In a colander, add the zucchini and lightly sprinkle with the salt. Let stand for 10 minutes.
2. Remove from the colander and pat the zucchini dry using a paper towel to gently press as much moisture out as you can.
3. In a large bowl, mix together the zucchini, Parmesan, flour, egg, garlic, and pepper and stir well.
4. Press the Sauté button on the Instant Pot. Add 2 tablespoons of the oil into the pot.
5. Working in batches, scoop out tablespoonfuls of the zucchini mixture and add to the Instant Pot, pressing down gently with the back of a spoon to create 2½ rounds.
6. Cook for 4 minutes per side until lightly browned on both sides.
7. Remove the zucchini fitters with a slotted spatula. Repeat with the remaining zucchini mixture, adding more oil, if needed, with each batch.
8. Allow to cool for 5 minutes before serving.

## Brussels Sprouts with Maple Glaze

**Prep time: 10 minutes | Cook time: 3 minutes | Serves 10**

2 pounds (907 g) fresh Brussels sprouts, sliced
$1/_3$ cup dried cranberries
2 large apples (Fuji or Braeburn), chopped
8 bacon strips, cooked and crumbled, divided

¼ cup maple syrup
2 tablespoons olive oil
$1/_3$ cup cider vinegar
1 teaspoon salt
½ teaspoon coarsely ground pepper
¾ cup chopped hazelnuts or pecans, toasted

1. In a large bowl, mix together the Brussels sprouts, cranberries, apples, and 4 slices of bacon.
2. In a small bowl, stir together the syrup, oil, vinegar, salt, and pepper. Pour this mixture over the Brussels sprouts mixture and toss until well coated.
3. Transfer to the Instant Pot. Secure the lid.
4. Press the Manual on the Instant Pot and set the cooking time for 3 minutes on High Pressure.
5. Once cooking is complete, use a quick pressure release. Carefully remove the lid.
6. Serve sprinkled with the remaining 4 slices of bacon and hazelnuts.

## Spaghetti Squash With Olives and Tomatoes

**Prep time: 15 minutes | Cook time: 10 minutes | Serves 10**

1 cup water
1 medium spaghetti squash, halved lengthwise and seeds removed
¼ cup sliced green olives with pimientos
1 can (14-ounce / 397-g) diced tomatoes, drained

1 teaspoon dried oregano
½ teaspoon salt
½ teaspoon pepper
½ cup shredded Cheddar cheese, for serving
¼ cup minced fresh basil, for serving

1. Pour the water into the Instant Pot and insert a trivet. Place the spaghetti squash on top of the trivet.

2. Secure the lid. Select the Manual mode and set the cooking time for 7 minutes at High Pressure.
3. Once cooking is complete, do a quick pressure release. Carefully open the lid.
4. Remove the spaghetti squash and trivet from the Instant Pot. Drain the cooking liquid from the pot.
5. Separate the squash into strands resembling spaghetti with a fork and discard the skin.
6. Return the squash to the Instant Pot. Add the olives, tomatoes, oregano, salt, and pepper and stir to combine.
7. Press the Sauté button on the Instant Pot and cook for about 3 minutes until heated through.
8. Serve topped with the cheese and basil.

## Chow-Chow Relish

**Prep time: 15 minutes | Cook time: 20 minutes | Serves 8**

2 large green bell peppers, deseeded and diced small
1 large red bell pepper, deseeded and diced small
2 cups finely diced cabbage
2 large green tomatoes, diced small
1 large sweet onion, peeled and diced small
1 cup water
1 cup apple cider

vinegar
½ cup granulated sugar
½ cup packed dark brown sugar
1 tablespoon ground mustard
1 tablespoon sea salt
2 teaspoons celery seed
2 teaspoons red pepper flakes
2 teaspoons ground ginger
1 teaspoon ground turmeric

1. Combine all the ingredients in the Instant Pot.
2. Secure the lid. Select the Manual mode and set the cooking time for 20 minutes at High Pressure.
3. Once cooking is complete, do a natural pressure release for 10 minutes, then release any remaining pressure. Carefully open the lid.
4. Give the mixture a good stir and transfer to a bowl. Serve warm.

## Steamed Leeks with Tomato and Orange

**Prep time: 10 minutes | Cook time: 2 minutes | Serves 6**

1 large tomato, chopped
1 small navel orange, peeled, sectioned, and chopped
2 tablespoons sliced Greek olives
2 tablespoons minced fresh parsley
1 teaspoon red wine vinegar
1 teaspoon capers, drained
1 teaspoon olive oil
½ teaspoon pepper
½ teaspoon grated orange zest
1 cup water
6 medium leeks (white part only), halved lengthwise, cleaned
Crumbled feta cheese, for serving

1. Stir together the tomato, orange, olives, parsley, vinegar, capers, olive oil, pepper, and orange zest in a large bowl and set aside.
2. Pour the water into the Instant Pot and insert a trivet. Place the leeks on top of the trivet.
3. Secure the lid. Select the Steam mode and set the cooking time for 2 minutes at High Pressure.
4. Once cooking is complete, do a quick pressure release. Carefully open the lid.
5. Transfer the leeks to a serving plate and spoon the tomato mixture over top. Scatter with the feta cheese and serve immediately.

## Easy Mushroom Rice Pilaf

**Prep time: 20 minutes | Cook time: 10 minutes | Serves 6**

¼ cup butter
1 cup medium grain rice
1 cup water
4 teaspoon beef base
2 garlic cloves, minced
6 green onions, chopped
½ pound (227 g) baby portobello mushrooms, sliced

1. Set your Instant Pot to Sauté and melt the butter.
2. Add the rice and cook for 3 to 5 minutes, stirring frequently, or until lightly browned.
3. Meanwhile, whisk together the water and beef base in a small bowl.

4. Add the garlic, green onions, and mushrooms to the Instant Pot and stir well. Pour the sauce over the top of the rice mixture.
5. Secure the lid. Select the Manual mode and set the cooking time for 4 minutes at High Pressure.
6. Once cooking is complete, do a natural pressure release for 10 minutes, then release any remaining pressure. Carefully open the lid.
7. Allow to cool for 5 minutes before serving.

## Instant Pot Pinto Beans

**Prep time: 10 minutes | Cook time: 20 minutes | Serves 4**

3 cups water
1 cup dried pinto beans, soaked for 8 hours and drained
2 cloves garlic, minced
½ yellow onion, chopped
1 teaspoon chili powder
1 teaspoon ground cumin
¼ teaspoon freshly ground black pepper
½ fine sea salt, or more to taste
Pinch of cayenne pepper (optional)
Chopped fresh cilantro, for garnish
Lime wedges, for garnish

1. In the Instant Pot, combine the water, beans, garlic, and onion.
2. Lock the lid. Select the Manual mode and set the cooking time for 20 minutes at High Pressure.
3. Once cooking is complete, do a natural pressure release for 10 minutes, then release any remaining pressure. Carefully open the lid.
4. Drain the beans and reserve the liquid.
5. Return the cooked beans to the pot and stir in ½ cup of the reserved liquid. Add the chili powder, cumin, black pepper, salt, and cayenne pepper (if desired) and stir well. Using a potato masher, mash the beans until smooth, leaving some texture if you like. If you prefer a more smooth texture, you can purée the beans with an immersion blender.
6. Taste and add more salt, if desired. Garnish with the cilantro and lime wedges and serve warm.

## Spicy Green Beans

**Prep time: 5 minutes | Cook time: 3 minutes | Serves 4 to 6**

1½ pounds (680 g) green beans, ends trimmed
¼ cup low-sodium soy sauce
¼ cup vegetable or garlic broth
3 cloves garlic, minced
2 tablespoons sriracha
2 tablespoons sesame oil
1 tablespoon paprika
1 tablespoon rice vinegar
2 teaspoons garlic powder
1 teaspoon onion powder
2 tablespoons chopped almonds (optional)
¼ teaspoon crushed red pepper flakes (optional)
¼ teaspoon cayenne pepper (optional)

1. Stir together all the ingredients in the Instant Pot.
2. Lock the lid. Select the Manual mode and set the cooking time for 3 minutes at High Pressure.
3. Once cooking is complete, do a quick pressure release. Carefully open the lid.
4. Serve warm.

## Artichokes with Mayonnaise Dip

**Prep time: 10 minutes | Cook time: 15 minutes | Serves 4**

2 large artichokes, rinsed
1 medium lemon, halved
¾ teaspoon salt, divided
3 cloves garlic, crushed
1 cup water

**Mayonnaise Dip:**

3 tablespoons mayonnaise
⅛ teaspoon black pepper
¼ teaspoon chili powder

1. Cut off top ½ inch of each artichoke.
2. Slice one half of the lemon into wedges and set the other half aside.
3. Add the lemon wedges, ½ teaspoon of salt, garlic, and water to your Instant Pot.
4. Put the trivet in the bottom of the pot and place the artichokes on top. Lock the lid. You may need to trim the artichoke stems to secure the lid.
5. Press the Manual button on your Instant Pot and set the cooking time for 15 minutes at High Pressure.
6. Once cooking is complete, do a quick pressure release. Carefully open the lid and remove the artichokes.
7. Meanwhile, make the mayonnaise dip by stirring together the juice from the remaining ½ lemon, the remaining ¼ teaspoon of salt, mayonnaise pepper, and chili powder in a small bowl.
8. Cut the artichokes in half and serve alongside the mayonnaise dip.

## Summer Squash and Tomatoes

**Prep time: 20 minutes | Cook time: 1 minute | Serves 8**

1 pound (454 g) medium yellow summer squash, cut into ¼-inch-thick slices
2 medium tomatoes, chopped
¼ cup thinly sliced green onions
1 cup vegetable broth
¼ teaspoon pepper
½ teaspoon salt
1½ cups coarsely crushed Caesar salad croutons, for serving
4 bacon strips, cooked and crumbled, for serving
½ cup shredded Cheddar cheese, for serving

1. Combine all the ingredients except the croutons, bacon, and cheese in the Instant Pot.
2. Secure the lid. Select the Manual mode and set the cooking time for 1 minute at High Pressure.
3. Once cooking is complete, do a quick pressure release. Carefully open the lid.
4. Remove the squash from the Instant Pot to a plate. Serve topped with the croutons, bacon, and cheese.

## Zucchini and Chickpea Tagine

**Prep time: 30 minutes | Cook time: 5 minutes | Serves 12**

2 tablespoons olive oil
2 garlic cloves, minced
2 teaspoons paprika
1 teaspoon ground cumin
1 teaspoon ground ginger
½ teaspoon salt
¼ teaspoon ground cinnamon
¼ teaspoon pepper
2 medium zucchini, cut into ½-inch pieces
1 small butternut squash, peeled and cut into ½-inch cubes
1 can (15-ounce /

425-g) chickpeas or garbanzo beans, rinsed and drained
12 dried apricots, halved
½ cup water
1 medium sweet red pepper, coarsely chopped
1 medium onion, coarsely chopped
2 teaspoon honey
2 to 3 teaspoon harissa chili paste
1 can (14.5-ounce / 411-g) crushed tomatoes, undrained
¼ cup chopped fresh mint leaves

1. Press the Sauté button on the Instant Pot and heat the olive oil until it shimmers.
2. Add the garlic, paprika, cumin, ginger, salt, cinnamon, and pepper and cook for about 1 minute until fragrant. Add the remaining ingredients except the tomatoes and mint to the Instant Pot and stir to combine.
3. Secure the lid. Select the Manual mode and set the cooking time for 3 minutes at High Pressure.
4. Once cooking is complete, do a quick pressure release. Carefully open the lid.
5. Stir in the tomatoes and mint until heated though. Serve warm.

## Sweet and Sour Beet Salad

**Prep time: 15 minutes | Cook time: 20 minutes | Serves 8**

1½ cups water
6 medium fresh beets (about 2 pounds / 907 g), scrubbed and tops trimmed

2 small red onions, halved and thinly sliced
2 large ruby red grapefruit, peeled and sectioned

**Sauce:**

¼ cup extra virgin olive oil
3 tablespoons lemon juice
2 tablespoons honey

2 tablespoons cider vinegar
¼ teaspoon pepper
¼ teaspoon salt

1. Pour the water into the Instant Pot and insert a trivet. Place the beets on top of the trivet.
2. Secure the lid. Select the Manual mode and set the cooking time for 20 minutes at High Pressure.
3. Once cooking is complete, do a natural pressure release for 10 minutes, then release any remaining pressure. Carefully open the lid.
4. Remove the beets from the Instant Pot and let cool to room temperature before peeling, halving and thinly slicing them. Transfer the beets to a salad bowl.
5. Whisk together all the ingredients for the sauce in a small bowl until smooth. Pour the sauce over the beets and add the red onions and grapefruit. Toss gently to coat and serve immediately.

## Black-Eyed Peas with Greens

**Prep time: 10 minutes | Cook time: 15 minutes | Serves 2**

1 tablespoon oil
½ yellow onion, diced
2 garlic cloves, minced
½ pound (227 g) dried black-eyed peas
2 cups chopped Swiss chard or kale
1 cup chicken stock
1½ teaspoons red pepper flakes
½ teaspoon dried thyme or 2 fresh thyme sprigs
½ tablespoon kosher salt
¼ teaspoon freshly ground black pepper
1 tablespoon apple cider vinegar
1 to 2 teaspoons hot sauce (optional)

1. Press the Sauté button on the Instant Pot and heat the oil until shimmering.
2. Add the onion and cook for 2 minutes until tender, stirring frequently.
3. Stir in the garlic and cook for about 1 minute until fragrant.
4. Add the peas, Swiss chard, chicken stock, red pepper flakes, thyme, salt, and pepper. Using a wooden spoon, scrape the bottom of the pot, then mix well.
5. Lock the lid. Select the Manual mode and set the cooking time for 10 minutes at High Pressure.
6. Once cooking is complete, do a natural pressure release for 10 minutes, then release any remaining pressure. Carefully open the lid.
7. Whisk in the vinegar and hot sauce, if desired. Taste and adjust the seasoning, if needed. Serve warm.

## Creamy Macaroni and Cheese

**Prep time: 5 minutes | Cook time: 7 minutes | Serves 2**

6 ounces (170 g) elbow macaroni
¾ cup vegetable stock, plus more as needed
½ teaspoon kosher salt
1 tablespoon unsalted butter
2 ounces (57 g) cream cheese
$1/_3$ cup whole milk
½ tablespoon Dijon mustard
½ tablespoon hot sauce (optional)
$1/_3$ cup shredded Gruyère cheese
$1/_3$ cup shredded fontina cheese
$1/_3$ cup shredded Cheddar cheese
Salt and freshly ground black pepper, to taste

1. Combine the macaroni, vegetable stock, and kosher salt in the Instant Pot.
2. Lock the lid. Select the Manual mode and set the cooking time for 5 minutes at High Pressure.
3. Once cooking is complete, do a quick pressure release. Carefully open the lid.
4. Set your Instant Pot to Sauté and stir in the butter until melted.
5. Add the cream cheese, milk, mustard, and hot sauce (if desired) and stir well.
6. Add the shredded cheeses, about $1/_3$ cup at a time, mixing well after each addition.
7. Sprinkle with the salt and pepper and serve.

## Ground Beef Quinoa

**Prep time: 10 minutes | Cook time: 14 to 15 minutes | Serves 4**

1 tablespoon olive oil
1 pound (454 g) ground beef
Salt and black pepper, to taste
1 cup fresh corn
1 onion, finely diced
1 red bell pepper, chopped
1 jalapeño pepper, minced
2 garlic cloves, minced
1 teaspoon ground cumin
1 tablespoon chili seasoning
1 (14-ounce / 397-g) can diced tomatoes
1 (8-ounce / 227-g) can black beans, rinsed
2½ cups chicken broth
1 cup quick-cooking quinoa
1 cup grated Cheddar cheese
2 tablespoons chopped cilantro
2 limes, cut into wedges for garnish

1. Press the Sauté button on the Instant Pot and heat the olive oil. Add the beef to the pot and sauté for 5 minutes, or until lightly browned. Season with salt and pepper.
2. Stir in the corn, onion, red bell pepper, jalapeño pepper and garlic. Cook for 5 minutes, or until the bell pepper is tender. Season with the cumin and chili seasoning. Stir in the tomatoes, black beans, chicken broth and quinoa.
3. Lock the lid. Select the Manual setting and set the cooking time for 1 minute at High Pressure. Once the timer goes off, use a quick pressure release. Carefully open the lid.
4. Select the Sauté mode. Sprinkle the food with the Cheddar cheese and 1 tablespoon of the cilantro. Cook for 3 to 4 minutes, or until cheese melts.
5. Spoon quinoa into serving bowls and garnish with the remaining 1 tablespoon of the cilantro and lime wedges. Serve warm.

## Buckwheat and Pork Cabbage Rolls

**Prep time: 10 minutes | Cook time: 40 minutes | Serves 4**

2 tablespoons butter
½ sweet onion, finely chopped
2 garlic cloves, minced
1 pound (454 g) ground pork
Salt and black pepper, to taste
1 cup buckwheat groats
2 cups beef stock
2 tablespoons chopped cilantro
1 head Savoy cabbage, leaves separated (scraps kept)
1 (23-ounce / 652-g) can chopped tomatoes

1. Set the Instant Pot to the Sauté mode and melt the butter. Add the onion and garlic to the pot and sauté for 4 minutes, or until slightly softened. Add the pork and season with salt and pepper. Cook for 5 minutes, or until the pork is no longer pink. Add the buckwheat groats and beef stock to the pot.
2. Set the lid in place. Select the Manual mode and set the cooking time for 6 minutes at High Pressure. Once the timer goes off, use a quick pressure release. Open the lid. Stir in the chopped cilantro.
3. On a clean work surface, lay the cabbage leaves. Scoop 3 to 4 tablespoons of mixture into the center of each leave and roll up tightly. Clean the pot and spread the cabbage scraps in the bottom. Pour in tomatoes with liquid and arrange cabbage rolls on top.
4. Lock the lid. Select the Manual mode and set the cooking time for 25 minutes on Low Pressure. Once the timer goes off, use a natural pressure release for 10 minutes, then release any remaining pressure. Carefully open the lid. Use a slotted spoon to transfer the cabbage rolls onto serving plates.
5. Serve immediately.

## Cheesy Chicken Kamut

**Prep time: 10 minutes | Cook time: 12 minutes | Serves 2**

| | |
|---|---|
| ½ pound (227 g) boneless and skinless chicken, chopped | 1 tablespoon butter, melted |
| ½ shallot, chopped | 1 teaspoon pressed fresh garlic |
| 1 sweet pepper, chopped | ½ teaspoon basil |
| 1 serrano pepper, chopped | ½ teaspoon thyme |
| ½ cup kamut | Sea salt and freshly ground black pepper, to taste |
| ½ cup tomato purée | 2 ounces (57 g) Colby cheese, shredded |
| ½ cup vegetable broth | |

1. Add all the ingredients, except for the Colby cheese, to the Instant Pot and stir to combine.
2. Lock the lid. Select the Manual setting and set the cooking time for 12 minutes on High Pressure. Once the timer goes off, do a quick pressure release. Carefully open the lid.
3. Sprinkle the shredded Colby cheese on top and lock the lid again. Let it sit in the residual heat until the cheese melts. Serve hot.

## Creamy Grits

**Prep time: 5 minutes | Cook time: 10 minutes | Serves 2**

| | |
|---|---|
| ¾ cup stone ground grits | ¼ cup milk |
| 1½ cups water | ½ teaspoon garlic powder |
| ½ teaspoon sea salt | ½ teaspoon paprika |
| ½ cup cream cheese, at room temperature | ¼ teaspoon porcini powder |

1. Add the grits, water and salt to the Instant Pot.
2. Lock the lid. Select the Manual mode and set the cooking time for 10 minutes on High Pressure. When the timer beeps, perform a natural pressure release for 10 minutes, then release any remaining pressure. Carefully open the lid.
3. Whisk in the remaining ingredients and serve warm.

## Sausage and Shrimp Grit Bowl

**Prep time: 15 minutes | Cook time: 28 minutes | Serves 4**

| | |
|---|---|
| 1 tablespoon olive oil | 1 tablespoon Cajun seasoning |
| 6 ounces (170 g) andouille sausage, diced | 1 teaspoon cayenne pepper |
| 1 yellow onion, diced | 1 tablespoon butter |
| 2 garlic cloves, minced | 1 pound (454 g) jumbo shrimp, peeled and deveined |
| 1 cup white wine | ¼ cup chopped chives |
| 1 cup corn grits | |
| 1 cup chicken broth | 1 tablespoon chopped parsley |
| 1 cup whole milk | |
| 1 (8-ounce / 227-g) can diced tomatoes | ¼ cup heavy cream |

1. Press the Sauté button on the Instant Pot and heat the olive oil. Add the sausage to the pot and fry for 5 minutes, or until slightly browned on all sides. Add the onion and garlic and sauté for 5 minutes, or until tender and fragrant. Pour in the white wine and cook for 3 minutes, or until it has a thick consistency and reduces about one-third.
2. In a medium heatproof bowl, stir together the grits, chicken broth, milk, tomatoes, Cajun seasoning and cayenne pepper.
3. Place a trivet over the sausage mixture and place the grit bowl on top of the trivet.
4. Lock the lid. Select the Manual mode and set the cooking time for 10 minutes at High Pressure. When the timer goes off, use a natural pressure release for 10 minutes, then release any remaining pressure. Carefully open the lid.
5. Remove the grit bowl from the pot. Mix in the butter and set aside.
6. Remove the trivet. Select the Sauté mode and stir in shrimp, chives and parsley. Cook for 5 minutes and stir in heavy cream. Let rest for 2 minutes.
7. Divide the grits among 4 bowls and spread the shrimp mixture on top. Serve immediately.

## Acorn Squash and Quinoa Pilaf

**Prep time: 5 minutes | Cook time: 4 minutes | Serves 2**

½ pound (227 g) acorn squash, peeled and sliced
1 sweet onion, thinly sliced
½ tablespoon coconut oil, melted
½ teaspoon chopped

fresh ginger
2 cups vegetable stock, divided
1 cup quinoa, rinsed
3 prunes, chopped
1 tablespoon roughly chopped fresh mint leaves

1. Add the acorn squash, sweet onion, coconut oil, ginger and 1 cup of the vegetable stock to the Instant Pot and stir to combine.
2. Lock the lid. Select the Manual mode and set the cooking time for 3 minutes on High Pressure. When the timer goes off, do a quick pressure release. Carefully open the lid.
3. Stir in the remaining 1 cup of the vegetable stock, quinoa and prunes.
4. Lock the lid. Select the Manual mode and set the cooking time for 1 minute on High Pressure. When the timer goes off, do a quick pressure release. Carefully open the lid.
5. Serve garnished with fresh mint leaves.

## Spicy Chicken Bulgur

**Prep time: 10 minutes | Cook time: 19 to 20 minutes | Serves 2**

½ tablespoon sesame oil
½ pound (227 g) chicken breasts, boneless and skinless, cut into bite-sized pieces
½ onion, chopped
1 teaspoon minced fresh garlic
1-inch ginger, peeled and sliced
1 Bird's-eye chili pepper, deseeded and minced

1 cup chicken stock
½ cup coconut milk
½ cup bulgur
1 teaspoon garam masala
½ teaspoon turmeric powder
½ teaspoon ground cumin
Sea salt and ground black pepper, to taste
1 tablespoon chopped fresh coriander

1. Set the Instant Pot to the Sauté mode and heat the sesame oil. Add the chicken breasts to the pot and sear for 3 to 4 minutes, or until lightly browned. Transfer to a plate and set aside.
2. Add the onion to the pot and sauté for 5 minutes, or until just softened and fragrant. Stir in the garlic and continue to sauté for 1 minute.
3. Return the cooked chicken breasts to the pot and stir in the remaining ingredients, except for the coriander.
4. Set the lid in place. Select the Manual setting and set the cooking time for 10 minutes on High Pressure. When the timer goes off, perform a natural pressure release for 10 minutes, then release any remaining pressure. Open the lid.
5. Transfer the chicken mixture to bowls and serve topped with fresh coriander

## Buckwheat Pilaf with Nuts

**Prep time: 10 minutes | Cook time: 11 minutes | Serves 4**

1 tablespoon olive oil
4 garlic cloves, minced
1 red bell pepper, diced
2¼ cups chicken broth
1 cup roasted buckwheat groats
½ cup yellow lentils
¾ teaspoon dried

thyme
Salt and black pepper, to taste
1 cup chopped dried figs
½ cup toasted walnuts
½ cup chopped dried apricots
½ cup chopped cilantro

1. Press the Sauté button on the Instant Pot and heat the oil. Add the garlic and bell pepper to the pot and sauté for 5 minutes. Stir in the chicken broth, buckwheat groats, lentils, thyme, salt and pepper.
2. Close and secure the lid. Select the Manual mode and set the cooking time for 6 minutes on High Pressure. Once the timer goes off, use a natural pressure release for 10 minutes, then release any remaining pressure. Carefully open the lid.
3. Stir in the figs, walnuts, apricots and cilantro. Spoon the pilaf into bowls and enjoy.

## Bulgur Wheat Bowl with Shallots

**Prep time: 5 minutes | Cook time: 14 minutes | Serves 2**

1 tablespoon butter
2 shallots, chopped
1 teaspoon minced fresh garlic
1 cup vegetable
broth
½ cup bulgur wheat
¼ teaspoon sea salt
¼ teaspoon ground black pepper

1. Set the Instant Pot to the Sauté mode and melt the butter. Add the shallots to the pot and sauté for 3 minutes, or until just tender and fragrant. Add the garlic and sauté for 1 minute, or until fragrant. Stir together the remaining ingredients in the pot.
2. Lock the lid. Select the Manual mode and set the cooking time for 10 minutes on High Pressure. When the timer beeps, perform a natural pressure release for 10 minutes, then release any remaining pressure. Carefully open the lid.
3. Fluff the bulgur wheat with a fork and serve immediately.

## Cheesy Mushroom Risotto

**Prep time: 10 minutes | Cook time: 20 minutes | Serves 4**

3 tablespoons butter, divided
1 small red onion, finely chopped
2 garlic cloves, thinly sliced
½ pound (227 g) baby Bella mushrooms, sliced
Salt and black
pepper, to taste
1 cup pearl barley
½ cup dry white wine
2½ cups beef broth, hot
2 teaspoons fresh thyme leaves
¼ cup grated Parmesan cheese, plus more for garnish

1. Set the Instant Pot on the Sauté mode and melt 2 tablespoons of the butter. Add the red onion and garlic to the pot and sauté for 5 minutes, or until softened.
2. Add the mushrooms and season with salt and pepper. Cook for 4 minutes, or until the mushrooms are tender.
3. Add the remaining 1 tablespoon of the butter, barley and wine. Cook for 4 minutes, or until the wine is absorbed. Pour the broth in the pot.

4. Lock the lid. Select the Manual mode and set the cooking time for 7 minutes at High Pressure. When the timer goes off, use a natural pressure release for 10 minutes, then release any remaining pressure. Carefully open the lid.
5. Mix in Parmesan cheese to melt and spoon the risotto into serving bowls. Garnish with Parmesan cheese and thyme. Serve warm.

## Onion-Artichoke Corn Risotto

**Prep time: 15 minutes | Cook time: 13 minutes | Serves 4**

2 tablespoons olive oil
2 large white onions, chopped
1 medium zucchini, chopped
4 garlic cloves, minced
Salt and black pepper, to taste
1 cup Arborio rice
½ cup white wine
2½ cups chicken
stock
2 cups corn kernels
1 (6-ounce / 170-g) can artichokes, drained and chopped
1 cup grated Parmesan cheese
3 tablespoons lemon juice
1 tablespoon lemon zest
¼ cup chopped basil, plus more for garnish

1. Set the Instant Pot on the Sauté function and heat the olive oil. Add the onions, zucchini and garlic to the pot and sauté for 5 minutes, or until tender. Season with salt and pepper. Stir in the rice and cook for 2 minutes, or until translucent.
2. Pour in the white wine and keep cooking until it has a thick consistency and reduces about one-third. Stir in the chicken stock, corn, salt and pepper.
3. Lock the lid. Select the Manual mode and set the cooking time for 6 minutes at High Pressure. When the timer goes off, use a natural pressure release for 15 minutes, then release any remaining pressure. Carefully open the lid.
4. Add the artichokes, cheese, lemon juice and zest and whisk until risotto is sticky. Stir in the chopped basil and transfer the risotto into bowls. Serve garnished with the basil.

## Cheesy Mushroom Farro Bowl

**Prep time: 10 minutes | Cook time: 18 to 19 minutes | Serves 2**

| | |
|---|---|
| 1 tablespoon olive oil | broth |
| 1 onion, chopped | ¾ cup farro |
| 1 cup sliced mushrooms | Sea salt and ground black pepper, to taste |
| 1 sweet pepper, chopped | $1/3$ cup grated Swiss cheese |
| 1 garlic clove, minced | 1 tablespoon chopped fresh parsley |
| ½ cup white wine | |
| 1½ cups vegetable | |

1. Set the Instant Pot on the Sauté mode and heat the oil. Add the onion to the pot and sauté for 3 to 4 minutes, or until softened. Add the mushrooms and pepper and sauté for 3 minutes. Stir in the garlic and continue to sauté for 1 minute.
2. Pour in the white wine to deglaze the pan. Stir in the vegetable broth, farro, salt and black pepper.
3. Lock the lid, select the Manual mode and set the cooking time for 11 minutes on High Pressure. When the timer goes off, do a natural pressure release for 10 minutes, then release any remaining pressure. Open the lid.
4. Transfer the dish to bowls and serve topped with the cheese and fresh parsley.

## Chickpea and Quinoa Salad

**Prep time: 10 minutes | Cook time: 1 minute | Serves 2**

| | |
|---|---|
| ½ cup quinoa, rinsed | 3 tablespoons extra-virgin olive oil, plus more for greasing the pot |
| 1 cup water | |
| 1 sweet pepper, deseeded and chopped | |
| 1 serrano pepper, deseeded and chopped | 1 tablespoon fresh lime juice |
| ½ onion, thinly sliced | ¼ teaspoon red pepper flakes |
| ½ cup boiled chickpeas | Sea salt and ground black pepper, to taste |

1. Grease the Instant Pot with the olive oil. Add the rinsed quinoa and water to the pot.

2. Lock the lid. Select the Manual mode and set the cooking time for 1 minute on High Pressure. When the timer goes off, do a natural pressure release for 10 minutes, then release any remaining pressure. Carefully open the lid.
3. Fluff the quinoa with a fork and let rest for 5 minutes. Toss the cooled quinoa with the remaining ingredients until well combined. Serve immediately.

## Corn and Bacon Casserole

**Prep time: 10 minutes | Cook time: 25 minutes | Serves 4**

| | |
|---|---|
| 8 bacon strips, chopped | 1 cup shredded Cheddar cheese |
| 2 eggs, beaten | ¾ cup heavy cream |
| 1 (15-ounce / 425-g) can corn, drained | ¼ cup salted butter, melted |
| 1 (10.5-ounce / 298-g) can sweet corn cream | 3 tablespoons chopped habanero chilies |
| 1 (8.5-ounce / 241-g) package corn muffin mix | Cooking spray |
| | 1 cup water |

1. Set the Instant Pot on the Sauté mode. Add the bacon to the pot and cook for 5 minutes, or until crispy and brown. Transfer the bacon to a large bowl and clean the pot.
2. In the bacon bowl, stir together all the remaining ingredients. Spritz a bundt pan with cooking spray. Pour the bacon mixture into the bundt pan and cover with the aluminum foil.
3. Pour the water in the pot, fit in a trivet and sit bundt pan on top. Lock the lid, select the Manual mode and set the cooking time for 20 minutes on High Pressure. Once cooking is complete, use a natural pressure release for 10 minutes, then release any remaining pressure.
4. Carefully open the lid and remove the bundt pan. Take off the aluminum foil and transfer the casserole to plates. Serve hot.

## Cheesy Egg Amaranth Pilaf

**Prep time: 5 minutes | Cook time: 7 minutes | Serves 2**

¾ cup amaranth
2 cups water
½ cup milk
Sea salt and freshly ground black pepper, to taste

1 tablespoon olive oil
2 eggs
½ cup shredded Cheddar cheese
2 tablespoons chopped fresh chives

1. Add the amaranth, water and milk to the Instant Pot.
2. Set the lid in place. Select the Manual mode and set the cooking time for 4 minutes on High Pressure. When the timer goes off, do a quick pressure release. Carefully open the lid. Sprinkle the salt and black pepper to season.
3. Heat the olive oil in a skillet over medium-high heat and fry the eggs for about 3 minutes, or until crispy on the edges.
4. Divide the cooked amaranth between 2 serving bowls. Place the fried eggs, cheese and chives on top. Serve immediately.

## White Bean Risotto

**Prep time: 10 minutes | Cook time: 15 minutes | Serves 4**

2 tablespoons olive oil
1 medium yellow onion, chopped
3 garlic cloves, minced
¼ teaspoon fresh thyme leaves
2 cups chicken stock
½ cup white wine

1 cup Arborio rice
½ cup grated Parmesan cheese
2 tablespoons butter
Salt and black pepper, to taste
1 (15-ounce / 425-g) can white beans, drained and rinsed

1. Press the Sauté button on the Instant Pot and heat the olive oil. Add the onion, garlic and thyme leaves to the pot and sauté for 2 minutes, or until fragrant. Stir in the chicken stock, white wine and Arborio rice.
2. Lock the lid. Select the Manual mode and set the cooking time for 10 minutes on Low Pressure. When the timer goes

off, do a natural pressure release for 10 minutes, then release any remaining pressure. Carefully open the lid.
3. Add the Parmesan cheese, butter, salt and black pepper to the pot and stir constantly until the cheese is melted. Whisk in the white beans. Select the Sauté mode and cook for 3 minutes, or until cooked through.
4. Divide the dish among 4 serving bowls and serve warm.

## Cheesy Chicken Quinoa

**Prep time: 10 minutes | Cook time: 12 minutes | Serves 4**

2 tablespoons butter
2 leeks, sliced
3 garlic cloves, minced
2 chicken breasts, cut into bite-size pieces
3 cups chicken broth
1½ cups quick-cooking quinoa
1 tablespoon chopped rosemary
1 teaspoon dried basil

Salt and black pepper, to taste
1½ cups green peas, thawed
1 cup ricotta cheese
1 cup grated Parmesan cheese
¼ cup chopped fresh parsley
2 tablespoons lemon juice
2 tablespoons lemon zest

1. Set the Instant Pot to the Sauté mode and melt the butter. Add the leeks to the pot and sauté for 3 minutes, or until bright green and tender. Add the garlic and sauté for 2 minutes, or until fragrant. Stir in the chicken breasts, chicken broth, quinoa, rosemary, basil, salt and black pepper.
2. Close and secure the lid. Select the Manual setting and set the cooking time for 1 minute at High Pressure. Once the timer goes off, use a quick pressure release. Carefully open the lid.
3. Whisk in all the remaining ingredients. Select the Sauté mode and cook for 6 minutes, or until the cheese is melted and the chicken is cooked through.
4. Divide the quinoa into bowls and serve immediately.

## Egg and Pepper Oatmeal Bowl

**Prep time: 5 minutes | Cook time: 6 to 7 minutes | Serves 2**

1½ cups vegetable broth
½ cup steel-cut oats
1 tomato, puréed
Kosher salt and freshly ground black

pepper, to taste
2 teaspoons olive oil
1 onion, chopped
2 bell peppers, deseeded and sliced
2 eggs, beaten

1. Add the vegetable broth, oats, tomato, salt and black pepper to the Instant Pot and stir to combine.
2. Set the lid in place. Select the Manual setting and set the cooking time for 3 minutes on High Pressure. When the timer goes off, perform a natural pressure release for 20 minutes, then release any remaining pressure. Open the lid. Transfer the oatmeal to bowls.
3. Heat the olive oil in a skillet over medium-high heat. Add the onion and peppers to the skillet and sauté for 3 to 4 minutes, or until tender. Add the beaten eggs and continue to cook until they are set.
4. Spread the egg mixture over the oatmeal and serve warm.

## Peppery Onion Pearl Barley

**Prep time: 5 minutes | Cook time: 25 minutes | Serves 2**

1 tablespoon sesame oil
½ yellow onion, chopped
1 garlic clove, minced
1 bell pepper, deseeded and chopped

1 jalapeño pepper, deseeded and chopped
1½ cups vegetable broth
¾ cup pearl barley, rinsed
2 tablespoons chopped chives

1. Set the Instant Pot to the Sauté mode and heat the oil. Add the onion to the pot and sauté for 3 minutes, or until just tender and fragrant. Add the garlic, bell pepper and jalapeño pepper to the pot and sauté for 2 minutes, or until fragrant. Stir in the vegetable broth and pearl barley.

2. Lock the lid. Select the Multigrain mode and set the cooking time for 20 minutes on High Pressure. When the timer goes off, perform a quick pressure release. Carefully open the lid.
3. Fluff the pearl barley mixture with a fork. Serve garnished with the chopped chives.

## Spicy Veggie Couscous

**Prep time: 10 minutes | Cook time: 7 minutes | Serves 2**

1 tablespoon butter, softened
1 carrot, trimmed and chopped
½ stalk celery, peeled and chopped
½ onion, chopped
1 piece ginger, peeled and grated
1 teaspoon pressed garlic
1 Peppadew pepper, chopped
2 cups water
1 cup couscous

½ cup tomato purée
½ tablespoon chicken bouillon granules
1 teaspoon cayenne pepper
1 teaspoon dried parsley flakes
½ teaspoon ground cumin
¼ teaspoon ground cinnamon
Sea salt and ground white pepper, to taste

1. Set the Instant Pot to the Sauté mode and melt the butter. Add the carrot, celery, onion, ginger and garlic to the pot and sauté for 4 minutes, or until softened.
2. Stir in the remaining ingredients until well combined.
3. Close and secure the lid. Select the Manual setting and set the cooking time for 3 minutes on High Pressure. When the timer beeps, do a quick pressure release. Carefully open the lid.
4. Transfer to the serving bowls and serve immediately.

## Quinoa with Shrimp and Broccoli

**Prep time: 10 minutes | Cook time: 11 minutes | Serves 4**

2 tablespoons butter
1 red bell pepper, chopped
1 medium white onion, finely diced
4 garlic cloves, minced
2 teaspoons smoked paprika
1½ cups quick-cooking quinoa

3 cups chicken broth
Salt and black pepper, to taste
1 pound (454 g) jumbo shrimp, peeled and deveined
2 cups broccoli florets
1 lemon, zested and juiced
3 scallions, chopped

1. Set the Instant Pot to the Sauté mode and melt the butter. Add the bell pepper and onion to the pot and sauté for 4 minutes. Add the garlic and paprika, and sauté for 1 minute. Stir in the quinoa, chicken broth, salt and pepper.
2. Lock the lid. Select the Manual mode and set the cooking time for 1 minute on High Pressure. Once cooking is complete, use a quick pressure release. Carefully open the lid.
3. Add the shrimp, broccoli, lemon zest and juice to the pot. Select the Sauté mode and cook for 5 minutes, or until shrimp are pink.
4. Garnish with the chopped scallions and serve.

## Rice and Lentils with Onions

**Prep time: 10 minutes | Cook time: 12 to 13 minutes | Serves 4**

1 tablespoon grapeseed oil
1 small onion, thinly sliced
2 cloves garlic, chopped
½ cup basmati rice, rinsed
½ cup brown lentils, sorted and rinsed
1½ cups water
¼ cup red cooking wine
1 tablespoon fresh

lemon juice
1 tablespoon fresh parsley
1 teaspoon turmeric powder
½ teaspoon ground ginger
½ teaspoon cumin
1 cinnamon stick
Kosher salt and red pepper, to taste
2 cups mustard greens

1. Set the Instant Pot to the Sauté mode and heat the grape seed oil until sizzling. Add the onion and garlic to the pot and sauté for 2 to 3 minutes, or until just tender and fragrant. Whisk in the remaining ingredients, except for the mustard greens.
2. Lock the lid. Select the Manual mode and set the cooking time for 10 minutes on High Pressure. When the timer beeps, perform a natural pressure release for 10 minutes, then release any remaining pressure. Carefully open the lid.
3. Stir in the mustard greens. Lock the lid again and let it sit in the residual heat for 10 minutes. Serve warm.

## Spicy Black Bean Quinoa

**Prep time: 10 minutes | Cook time: 45 minutes | Serves 4**

1 cup dried black beans, soaked
4 cups vegetable broth
1 cup white quinoa, rinsed
3 sweet potatoes, peeled and cubed
1 cup corn kernels
1 teaspoon coriander powder
1 teaspoon garlic

powder
1 teaspoon cumin powder
1 teaspoon cayenne pepper
½ teaspoon dried thyme
Salt and black pepper, to taste
½ cup chopped scallions

1. Add the black beans and vegetable broth to the Instant Pot.
2. Lock the lid. Select the Manual setting and set the cooking time for 30 minutes at High Pressure. Once the timer goes off, use a quick pressure release. Open the lid.
3. Stir in the quinoa and potatoes.
4. Lock the lid again. Select the Manual setting and set the cooking time for 10 minutes at High Pressure. When the timer beeps, do a quick pressure release. Open the lid.
5. Select the Sauté mode. Add the remaining ingredients, except for the scallions, to the pot and cook for 5 minutes.
6. Serve garnished with the chopped scallions.

## Spicy Manchego Buckwheat

**Prep time: 5 minutes | Cook time: 8 to 9 minutes | Serves 2**

| | |
|---|---|
| 1 teaspoon olive oil | chopped |
| 1 shallot, chopped | 1 cup buckwheat |
| 1 teaspoon minced garlic | 1 cup chicken broth |
| 1 bell pepper, chopped | 1 cup water |
| 1 Chile de árbol, | 1/3 cup grated Manchego curado |

1. Set the Instant Pot to the Sauté mode and heat the oil. Add the shallot to the pot and sauté for 3 minutes, or until just softened. Add the garlic, bell pepper and Chile de árbol and sauté for 2 to 3 minutes, or until fragrant. Stir in the buckwheat, chicken broth and water to the pot.
2. Set the lid in place. Select the Manual mode and set the cooking time for 3 minutes on High Pressure. When the timer goes off, perform a quick pressure release. Carefully open the lid.
3. Serve garnished with cheese.

## Wheat Berry Salad with Olives

**Prep time: 5 minutes | Cook time: 35 minutes | Serves 2**

| | |
|---|---|
| ½ cup wheat berries | 2 tablespoons red wine vinegar |
| 2 cups water | 2 tablespoons olive oil |
| 1 tomato, sliced | |
| ½ red onion, sliced | |
| ½ cucumber, sliced | ½ teaspoon basil |
| ¼ cup Kalamata olives | ½ teaspoon oregano |

1. Add the wheat berries and water to the Instant Pot.
2. Set the lid in place. Select the Manual mode and set the cooking time for 35 minutes on High Pressure. When the timer goes off, perform a quick pressure release. Carefully open the lid.
3. Fluff the wheat berries with a fork and transfer to a large bowl. Stir in the remaining ingredients. Cover in plastic and set in a refrigerator. Serve cold.

## Braised Pinto Beans with Pancetta

**Prep time: 10 minutes | Cook time: 45 minutes | Serves 6**

| | |
|---|---|
| 4 ounces (113 g) pancetta, chopped | soaked |
| 1 tablespoon olive oil | 4 cups water |
| 1 onion, finely chopped | ½ teaspoon ground cumin |
| 1 garlic clove, minced | Salt and black pepper, to taste |
| 1 pound (454 g) dried pinto beans, | 3 tablespoons chopped parsley |

1. Set the Instant Pot to the Sauté mode and heat the olive oil. Add the pancetta, onion and garlic to the pot and sauté for 5 minutes. Whisk in the beans, water, cumin, salt and pepper.
2. Lock the lid. Select the Manual mode and set the cooking time for 40 minutes at High Pressure. When the timer beeps, perform a natural pressure release for 10 minutes, then release any remaining pressure. Carefully open the lid.
3. Serve topped with the chopped parsley.

## Pinto Bean and Beet Hummus

**Prep time: 5 minutes | Cook time: 13 minutes | Serves 4**

| | |
|---|---|
| 2 large beets, peeled and chopped | 1 teaspoon garlic powder |
| 2 cups canned pinto beans, rinsed | Salt, to taste |
| 2 cups vegetable stock | ¼ cup olive oil |
| | Juice of ½ lemon |

1. Add the beets, pinto beans, vegetable stock, garlic powder, and salt to the Instant Pot and stir to combine.
2. Set the lid in place. Select the Manual mode and set the cooking time for 13 minutes at High Pressure. When the timer goes off, perform a quick pressure release. Carefully open the lid.
3. Transfer the mixture to a food processor and pulse until creamy and smooth. Pour in the olive oil and lemon juice. Process again to mix well.
4. Pour the mixture into bowls and serve.

## Sweet and Savory Soybeans

**Prep time: 5 minutes | Cook time: 35 minutes | Serves 4**

1 cup dried soybeans, soaked
4 cups water
½ cup soy sauce
¼ cup brown sugar
1 tablespoon rice vinegar

1 teaspoon sesame oil
2 garlic cloves, minced
2 teaspoons sesame seeds

1. Add the soybeans and water to the Instant Pot.
2. Set the lid in place. Select the Manual mode and set the cooking time for 20 minutes at High Pressure. When the timer goes off, do a natural pressure release for 10 minutes, then release any remaining pressure. Carefully open the lid.
3. Stir in the remaining ingredients, except for the sesame seeds. Select the Sauté mode and cook for 15 minutes.
4. Divide the dish among 4 platters and sprinkle the sesame seeds on top. Serve immediately.

## Navy Beans with Mushrooms

**Prep time: 10 minutes | Cook time: 13 minutes | Serves 2**

1 pound (454 g) white button mushrooms, quartered
1 tablespoon olive oil
1 medium butternut squash, chopped
1 medium white onion, diced
¼ teaspoon dried rosemary

Salt and black pepper, to taste
3 cups chicken broth
1 cup chopped tomatoes
1 (15-ounce / 425-g) can navy beans, rinsed
2 cups baby spinach
Juice of 1 lemon

1. Press the Sauté button on the Instant Pot and heat the olive oil. Add the mushrooms, squash and onion to the pot and sauté for 6 minutes, or until tender. Sprinkle with the rosemary, salt and pepper and continue to sauté for 1 minute. Stir in chicken broth and tomatoes.

2. Lock the lid. Select the Manual mode and set the cooking time for 3 minutes at High Pressure. When the timer goes off, use a natural pressure release for 10 minutes, then release any remaining pressure. Carefully open the lid.
3. Select the Sauté mode. Add the navy beans, spinach and sauté for 3 minutes, or until the spinach is wilted.
4. Drizzle with the lemon juice and serve immediately.

## Tofu and Black Bean Scramble

**Prep time: 10 minutes | Cook time: 23 minutes | Serves 2**

1 cup canned black beans
2 cups vegetable broth
1 tablespoon ghee
3 tomatoes, chopped
1 small red onion, finely chopped
3 garlic cloves, minced
1 (14-ounce / 397-

g) extra-firm tofu, crumbled
1 teaspoon turmeric powder
1 teaspoon cumin powder
1 teaspoon smoked paprika
Salt and black pepper, to taste

1. Add the black beans and vegetable broth to the Instant Pot.
2. Close and secure the lid. Select the Manual setting and set the cooking time for 10 minutes at High Pressure. When the timer beeps, use a quick pressure release. Carefully open the lid.
3. Drain the beans and transfer to a bowl. Clean the pot.
4. Select the Sauté mode and melt the ghee. Add the tomatoes, onion and garlic to the pot and sauté for 4 minutes, or until tender. Fold in the tofu and cook for 5 minutes.
5. Sprinkle the tofu mixture with the turmeric, cumin, paprika, salt and black pepper to season. Cook for 1 minute. Stir in the cooked black beans and cook for additional 3 minutes.
6. Serve immediately.

## Creamy Coconut Lentil Curry

**Prep time: 10 minutes | Cook time: 13 minutes | Serves 4**

2 tablespoons coconut oil
1 large carrot, finely chopped
1 medium onion, finely chopped
1 leek, chopped
Salt, to taste
1 cup chopped tomatoes
2 teaspoons turmeric powder
2 garlic cloves
1 cup dried green lentils, rinsed
½ cup coconut milk
2½ cups vegetable stock
½ lemon, juiced
2 tablespoons chopped cilantro

1. Set the Instant Pot to the Sauté mode and heat the coconut oil. Add the carrot, onion, leek and salt to the pot and sauté for 5 minutes, or until tender. Stir in the tomatoes, turmeric and garlic. Cook for 3 minutes, or until the tomatoes are softened. Pour in the green lentils, coconut milk and vegetable stock.
2. Close and secure the lid. Select the Manual setting and set the cooking time for 5 minutes at High Pressure. Once the timer goes off, use a natural pressure release for 10 minutes, then release any remaining pressure. Carefully open the lid.
3. Drizzle with the lemon juice and stir. Serve topped with the chopped cilantro.

## Stir-Fried Lentils with Zucchinis

**Prep time: 10 minutes | Cook time: 20 minutes | Serves 4**

2 tablespoons olive oil
2 large zucchinis, chopped
4 garlic cloves, minced
½ tablespoon curry powder
½ tablespoon dried oregano
Salt and black pepper, to taste
2 cups canned beluga lentils, drained
½ cup chopped basil
¼ cup chopped parsley
1 small red onion, diced
2 tablespoons balsamic vinegar
1 teaspoon Dijon mustard

1. Press the Sauté button on the Instant Pot and heat the olive oil. Add the zucchinis to the pot and sauté for 10 minutes, or until softened. Add the garlic and sauté for 1 minute, or until fragrant.
2. Sprinkle the curry powder, oregano, salt and pepper on top and cook for 1 minute, stirring constantly until well combined.
3. Whisk in the lentils and cook for 3 minutes. Stir in the basil, ⅛ cup of the parsley and onion. Sauté for 5 minutes, or until onion is tender.
4. In a bowl, whisk together the vinegar and mustard. Spread the vinegar mixture over the lentil mixture.
5. Serve topped with the remaining ⅛ cup of the parsley.

## Cannellini Beans with Bacon

**Prep time: 5 minutes | Cook time: 14 minutes | Serves 4**

3 bacon slices, chopped
2 (15-ounce / 425-g) cans cannel in beans, rinsed and drained
1 cup water
½ cup canned tomatoes
1 tablespoon ground mustard
1 teaspoon chili powder
1 cup cooked white rice
¼ cup chopped mint

1. Set the Instant Pot on the Sauté mode. Add the bacon to the pot and cook for 6 minutes, or until crispy and browned. Transfer the bacon to a plate with paper towels to soak up excess fat.
2. Add the cannellini beans, water, tomatoes, mustard and chili powder to the pot. Place the bacon back in the pot.
3. Lock the lid. Select the Manual mode and set the cooking time for 8 minutes at High Pressure. When the timer goes off, use a natural pressure release for 10 minutes, then release any remaining pressure. Carefully open the lid.
4. Stir in the cooked white rice and serve garnished with the chopped mint.

## Steamed Corn in Cilantro Butter

**Prep time: 5 minutes | Cook time: 7 to 8 minutes | Serves 2**

2 large ears corn, husked and halved
1 cup water
2 tablespoons butter
1 tablespoon

chopped cilantro
½ teaspoon paprika
Sea salt and ground black pepper, to taste

1. Pour the water into the Instant Pot and place a trivet over it. Place the corn into the trivet.
2. Close and secure the lid. Select the Manual setting and set the cooking time for 6 minutes at High Pressure. Once the timer goes off, do a quick pressure release. Carefully open the lid. Remove the water and transfer the corn to a plate.
3. Select the Sauté mode and melt the butter. Add the cilantro, paprika, salt and black pepper to the pot. Stir for 1 to 2 minutes, or until the butter is melted and everything is well combined.
4. Spread the butter mixture over the steamed corn and serve immediately.

## Green Lentil Salad with Cucumber

**Prep time: 10 minutes | Cook time: 8 minutes | Serves 4**

1 cup green lentils, rinsed
2 cups water
1 cucumber, sliced
½ carrot, julienned
1 bell pepper, deseeded and sliced
½ cup grape tomatoes, halved
¹/₃ cup chopped

scallions
4 tablespoons extra-virgin olive oil
½ teaspoon red pepper flakes
½ fresh lemon, juiced
Sea salt and ground white pepper, to taste

1. Add the lentils and water to the Instant Pot.
2. Lock the lid. Select the Manual mode and set the cooking time for 8 minutes on High Pressure. When the timer goes off, perform a natural pressure release for 15 minutes, then release any remaining pressure. Carefully open the lid.
3. Transfer the cooked lentils to a large mixing bowl. Stir in the remaining ingredients. Toss to combine well. Serve immediately.

## Traditional Greek Green Beans

**Prep time: 10 minutes | Cook time: 6 minutes | Serves 4**

1 tablespoon olive oil
2 garlic cloves, chopped
1 pound (454 g) fresh green beans
4 tomatoes, puréed
Sea salt and freshly ground black pepper, to taste

½ cup bone broth
½ teaspoon paprika
½ teaspoon dried oregano
½ teaspoon dried basil
½ dried dill
3 ounces (85 g) Feta cheese, crumbled

1. Set the Instant Pot on the Sauté mode and heat the olive oil. Add the garlic to the pot and sauté for about 1 minute, or until fragrant. Stir in the remaining ingredients, except for the Feta cheese.
2. Lock the lid. Select the Manual setting and set the cooking time for 5 minutes on High Pressure. When the timer beeps, do a quick pressure release. Carefully open the lid.
3. Divide the dish among 4 serving bowls and serve with the Feta cheese on the side.

## Cheesy Black Beans

**Prep time: 10 minutes | Cook time: 15 minutes | Serves 2**

1 teaspoon olive oil
1 large white onion, chopped
1 teaspoon grated garlic
3 cups vegetable broth
1 cup dried black

beans, soaked
1 teaspoon Mexican seasoning
Salt, to taste
½ cup Cotija cheese
¼ cup chopped cilantro

1. Set the Instant Pot to the Sauté mode and heat the olive oil. Add the onion and garlic to the pot and sauté for 3 minutes, or until tender. Stir in the vegetable broth, black beans, Mexican seasoning and salt.
2. Set the lid in place. Select the Manual mode and set the cooking time for 12 minutes at High Pressure. When the timer goes off, perform a quick pressure release. Carefully open the lid.
3. Divide the beans between 2 plates and serve topped with the Cotija cheese and cilantro.

## Pinto Bean and Pork Casserole

**Prep time: 10 minutes | Cook time: 14 minutes | Serves 4**

2 tablespoons olive oil
1 pound (454 g) pork roast, cubed
Salt and black pepper, to taste
2 green chilies, chopped
1 small red onion, chopped
3 cups chicken broth
1 cup dried pinto beans, soaked overnight and rinsed
1 cup tomato sauce
1 teaspoon chili powder
1 teaspoon garlic powder
¼ cup chopped parsley

1. Press the Sauté button on the Instant Pot and heat the olive oil. Add the pork to the pot and season with salt and pepper. Sear the pork for 4 minutes, or until browned. Stir in the remaining ingredients, except for the parsley.
2. Close and secure the lid. Select the Manual mode and set the cooking time for 10 minutes at High Pressure. When the timer goes off, use a quick pressure release. Carefully open the lid.
3. Stir in the chopped parsley and serve immediately.

## Scarlet Runner Beans with Turkey

**Prep time: 10 minutes | Cook time: 31 to 32 minutes | Serves 2**

1 tablespoon olive oil
½ onion, chopped
1 bell pepper, sliced
1 garlic clove, minced
¼ pound (113 g) Scarlet Runner beans
2 ounces (57 g) smoked turkey, boneless and
shredded
1 tablespoon sherry wine
1 cup turkey broth
1 bay leaf
1 sprig thyme
1 sprig rosemary
Kosher salt and ground black pepper, to taste

1. Set the Instant Pot to the Sauté mode and heat the olive oil. Add the onion to the pot and sauté for 5 minutes, or until softened and translucent. Add the bell pepper and garlic to the pot and sauté for 1 to 2 minutes, or until fragrant. Stir in the remaining ingredients.

2. Lock the lid. Select the Bean/Chili mode and set the cooking time for 25 minutes on High Pressure. When the timer beeps, perform a natural pressure release for 10 minutes, then release any remaining pressure. Carefully open the lid.
3. Serve warm.

## Spicy Chickpea Hummus

**Prep time: 5 minutes | Cook time: 35 minutes | Serves 2**

½ cup dried chickpeas, rinsed
6 cups water
½ teaspoon baking soda
½ teaspoon sea salt
4 tablespoons olive oil
1 tablespoon tahini
1 tablespoon fresh lemon juice
½ teaspoon cayenne pepper
¼ teaspoon hot pepper sauce
1 garlic clove

1. Add the chickpeas, water, baking soda and salt to the Instant Pot and stir to combine.
2. Set the lid in place. Select the Manual mode and set the cooking time for 35 minutes on High Pressure. When the timer goes off, do a natural pressure release for 20 minutes, then release any remaining pressure. Carefully open the lid. Drain the chickpeas and reserve the cooking liquid.
3. Transfer the drained chickpeas to a blender. Stir in the remaining ingredients and blend until smooth. Stop to pour in the reserved cooking liquid to reach the desired consistency.
4. Serve immediately.

## Yellow Lentil Pancake with Arugula

**Prep time: 10 minutes | Cook time: 35 minutes | Serves 2**

1 cup split yellow lentils, soaked
3 eggs, beaten
2 garlic cloves, whole
½ teaspoon smoked paprika
¼ teaspoon cumin powder
¼ teaspoon coriander
powder
⅛ teaspoon turmeric
Salt, to taste
½ cup water, plus 1 cup water for steaming
2 cups chopped arugula

1. Line a cake pan with the parchment paper and set aside.
2. In a food processor, combine all the ingredients, except for the arugula, and process until smooth. Pour the mixture into the cake pan and stir in the arugula. Cover with the aluminium foil.
3. Pour 1 cup of the water into the pot, fit in a trivet and place the cake pan on top.
4. Close and secure the lid. Select the Manual mode and set the cooking time for 35 minutes at High Pressure. When the timer goes off, use a quick pressure release. Carefully open the lid.
5. Slice and serve.

## Pumpkin Risotto

**Prep time: 10 minutes | Cook time: 11 to 12 minutes | Serves 4 to 6**

2 ounces (57 g) extra virgin olive oil
1 small yellow onion, chopped
2 cloves garlic, minced
4 cups chicken stock
2 cups Arborio rice
¾ cup pumpkin purée
1 teaspoon thyme, chopped
½ teaspoon grated ginger
½ teaspoon cinnamon
½ teaspoon nutmeg
½ cup heavy cream
Salt, to taste

1. Press the Sauté button on your Instant Pot Add and heat the oil.
2. Add the onion and garlic and sauté for 1 to 2 minutes.
3. Stir in the chicken stock, rice, pumpkin purée, thyme, ginger, cinnamon, and nutmeg.
4. Lock the lid. Press the Manual button and cook for 10 minutes at High Pressure.
5. Once cooking is complete, do a quick pressure release. Carefully open the lid.
6. Mix in the heavy cream and salt. Stir well.
7. Serve.

## Basmati Rice

**Prep time: 5 minutes | Cook time: 6 minutes | Serves 4**

1 cup white basmati rice, rinsed
1¼ cups water
¼ teaspoon salt
Butter to taste (optional)

1. Combine all the ingredients except the butter in the Instant Pot.
2. Lock the lid. Select the Manual mode and set the cooking time for 6 minutes at High Pressure.
3. Once cooking is complete, do a natural pressure release for 10 minutes, then release any remaining pressure. Carefully remove the lid.
4. Fluff the rice with a fork. You can stir in the butter, if desired. Serve warm.

## Cheesy Ground Beef Pasta

**Prep time: 5 minutes | Cook time: 12 to 13 minutes | Serves 4 to 6**

| | |
|---|---|
| 1 teaspoon olive oil | 1 pound (454 g) |
| 1¼ pound (567 g) | elbow macaroni |
| ground beef | 8 ounces (227 g) |
| 1 packet onion soup | sharp Cheddar |
| mix | cheese, grated |
| 3½ cups hot water | Salt and ground |
| 3 beef bouillon cubes | black pepper, to taste |

1. Press the Sauté button on your Instant Pot. Pour in the oil and let heat for 1 minute.
2. Add the ground beef and sauté for 4 to 5 minutes until browned.
3. Mix together the onion soup mix, water, and bouillon cubes in a bowl.
4. Add the mixture and macaroni to the pot and stir to combine.
5. Press the Manual button on your Instant Pot and cook for 7 minutes at High Pressure.
6. When the timer goes off, perform a quick pressure release. Carefully open the lid.
7. Stir in the Cheddar cheese and let stand for 5 minutes.
8. Taste and sprinkle with salt and pepper if needed.
9. Serve.

## Rice Medley

**Prep time: 5 minutes | Cook time: 23 minutes | Serves 4**

| | |
|---|---|
| ¾ cup (or more) | red, wild or black |
| short grain brown | rice, rinsed |
| rice, rinsed | 1½ cups water |
| 3 to 4 tablespoons | ¼ teaspoon sea salt |

1. Combine all the ingredients in the Instant Pot.
2. Lock the lid. Select the Multigrain mode and set the cooking time for 23 minutes at High Pressure.
3. Once cooking is complete, do a natural pressure release for 15 minutes, then release any remaining pressure. Carefully open the lid.
4. Fluff the rice with a fork and serve.

## Jasmine Rice

**Prep time: 5 minutes | Cook time: 4 minutes | Serves 4 to 6**

| | |
|---|---|
| 2 cups jasmine rice, | ½ teaspoon salt |
| rinsed | 2 cups water |
| 2 teaspoons olive oil | |

1. Place all the ingredients into the Instant Pot and give a good stir.
2. Lock the lid. Select the Manual mode and set the cooking time for 4 minutes at High Pressure.
3. Once cooking is complete, do a natural pressure release for 10 minutes, then release any remaining pressure. Remove the lid.
4. Fluff the rice with a fork and serve.

## Breaded Chicken Parmesan Pasta

**Prep time: 10 minutes | Cook time: 20 minutes | Serves 2 to 4**

| | |
|---|---|
| 8 ounces (227 g) | chopped |
| linguine noodles, | ¼ cup parsley, |
| halved | chopped |
| ½ jar spaghetti | ½ teaspoon Italian |
| sauce | seasoning |
| 1 cup water | Salt and crushed red |
| 2 chicken breasts, | pepper, to taste |
| skinless and boneless | 1 tablespoon butter |
| 8 ounces (227 g) | ½ cup Italian bread |
| cherry tomatoes, | crumbs |
| halved | 1 cup Parmesan |
| 3 cloves garlic, | cheese, grated |

1. Stir together the noodles, jar of spaghetti sauce, and water in your Instant Pot.
2. Mix in the chicken breasts, tomatoes, garlic, parsley, Italian seasoning, salt and pepper and stir well.
3. Secure the lid. Press the Manual button on your Instant Pot and cook for 20 minutes on High Pressure.
4. Meantime, melt the butter in a pan and toast the bread crumbs.
5. When the timer goes off, do a quick pressure release. Carefully remove the lid.
6. Stir the dish well. Sprinkle with the bread crumbs and cheese and let sit for 5 minutes.
7. Serve.

## Vegetable Pasta

**Prep time: 10 minutes | Cook time: 7 minutes | Serves 4 to 6**

2 cups dried pasta
1 cup water
½ jar spaghetti sauce
½ can chickpeas, rinsed and drained
½ can black olives, rinsed and drained
½ cup frozen spinach

½ cup frozen lima beans
½ squash, shredded
½ zucchini, sliced
½ tablespoon Italian seasoning
½ teaspoon cumin
½ teaspoon garlic powder

1. Add all the ingredients to the Instant Pot and stir to combine.
2. Press the Manual button on the Instant Pot and set the cooking time for 7 minutes on High Pressure.
3. Once cooking is complete, perform a natural pressure release for 10 minutes and then release any remaining pressure. Carefully open the lid.
4. Transfer to a serving dish and serve immediately.

## Chicken Fettuccine Alfredo

**Prep time: 5 minutes | Cook time: 3 minutes | Serves 2**

8 ounces (227 g) fettuccine, halved
2 cups water
2 teaspoons chicken seasoning
1 cup cooked and

diced chicken
1 jar (15-ounce / 425-g) Alfredo sauce
Salt and ground black pepper, to taste

1. Add the pasta, water, and chicken seasoning to the Instant Pot and stir to combine.
2. Secure the lid. Press the Manual button on the Instant Pot and set the cooking time for 3 minutes at High Pressure.
3. When the timer goes off, perform a quick pressure release. Carefully remove the lid.
4. Drain the pasta and transfer to a serving bowl.
5. Add the cooked chicken and drizzle the sauce over the top. Sprinkle with salt and pepper.
6. Stir until well mixed and serve.

## Broccoli Pasta

**Prep time: 5 minutes | Cook time: 6 minutes | Serves 4**

2 cups water
½ pound (227 g) pasta
½ cup broccoli
½ cup half and half

8 ounces (227 g) grated Cheddar cheese
Salt, to taste

1. Place the water and pasta in the Instant Pot and insert a steamer basket.
2. Add the broccoli to the basket. Secure the lid.
3. Press the Manual button on the Instant Pot and set the cooking time for 4 minutes on High Pressure.
4. Once cooking is complete, do a quick pressure release. Carefully remove the lid.
5. Take out the broccoli and drain the pasta.
6. Press the Sauté button on the Instant Pot. Add the cooked pasta, broccoli, half and half, and cheese. Stir well. Sprinkle with the salt. Cook the dish for 2 minutes, stirring occasionally.
7. Transfer to a serving dish and serve.

## Jasmine Rice with Cauliflower and Pineapple

**Prep time: 5 minutes | Cook time: 20 minutes | Serves 4 to 6**

4 cups water
2 cups jasmine rice
1 cauliflower, florets separated and chopped
½ pineapple, peeled

and chopped
2 teaspoons extra virgin olive oil
Salt and ground black pepper, to taste

1. Stir together all the ingredients in the Instant Pot.
2. Lock the lid. Select the Manual mode and set the cooking time for 20 minutes at Low Pressure.
3. When the timer beeps, perform a natural pressure release for 10 minutes, then release any remaining pressure. Carefully remove the lid.
4. Fluff with the rice spatula or fork, then serve.

## Ground Beef and Pasta

**Prep time: 5 minutes | Cook time: 11 to 13 minutes | Serves 4**

| | |
|---|---|
| 1 teaspoon olive oil | pasta sauce |
| 1 pound (454 g) ground beef | 1½ cup water |
| 8 ounces (227 g) dried pasta | Salt and ground black pepper, to taste |
| 24 ounces (680 g) | Italian seasoning, to taste |

1. Press the Sauté button on the Instant Pot. Add the oil and let heat for 1 minute.
2. Fold in the ground beef and cook for 3 to 5 minutes until browned, stirring frequently.
3. Mix in the pasta, sauce and water and stir to combine.
4. Secure the lid. Press the Manual button on the Instant Pot and set the cooking time for 7 minutes on High Pressure.
5. Once cooking is complete, do a quick pressure release. Carefully remove the lid.
6. Stir in salt, pepper, and Italian seasoning and stir well.
7. Transfer to a serving dish and serve immediately.

## Chipotle Styled Rice

**Prep time: 10 minutes | Cook time: 30 minutes | Serves 4 to 6**

| | |
|---|---|
| 2 cups brown rice, rinsed | 1½ tablespoons olive oil |
| 2¾ cups water | 1 teaspoon salt |
| 4 small bay leaves | ½ cup chopped cilantro |
| 1 lime, juiced | |

1. Place the rice, water, and bay leaves into the Instant Pot and stir.
2. Lock the lid. Select the Rice mode and set the cooking time for 30 minutes at High Pressure.
3. When the timer beeps, perform a natural pressure release for 10 minutes, then release any remaining pressure. Carefully remove the lid.
4. Add the lime juice, olive oil, salt, and cilantro and stir to mix well. Serve immediately.

## Stick of Butter Rice

**Prep time: 5 minutes | Cook time: 24 minutes | Serves 4 to 6**

| | |
|---|---|
| 1 stick (½ cup) butter | onion soup |
| 2 cups brown rice | 1 cups vegetable stock |
| 1½ cups French | |

1. Set your Instant Pot to Sauté and melt the butter.
2. Add the rice, onion soup, and vegetable stock to the Instant Pot and stir until combined.
3. Lock the lid. Select the Manual mode and set the cooking time for 22 minutes at High Pressure.
4. When the timer beeps, perform a natural pressure release for 10 minutes, then release any remaining pressure. Carefully remove the lid.
5. Serve warm.

## Pasta with Capers and Olives

**Prep time: 10 minutes | Cook time: 5 minutes | Serves 4**

| | |
|---|---|
| 3 cloves garlic, minced | 1 tablespoon of capers |
| 4 cups of pasta such as penne or fusilli (short pasta) | ½ cup of Kalamata olives, sliced |
| 4 cups of pasta sauce (homemade or store-bought) | ¼ teaspoon. of crushed red pepper flakes |
| 3 cups of water, plus more as needed | Salt and pepper, to taste |

1. Press the Sauté button on your Instant Pot and add the garlic.
2. Add a splash of water and cook for about 30 seconds until fragrant.
3. Mix in the pasta, pasta sauce, water, capers, olives, and crushed red pepper flakes and stir to combine.
4. Lock the lid. Press the Manual button on the Instant Pot and set the cooking time for 5 minutes on High Pressure.
5. Once the timer goes off, use a quick pressure release. Carefully remove the lid.
6. Fold in the pasta and sprinkle with salt and pepper. Stir well.
7. Serve immediately.

## Cheesy Pizza Pasta

**Prep time: 5 minutes | Cook time: 5 to 8 minutes | Serves 6**

| | |
|---|---|
| 4 cups of noodles such as ziti or rigatoni | sauce |
| 8 cups of water | 1½ cup of shredded mozzarella cheese |
| 2 cups of spaghetti | 10 pepperoni, cut in half |

1. Add the noodles and water to the Instant Pot.
2. Lock the lid. Press the Manual button on the Instant Pot and cook for 3 minutes at High Pressure.
3. Once cooking is complete, perform a quick pressure release. Carefully remove the lid. Drain the cooking liquid.
4. Return the pasta to the Instant Pot. Fold in the spaghetti sauce, shredded cheese, and sliced pepperoni. Stir well.
5. Press the Sauté button on the Instant Pot. Cook for 2 to 3 minutes, or until the sauce starts to bubble and the cheese has melted, stirring occasionally.
6. Serve immediately.

## Mexican Rice

**Prep time: 5 minutes | Cook time: 14 to 16 minutes | Serves 4 to 6**

| | |
|---|---|
| 1 tablespoon olive oil | 1 cup salsa |
| ¼ cup diced onion | 2¹/₃ cups chicken stock |
| 2 cups long grain white rice | 1 teaspoon salt |

1. Press the Sauté button on the Instant Pot and heat the olive oil.
2. Add the diced onion and sauté for 2 to 3 minutes until translucent.
3. Add the white rice and cook for an additional 2 to 3 minutes. Stir in the remaining ingredients.
4. Lock the lid. Select the Manual mode and set the cooking time for 10 minutes at High Pressure.
5. Once cooking is complete, do a natural pressure release for 10 minutes, then release any remaining pressure. Carefully open the lid.
6. Fluff the rice with the rice spatula or fork. Serve warm.

## Spanish Rice

**Prep time: 5 minutes | Cook time: 14 minutes | Serves 4 to 6**

| | |
|---|---|
| 2 tablespoons butter | powder |
| 2 cups long grain rice | 1 teaspoon cumin |
| 8 ounces (227 g) tomato sauce | ½ teaspoon onion powder |
| 1½ cups chicken stock or water | ½ teaspoon garlic powder |
| 1 teaspoon chili | ½ teaspoon salt |

1. Set your Instant Pot to Sauté and melt the butter.
2. Add the rice and sauté for about 4 minutes, stirring occasionally.
3. Add the remaining ingredients to the Instant Pot and stir.
4. Secure the lid. Select the Manual mode and set the cooking time for 10 minutes at High Pressure.
5. When the timer beeps, perform a natural pressure release for 10 minutes, then release any remaining pressure. Carefully remove the lid.
6. Fluff the rice with the rice spatula or fork. Serve warm.

## Shawarma Rice

**Prep time: 10 minutes | Cook time: 15 minutes | Serves 6 to 8**

| | |
|---|---|
| 1½ cups basmati rice, rinsed and drained | 1 cup chopped onion |
| 4 cups shredded cabbage | 5 cloves garlic, minced |
| 1 pound (454 g) ground beef (chicken, fish, pork, optional), cooked | 3 tablespoons shawarma spice |
| 1½ cups water | 1 tablespoon olive oil |
| | 1 teaspoon salt |
| | ¼ cup chopped cilantro |

1. Combine all the ingredients except the cilantro in the Instant Pot.
2. Lock the lid. Select the Manual mode and set the cooking time for 15 minutes at High Pressure.
3. When the timer beeps, perform a natural pressure release for 10 minutes, then release any remaining pressure. Carefully remove the lid.
4. Stir in the cilantro and serve immediately.

## Pasta Salad with Feta and Arugula

**Prep time: 10 minutes | Cook time: 8 minutes | Serves 4 to 6**

1 pound (454 g) dry rotini pasta
Water as needed, to cover the pasta
2 cups arugula or spinach, chopped
1 cup feta cheese, diced
2 Roma or plum tomatoes, diced

2 garlic cloves, minced
1 red bell pepper, diced
2 tablespoons white wine vinegar
$1/3$ cup extra-virgin olive oil
Salt and ground black pepper, to taste

1. Place the pasta and water in your Instant Pot.
2. Secure the lid. Press the Manual button on your Instant Pot and set the cooking time for 8 minutes on High Pressure.
3. Once the timer goes off, do a quick pressure release. Carefully open the lid.
4. Drain the pasta and set aside.
5. Mix together the arugula, feta, tomatoes, garlic, bell pepper, vinegar, and olive oil in a large bowl.
6. Fold in the pasta. Sprinkle with salt and pepper. Stir well.
7. Serve immediately.

## Seafood Pasta with Tomatoes

**Prep time: 15 minutes | Cook time: 14 minutes | Serves 4 to 6**

1 tablespoon olive oil
2 cloves garlic, chopped
1 medium onion, chopped
1 red bell pepper, chopped
2 tomatoes, chopped
½ cup dry white wine
2 cups macaroni
2 cups vegetable stock

1½ cups frozen mixed seafood
1 tablespoon tomato purée
1 teaspoon mixed herbs
½ teaspoon salt
½ teaspoon ground black pepper
½ cup grated Parmesan cheese

1. Press the Sauté button on your Instant Pot. Add and heat the oil.
2. Add the garlic and onion and cook for 2 minutes, stirring occasionally.
3. Fold in the bell pepper and tomatoes and cook for an additional 2 minutes.

4. Add the wine and stir well. Let simmer for 5 minutes.
5. Add the macaroni, stock, seafood, tomato purée, and herbs. Sprinkle with salt and pepper. Stir until well mixed.
6. Select the Manual mode and cook for 5 minutes on High Pressure.
7. Once the timer goes off, perform a quick pressure release. Carefully remove the lid.
8. Serve topped with the cheese.

## Instant Pot Pasta Carbonara

**Prep time: 10 minutes | Cook time: 8 to 9 minutes | Serves 4**

1 pound (454 g) pasta dry such as rigatoni, penne or cavatappi)
4 cups water
¼ teaspoon kosher salt
4 large eggs
1 cup grated

Parmesan cheese
Ground black pepper, to taste
8 ounces (227 g) bacon pancetta or guanciale
4 tablespoons heavy cream

1. Place the pasta, water, and salt in your Instant Pot.
2. Secure the lid. Press the Manual button and cook for 5 minutes at High Pressure.
3. Meantime, beat together the eggs, cheese and black pepper in a mixing bowl until well mixed.
4. Cook the bacon on medium heat in a frying pan for 3 minutes until crispy.
5. Once cooking is complete, do a quick pressure release. Carefully remove the lid.
6. Select the Sauté mode. Transfer the bacon to the pot and cook for 30 seconds.
7. Stir in the egg mixture and heavy cream.
8. Secure the lid and let stand for 5 minutes.
9. Transfer to a serving dish and serve.

## Tomato Pasta with Capers and Tuna

**Prep time: 10 minutes | Cook time: 10 to 11 minutes | Serves 4 to 6**

2 tablespoons olive oil
2 cloves garlic, sliced
2 cups pasta of your choice
1½ cups tomatoes, diced
⅛ teaspoon oregano
⅛ teaspoon chili pepper
¾ cup red wine
2 cups water
Salt and ground black pepper, to taste
2 tablespoons capers
1 small can tuna in oil
½ cup grated Parmesan cheese

1. Press the Sauté button on your Instant Pot. Add and heat the oil.
2. Add the garlic and sauté for 1 minute until fragrant.
3. Fold in the pasta and tomatoes and stir well. Season with oregano and chilies.
4. Add the red wine and water. Season with the salt and pepper. Stir to combine.
5. Secure the lid. Press the Manual button on your Instant Pot and cook for 6 minutes on High Pressure.
6. Once the timer beeps, do a quick pressure release. Carefully open the lid.
7. Select the Sauté mode. Stir in the capers and tuna. Sauté for 3 to 4 minutes.
8. Serve topped with the cheese.

## Mustard Macaroni and Cheese

**Prep time: 10 minutes | Cook time: 6 minutes | Serves 4 to 6**

1 pound (454 g) elbow macaroni
4 cups chicken broth or vegetable broth, low sodium
3 tablespoons unsalted butter
½ cup sour cream
3 cups shredded Cheddar cheese,
about 12 ounces (340 g)
½ cup shredded Parmesan cheese, about 2 ounces (57 g)
1½ teaspoons yellow mustard
⅛ teaspoon cayenne pepper

1. Add the macaroni, broth, and butter to your Instant Pot.
2. Secure the lid. Press the Manual button on the Instant Pot and set the cooking time for 6 minutes on High Pressure.

3. Once cooking is complete, perform a quick pressure release. Carefully remove the lid.
4. Stir in the sour cream, cheese, mustard, and cayenne pepper.
5. Let stand for 5 minutes. Stir well.
6. Serve immediately.

## Lemony Parmesan Risotto with Peas

**Prep time: 10 minutes | Cook time: 15 minutes | Serves 4**

1 tablespoon extra-virgin olive oil
2 tablespoons butter, divided
1 yellow onion, chopped
1½ cups Arborio rice
2 tablespoons lemon juice
3½ cups chicken stock, divided
1½ cups frozen peas,
thawed
2 tablespoons parsley, finely chopped
2 tablespoons parmesan, finely grated
1 teaspoon grated lemon zest
Salt and ground black pepper, to taste

1. Press the Sauté button on your Instant Pot. Add and heat the oil and 1 tablespoon of butter.
2. Add the onion and cook for 5 minutes, stirring occasionally. Mix in the rice and cook for an additional 3 minutes, stirring occasionally.
3. Stir in the lemon juice and 3 cups of stock.
4. Lock the lid. Select the Manual function and set the cooking time for 5 minutes at High Pressure.
5. Once cooking is complete, do a quick pressure release. Carefully open the lid.
6. Select the Sauté function again. Fold in the remaining ½ cup of stock and the peas and sauté for 2 minutes.
7. Add the remaining 1 tablespoon of butter, parsley, parmesan, lemon zest, salt, and pepper and stir well.
8. Serve.

## Cheesy Spaghetti with Ground Turkey

**Prep time: 10 minutes | Cook time: 16 minutes | Serves 4 to 6**

1 teaspoon olive oil
1 pound (454 g) ground turkey
1 clove garlic, minced
¼ onion, diced
8 ounces (227 g) whole wheat spaghetti, halved
1 jar (25-ounce

/ 709-g) Delallo Pomodoro Tomato-Basil Sauce (or of your choice)
¾ teaspoon kosher salt
2 cups water
shredded Parmesan cheese (optional)

1. Set your Instant Pot to Sauté. Add and heat the oil.
2. Add the ground turkey and sauté for 3 minutes.
3. Fold in the garlic and onion. Sauté for another 4 minutes.
4. Mix in the spaghetti, sauce and salt. Add the water to the pot and stir to combine.
5. Secure the lid. Press the Manual button on the Instant Pot and cook for 9 minutes on High Pressure.
6. Once the cooking is complete, do a quick pressure release. Carefully remove the lid.
7. Serve topped with the shredded cheese.

## Tuna Noodle Casserole with Cheese

**Prep time: 10 minutes | Cook time: 3 minutes | Serves 6**

12 ounces (340 g) egg noodles
1 (8- to 12-ounce / 227- to 340-g) can tuna albacore chunk preferred, drained
1 cup of frozen peas
1 cup of mushrooms, sliced
3 cup of chicken

broth
1 teaspoon of salt
1 teaspoon of garlic powder
½ teaspoon of pepper (optional)
1.5 cup of cheese
1 cup half and half
Hot water and cornstarch as needed

1. Stir together all the ingredients except the cheese and half and half in your Instant Pot.
2. Lock the lid. Press the Manual button and cook for 3 minutes at High Pressure.

3. Once cooking is complete, use a quick pressure release. Carefully remove the lid.
4. Add the cheese and half and half and stir until the cheese has melted. Let stand for about 5 minutes until thickened.
5. Combine some hot water and some cornstarch in a medium bowl and add to the pot to thicken quicker.
6. Serve.

## Chicken and Broccoli Rice

**Prep time: 5 minutes | Cook time: 20 minutes | Serves 4 to 6**

2 tablespoons butter
2 cloves garlic, minced
1 onion, chopped
1½ pounds (680 g) boneless chicken breasts, sliced
Salt and ground black pepper, to taste

$1^{1}/_{3}$ cups chicken broth
$1^{1}/_{3}$ cups long grain rice
½ cup milk
1 cup broccoli florets
½ cup grated Cheddar cheese

1. Set your Instant Pot to Sauté and melt the butter.
2. Add the garlic, onion, and chicken pieces to the pot. Season with salt and pepper to taste.
3. Sauté for 5 minutes, stirring occasionally, or until the chicken is lightly browned.
4. Stir in the chicken broth, rice, milk, broccoli, and cheese.
5. Lock the lid. Select the Manual mode and set the cooking time for 15 minutes at High Pressure.
6. When the timer beeps, perform a natural pressure release for 10 minutes, then release any remaining pressure. Carefully remove the lid.
7. Divide into bowls and serve.

## Pesto Farfalle with Cherry Tomatoes

**Prep time: 5 minutes | Cook time: 8 to 9 minutes | Serves 2 to 4**

| | |
|---|---|
| 1½ cup farfalle | sauce |
| 4 cups water | 1 cup cherry |
| ¾ cup vegan pesto | tomatoes, quartered |

1. Place the farfalle and water in your Instant Pot.
2. Secure the lid. Press the Manual button and cook for 7 minutes at High Pressure.
3. Once cooking is complete, do a quick pressure release. Carefully remove the lid.
4. Drain the pasta and transfer it back to the pot.
5. Stir in the sauce.
6. Press the Sauté button on your Instant Pot and cook for 1 to 2 minutes.
7. Fold in the tomatoes and stir to combine.
8. Transfer to a serving dish and serve immediately.

## Breakfast Risotto with Apples

**Prep time: 5 minutes | Cook time: 11 minutes | Serves 4 to 6**

| | |
|---|---|
| 2 tablespoons butter | 1 cup apple juice |
| 1½ cups Arborio rice | 1½ teaspoons |
| 2 apples, cored and sliced | cinnamon powder |
| | Salt, to taste |
| $1/_3$ cup brown sugar | ½ cup dried cherries |
| 3 cups milk | |

1. Set the Instant Pot to Sauté. Add and melt the butter.
2. Add the rice and cook for 5 minutes, stirring occasionally.
3. Stir in the apples, sugar, milk, apple juice, cinnamon and salt.
4. Lock the lid. Press the Manual button and cook for 6 minutes at High Pressure.
5. Once cooking is complete, use a natural pressure release for 6 minutes and then release any remaining pressure. Carefully remove the lid.
6. Fold in the cherries and stir well. Secure the lid and let stand for another 5 minutes.
7. Serve.

## Carrot and Pea Rice

**Prep time: 10 minutes | Cook time: 23 minutes | Serves 4 to 6**

| | |
|---|---|
| 1 tablespoon olive oil | 1 cup frozen peas |
| 1 clove garlic, minced | ½ cup chopped carrots |
| ¼ cup chopped shallots | 2 teaspoons curry powder |
| 2 cups chicken broth | Salt and ground black pepper, to taste |
| 1½ cups basmati rice, rinsed | |

1. Set your Instant Pot to Sauté and heat the olive oil.
2. Add the garlic and shallots and sauté for about 3 minutes until fragrant, stirring occasionally.
3. Add the remaining ingredients to the Instant Pot and stir to incorporate.
4. Lock the lid. Select the Rice mode and set the cooking time for 20 minutes at High Pressure.
5. Once cooking is complete, do a natural pressure release for 10 minutes, then release any remaining pressure. Carefully remove the lid.
6. Fluff the rice with the rice spatula or fork. Serve warm.

## Brown Rice and Black Bean Casserole

**Prep time: 5 minutes | Cook time: 28 minutes | Serves 4 to 6**

| | |
|---|---|
| 2 cups uncooked brown rice | 1 teaspoon garlic |
| 1 cup black beans, soaked for at least 2 hours and drained | 2 teaspoons chili powder |
| 6 ounces (170 g) tomato paste | 2 teaspoons onion powder |
| 5 cups water | 1 teaspoon salt, or more to taste |

1. Place all the ingredients into the Instant Pot and stir to mix well.
2. Lock the lid. Select the Manual mode and set the cooking time for 28 minutes at High Pressure.
3. When the timer beeps, perform a quick pressure release. Carefully remove the lid.
4. Taste and add more salt, if needed. Serve immediately.

## Vegetable Basmati Rice

**Prep time: 10 minutes | Cook time: 9 to 10 minutes | Serves 6 to 8**

3 tablespoons olive oil
3 cloves garlic, minced
1 large onion, finely chopped
3 tablespoons chopped cilantro stalks
1 cup garden peas, frozen
1 cup sweet corn, frozen
2 cups basmati rice, rinsed
1 teaspoon turmeric powder
¼ teaspoon salt
3 cups chicken stock
2 tablespoons butter (optional)

1. Press the Sauté button on the Instant Pot and heat the olive oil.
2. Add the garlic, onion, and cilantro and sauté for 5 to 6 minutes, stirring occasionally, or until the garlic is fragrant.
3. Stir in the peas, sweet corn, and rice. Scatter with the turmeric and salt. Pour in the chicken stock and stir to combine.
4. Lock the lid. Select the Manual mode and set the cooking time for 4 minutes at High Pressure.
5. Once cooking is complete, do a quick pressure release. Carefully open the lid.
6. You can add the butter, if desired. Serve warm.

## Beef Congee

**Prep time: 5 minutes | Cook time: 10 minutes | Serves 4**

1 tablespoon olive oil
5 cloves garlic, minced
1 cup diced onion
1 pound (454 g) ground beef
1½ cups basmati rice, rinsed
1½ cups chicken or vegetable stock
Salt, to taste

1. Press the Sauté button on the Instant Pot and heat the olive oil.
2. Add the garlic and sauté for 30 seconds until fragrant.
3. Stir in the diced onion and beef and sauté for about 3 minutes, stirring occasionally, or until the beef begins to brown.

4. Add the basmati rice, stock, and salt to the Instant Pot. Stir well.
5. Lock the lid. Select the Manual mode and set the cooking time for 5 minutes at High Pressure.
6. When the timer beeps, perform a natural pressure release for 10 minutes, then release any remaining pressure. Carefully remove the lid.
7. Serve warm.

## Rice Bowl with Raisins and Almonds

**Prep time: 5 minutes | Cook time: 20 minutes | Serves 4**

1 cup brown rice
1 cup water
1 cup coconut milk
½ cup coconut chips
½ cup maple syrup
¼ cup raisins
¼ cup almonds
A pinch of cinnamon powder
Salt, to taste

1. Place the rice and water into the Instant Pot and give a stir.
2. Secure the lid. Select the Manual mode and set the cooking time for 15 minutes at High Pressure.
3. When the timer beeps, perform a quick pressure release. Carefully remove the lid.
4. Stir in the coconut milk, coconut chips, maple syrup, raisins, almonds, cinnamon powder, and salt.
5. Lock the lid. Select the Manual mode and set the cooking time for 5 minutes at High Pressure.
6. Once cooking is complete, do a quick pressure release. Open the lid.
7. Serve warm.

# Chapter 7 Fish and Seafood

## Fast Salmon with Broccoli

**Prep time: 5 minutes | Cook time: 5 minutes | Serves 2**

| | |
|---|---|
| 1 cup water | broccoli, cut into florets |
| 8 ounces (227 g) salmon fillets | Salt and ground black pepper, to taste |
| 8 ounces (227 g) | |

1. Pour the water into the Instant Pot and insert a trivet.
2. Season the salmon and broccoli florets with salt and pepper. Put them on the trivet.
3. Secure the lid. Select the Steam mode and set the cooking time for 5 minutes at High Pressure.
4. Once cooking is complete, do a natural pressure release for 10 minutes, then release any remaining pressure. Carefully open the lid.
5. Serve hot.

## Teriyaki Salmon

**Prep time: 5 minutes | Cook time: 0 minutes | Serves 4**

| | |
|---|---|
| 1 pound (454 g) salmon fillets | 1 tablespoon cornstarch |
| ½ cup packed light brown sugar | 1 teaspoon minced ginger |
| ½ cup rice vinegar | ¼ teaspoon garlic powder |
| ½ cup soy sauce | |

1. Place the salmon fillets into the Instant Pot.
2. Whisk together the remaining ingredients in a small bowl until well combined. Pour the mixture over the salmon fillets, turning to coat.
3. Secure the lid. Select the Manual mode and set the cooking time for 0 minutes at High Pressure.
4. Once cooking is complete, do a natural pressure release for 10 minutes, then release any remaining pressure. Carefully open the lid.
5. Serve hot.

## Easy Steamed Salmon

**Prep time: 5 minutes | Cook time: 10 minutes | Serves 2**

| | |
|---|---|
| 1 cup water | Salt and ground black pepper, to taste |
| 2 salmon fillets | |

1. Pour the water into the Instant Pot and add a trivet.
2. Season the salmon fillets with salt and black pepper to taste. Put the salmon fillets on the trivet.
3. Secure the lid. Select the Steam mode and set the cooking time for 10 minutes at High Pressure.
4. Once cooking is complete, do a natural pressure release for 10 minutes, then release any remaining pressure. Carefully open the lid.
5. Serve hot.

## Crabs with Coconut Milk

**Prep time: 10 minutes | Cook time: 9 minutes | Serves 2 to 4**

| | |
|---|---|
| 1 tablespoon olive oil | 1 can coconut milk |
| 1 onion, chopped | 1 lemongrass stalk |
| 3 cloves garlic, minced | 1 thumb-size ginger, sliced |
| 1 pound (454 g) crabs, halved | Salt and ground black pepper, to taste |

1. Set the Instant Pot to Sauté. Add and heat the oil.
2. Add the onion and sauté for 2 minutes until tender.
3. Mix in the garlic and sauté for another 1 minute until fragrant.
4. Add the crabs, coconut milk, lemongrass stalk, ginger, salt, and pepper.
5. Secure the lid. Select the Manual function and set the cooking time for 6 minutes at High Pressure.
6. Once the timer beeps, do a quick pressure release. Carefully remove the lid.
7. Transfer to a serving plate and serve immediately.

## Almond-Crusted Tilapia

**Prep time: 5 minutes | Cook time: 5 minutes | Serves 4**

| | |
|---|---|
| 1 cup water | pepper |
| 2 tablespoons Dijon mustard | 4 tilapia fillets |
| 1 teaspoon olive oil | $2/3$ cup sliced almonds |
| ¼ teaspoon lemon | |

1. Pour the water into the Instant Pot and add a trivet.
2. Whisk together the Dijon mustard, olive oil, and lemon pepper in a small bowl. Brush both sides of the tilapia fillets with the mixture.
3. Spread the almonds on a plate. Roll the fillets in the almonds until well coated. Place the fillets on top of the trivet.
4. Secure the lid. Select the Manual mode and set the cooking time for 5 minutes at High Pressure.
5. Once cooking is complete, do a quick pressure release. Carefully open the lid.
6. Divide the fillets among the plates and serve.

## Lime Tilapia Fillets

**Prep time: 10 minutes | Cook time: 2 minutes | Serves 4**

| | |
|---|---|
| 1 cup water | powder |
| 4 tablespoons lime juice | ½ teaspoon salt |
| 3 tablespoons chili | 1 pound (454 g) tilapia fillets |

1. Pour the water into Instant Pot and insert a trivet.
2. Whisk together the lime juice, chili powder, and salt in a small bowl until combined. Brush both sides of the tilapia fillets generously with the sauce. Put the tilapia fillets on top of the trivet.
3. Secure the lid. Select the Manual mode and set the cooking time for 2 minutes at High Pressure.
4. Once cooking is complete, do a quick pressure release. Carefully open the lid.
5. Remove the tilapia fillets from the Instant Pot to a plate and serve.

## Tuna Noodle Casserole

**Prep time: 5 minutes | Cook time: 4 minutes | Serves 4**

| | |
|---|---|
| 3 cups water | 1 cup frozen peas |
| 28 ounces (794 g) cream of mushroom soup | Salt and ground black pepper, to taste |
| 14 ounces (397 g) canned tuna, drained | 4 ounces (113 g) grated Cheddar cheese |
| 20 ounces (567 g) egg noodles | ¼ cup bread crumbs (optional) |

1. Combine the water and mushroom soup in the Instant Pot.
2. Stir in the tuna, egg noodles, and peas. Season with salt and pepper.
3. Secure the lid. Select the Manual mode and set the cooking time for 4 minutes at High Pressure.
4. When the timer beeps, perform a quick pressure release. Carefully remove the lid.
5. Scatter the grated cheese and bread crumbs (if desired) on top. Lock the lid and allow to sit for 5 minutes.
6. Serve warm.

## Dijon Salmon

**Prep time: 5 minutes | Cook time: 5 minutes | Serves 2**

| | |
|---|---|
| 1 cup water | Salt and ground black pepper, to taste |
| 2 fish fillets or steaks, such as salmon, cod, or halibut (1-inch thick) | 2 teaspoons Dijon mustard |

1. Add the water to the Instant Pot and insert a trivet.
2. Season the fish with salt and pepper to taste. Put the fillets, skin-side down, on the trivet and top with the Dijon mustard.
3. Secure the lid. Select the Manual mode and set the cooking time for 5 minutes at High Pressure.
4. Once cooking is complete, do a quick pressure release. Carefully open the lid.
5. Divide the fish between two plates and serve.

## Salmon Cakes

**Prep time: 15 minutes | Cook time: 9 minutes | Serves 4**

½ pound (227 g) cooked salmon, shredded
2 medium green onions, sliced
2 large eggs, lightly beaten
1 cup bread crumbs
½ cup chopped flat leaf parsley
¼ cup soy sauce
1 tablespoon Worcestershire sauce
1 teaspoon salt
½ tablespoon garlic powder
½ teaspoon cayenne pepper
¼ teaspoon celery seed
4 tablespoons olive oil, divided

1. Stir together all the ingredients except the olive oil in a large mixing bowl until combined.
2. Set your Instant Pot to Sauté and heat 2 tablespoons of olive oil.
3. Scoop out golf ball-sized clumps of the salmon mixture and roll them into balls, then flatten to form cakes.
4. Working in batches, arrange the salmon cakes in an even layer in the Instant Pot.
5. Cook each side for 2 minutes until golden brown. Transfer to a paper towel-lined plate. Repeat with the remaining 2 tablespoons of olive oil and salmon cakes.
6. Serve immediately.

## Steamed Cod and Veggies

**Prep time: 5 minutes | Cook time: 2 to 4 minutes | Serves 2**

½ cup water
Kosher salt and freshly ground black pepper, to taste
2 tablespoons freshly squeezed lemon juice, divided
2 tablespoons melted butter
1 garlic clove, minced
1 zucchini or yellow summer squash, cut
into thick slices
1 cup cherry tomatoes
1 cup whole Brussels sprouts
2 (6-ounce / 170-g) cod fillets
2 thyme sprigs or ½ teaspoon dried thyme
Hot cooked rice, for serving

1. Pour the water into your Instant Pot and insert a steamer basket.
2. Sprinkle the fish with the salt and pepper. Mix together 1 tablespoon of the lemon juice, the butter, and garlic in a small bowl. Set aside.
3. Add the zucchini, tomatoes, and Brussels sprouts to the basket. Sprinkle with the salt and pepper and drizzle the remaining 1 tablespoon of lemon juice over the top.
4. Place the fish fillets on top of the veggies. Brush with the mixture and then turn the fish and repeat on the other side. Drizzle any remaining mixture all over the veggies. Place the thyme sprigs on top.
5. Lock the lid. Select the Steam mode and set the cooking time for 2 to 4 minutes on High Pressure, depending on the thickness of the fish.
6. Once cooking is complete, use a quick pressure release. Carefully open the lid.
7. Serve the cod and veggies over the cooked rice.

## Tilapia with Pineapple Salsa

**Prep time: 10 minutes | Cook time: 2 minutes | Serves 4**

1 pound (454 g) tilapia fillets
¼ teaspoon salt
⅛ teaspoon black
pepper
½ cup pineapple salsa
1 cup water

1. Put the tilapia fillets in the center of a 1½ piece of aluminum foil. Sprinkle the salt and pepper to season.
2. Fold the sides of the aluminum foil up to resemble a bowl and pour in the pineapple salsa. Fold foil over top of tilapia fillets and crimp the edges.
3. Pour the water into the Instant Pot and insert a trivet, then put the foil packet on top of the trivet.
4. Secure the lid. Select the Manual mode and set the cooking time for 2 minutes at High Pressure.
5. Once cooking is complete, do a quick pressure release. Carefully open the lid.
6. Remove the foil packet and carefully open it. Serve the tilapia fillets hot with the salsa as garnish.

## Tilapia Fish Cakes

**Prep time: 15 minutes | Cook time: 15 minutes | Serves 4**

½ pound (227 g) cooked tilapia fillets, shredded
1½ cups bread crumbs
2 large eggs, lightly beaten
1 cup peeled and shredded russet potato
2 teaspoons lemon juice
2 tablespoons full-fat sour cream
1 teaspoon salt
¼ teaspoon black pepper
½ teaspoon chili powder
⅛ teaspoon cayenne pepper
4 tablespoons olive oil, divided

1. Mix together all the ingredients except the olive oil in a large bowl and stir until well incorporated.
2. Scoop out golf ball-sized clumps of the tilapia mixture and roll them into balls, then flatten to form cakes.
3. Set your Instant Pot to Sauté and heat 2 tablespoons of olive oil.
4. Put the tilapia cakes in the Instant Pot in an even layer. You'll need to work in batches to avoid overcrowding.
5. Sear for 2 minutes per side until golden brown. Transfer to a paper towel-lined plate. Repeat with the remaining 2 tablespoons of olive oil and tilapia cakes.
6. Serve immediately.

## Shrimp Paella with Saffron

**Prep time: 10 minutes | Cook time: 8 minutes | Serves 4**

1¾ cups store-bought chicken or vegetable broth
2 big pinches of saffron
3 tablespoons olive oil
1 medium yellow onion, chopped
1½ cups long-grain rice
1 cup drained,
chopped roasted bell peppers
1 cup drained canned fire-roasted tomatoes with garlic
Salt and freshly ground black pepper, to taste
1 pound (454 g) frozen large/jumbo shell-on, deveined shrimp

1. Mix together the broth and saffron in a mixing bowl and set aside.
2. Set your Instant Pot to Sauté. Add and heat the oil.
3. Add the onion and sauté for 4 minutes until tender. Mix in the rice and stir to coat.
4. Stir in the broth-saffron mixture, roasted peppers, tomatoes, ¾ teaspoon of salt, and pepper. Arrange the frozen shrimp on the rice mixture.
5. Secure the lid. Select the Manual mode and cook for 4 minutes on High Pressure.
6. When the timer beeps, do a natural pressure release for 10 minutes and then release any remaining pressure. Carefully open the lid.
7. Transfer the paella to a serving dish. Serve immediately.

## White Fish and Vegetables

**Prep time: 15 minutes | Cook time: 15 minutes | Serves 2**

1 cup water
2 fillets white fish
½ pound (227 g) frozen vegetables of your choice
2 teaspoons grated ginger
1 clove garlic,
minced
¼ long red chili, sliced
2 tablespoons soy sauce
1 tablespoon honey
Salt and ground black pepper, to taste

1. Pour the water into the Instant Pot and place the trivet in the bottom of the pot.
2. Place the vegetables in a pan. Put the pan on the trivet.
3. Stir together the ginger, garlic, red chili, soy sauce, honey, salt, and pepper in a bowl. Add the fillets and stir until well coated.
4. Lay the fish fillets on the vegetables.
5. Secure the lid. Select the Steam function and cook for 15 minutes at Low Pressure.
6. When the timer goes off, do a natural pressure release for 10 minutes and then release any remaining pressure. Carefully open the lid.
7. Transfer to a serving plate and serve.

## Mayonnaise Salmon

**Prep time: 5 minutes | Cook time: 15 minutes | Serves 4 to 6**

| | |
|---|---|
| ½ cup mayonnaise | salmon fillets |
| 4 cloves garlic, minced | Salt and ground pepper, to taste |
| 1 tablespoon lemon juice | 2 tablespoons olive oil |
| 1 teaspoon dried basil leaves | Chopped green onion, for garnish |
| 2 pounds (907 g) | |

1. Stir together the mayo, garlic, lemon juice, and basil in a bowl. Set aside.
2. Season the salmon fillets with salt and pepper to taste.
3. Press the Sauté button on the Instant Pot and heat the olive oil.
4. Add the seasoned fillets and brown each side for 5 minutes. Add the mayo mixture to the Instant Pot and coat the fillets. Continue cooking for another 5 minutes, flipping occasionally.
5. Remove from the Instant Pot to a plate and serve garnished with the green onions.

## Fish Tacos with Cabbage

**Prep time: 15 minutes | Cook time: 5 minutes | Serves 4**

| | |
|---|---|
| 1 cup water | mayonnaise |
| 3 tablespoons olive oil | 1 tablespoon lime juice |
| 1 (1-ounce / 28-g) packet taco seasoning | 1 teaspoon sriracha |
| 1 pound (454 g) cod fillets | ⅛ teaspoon cumin |
| 3 tablespoons full-fat sour cream | ⅛ teaspoon garlic powder |
| 3 tablespoons | 8 small corn tortillas |
| | 1 cup shredded red cabbage |

1. Add the water to your Instant Pot and place the trivet inside the pot.
2. Combine the oil and taco seasoning in a small bowl. Brush the cod with the mixture. Lay the seasoned cod on the trivet.
3. Lock the lid. Select the Manual mode and cook for 5 minutes at Low Pressure.

4. Once cooking is complete, perform a quick pressure release. Carefully open the lid.
5. Meanwhile, stir together the sour cream, mayonnaise, lime juice, sriracha, cumin, and garlic powder in another small bowl.
6. Serve the cod wrapped in the tortillas with the sauce and cabbage.

## Braised Squid in Tomato Sauce

**Prep time: 5 minutes | Cook time: 27 minutes | Serves 4**

| | |
|---|---|
| 2 tablespoons olive oil | sliced squid |
| 1 medium yellow onion, chopped | 1 (14-ounce / 397-g) can diced tomatoes with Italian herbs, with juice |
| 1 teaspoon dried oregano | Salt and freshly ground black pepper, to taste |
| 4 medium garlic cloves, chopped | Lemon wedges, for garnish |
| ¼ cup dry red wine | |
| 1 pound (454 g) frozen cleaned and | |

1. Set your Instant Pot to Sauté. Add and heat the oil.
2. Add the onion and sauté for 6 minutes until slightly browned. Fold in the oregano and garlic and cook for 45 seconds until fragrant.
3. Pour in the wine and let simmer for 1 minute, scraping any browned bits out of the bottom of the pot.
4. Mix in the squid, tomatoes, and several grinds of pepper. Secure the lid. Select the Manual setting and cook for 20 minutes at High Pressure.
5. Once cooking is complete, do a quick pressure release. Carefully remove the lid. Sprinkle with the salt and pepper.
6. Transfer to a serving plate and serve with the lemon wedges, if desired.

## Shrimp Scampi with Tomatoes

**Prep time: 10 minutes | Cook time: 3 minutes | Serves 2 to 4**

2 tablespoons olive oil
1 clove garlic, minced
1 pound (454 g) shrimp, peeled and deveined
10 ounces (284 g) canned tomatoes, chopped
$1/_3$ cup tomato paste
$1/_3$ cup water
1 tablespoon parsley, finely chopped
¼ teaspoon dried oregano
½ teaspoon kosher salt
½ teaspoon ground black pepper, to taste
1 cup grated Parmesan Cheese

1. Set the Instant Pot to Sauté. Add and heat the oil.
2. Add the garlic and sauté for 1 minute until fragrant.
3. Stir in the shrimp, tomatoes, tomato paste, water, parsley, oregano, salt and pepper.
4. Secure the lid. Select the Manual function and cook for 3 minutes on High Pressure.
5. When the timer beeps, do a quick pressure release. Carefully remove the lid.
6. Serve scattered with the Parmesan Cheese.

## Fast Salmon with Broccoli

**Prep time: 5 minutes | Cook time: 8 minutes | Serves 2**

2 cup water
8 ounces (227 g) salmon fillets
8 ounces (227 g)
broccoli, cut into florets
Salt and ground black pepper, to taste

1. Pour the water into the Instant Pot and insert a trivet.
2. Season the salmon and broccoli florets with salt and pepper. Put them on the trivet.
3. Secure the lid. Select the Steam mode and set the cooking time for 8 minutes at High Pressure.
4. Once cooking is complete, do a natural pressure release for 10 minutes, then release any remaining pressure. Carefully open the lid.
5. Serve hot.

## Wild Alaskan Cod with Cherry Tomatoes

**Prep time: 5 minutes | Cook time: 8 minutes | Serves 2**

1 large fillet wild Alaskan Cod
1 cup cherry tomatoes, chopped
Salt and ground black pepper, to taste
2 tablespoons butter

1. Add the tomatoes to your Instant Pot. Top with the cod fillet. Sprinkle with the salt and pepper.
2. Secure the lid. Press the Manual button on your Instant Pot and set the cooking time for 8 minutes on High Pressure.
3. Once the timer goes off, perform a quick pressure release. Carefully remove the lid.
4. Add the butter to the cod fillet. Secure the lid and let stand for 1 minute.
5. Transfer to a serving plate and serve.

## Garlic and Lemon Cod

**Prep time: 10 minutes | Cook time: 5 minutes | Serves 4**

1 pound (454 g) cod fillets
4 cloves garlic, smashed
1 medium lemon, cut into wedges
½ teaspoon salt
¼ teaspoon black pepper
1 tablespoon olive oil
1 cup water

1. Place the cod, garlic, and lemon in the center of aluminum foil. Sprinkle with the salt and pepper. Drizzle the oil over the top. Fold the foil up on all sides and crimp the edges tightly.
2. Place the trivet in the bottom of your Instant Pot. Pour in the water. Carefully lower the foil packet into the pot.
3. Secure the lid. Select the Manual mode and cook for 5 minutes on Low Pressure.
4. Once the timer goes off, do a quick release pressure. Carefully open the lid.
5. Lift the foil packet out of your Instant Pot. Carefully open the foil packet.
6. Squeeze fresh lemon juice over the cod and serve.

## Cod Fillets with Lemon and Dill

**Prep time: 5 minutes | Cook time: 5 minutes | Serves 2**

1 cup water
2 cod fillets
¼ teaspoon garlic powder
Salt and ground

black pepper, to taste
2 sprigs fresh dill
4 slices lemon
2 tablespoons butter

1. Add the water to the Instant Pot and put the trivet in the bottom of the pot.
2. Arrange the cod fillets on the trivet. Sprinkle with the garlic powder, salt, and pepper.
3. Layer 1 sprig of dill, 2 lemon slices, and 1 tablespoon of butter on each fillet.
4. Secure the lid. Select the Manual mode and set the cooking time for 5 minutes on High Pressure.
5. Once the timer beeps, use quick pressure release. Carefully remove the lid.
6. Serve.

## Shrimp and Sausage Boil

**Prep time: 5 minutes | Cook time: 4 minutes | Serves 2**

½ pound (227 g) red potatoes, halved
1 cup water
2 ears of corn, shucked and broken in half
1 medium sweet onion, chopped
½ pound (227 g) fully cooked kielbasa sausage, cut into 2-inch slices

2 tablespoons crab boil seasoning (optional)
2 tablespoons Old Bay seasoning, plus more for seasoning
½ teaspoon kosher salt
1 pound (454 g) peel-on large raw shrimp, deveined

1. Mix together the potatoes, water, corn, onion, kielbasa, the crab boil seasoning (if desired), 2 tablespoons of Old Bay, and salt in your Instant pot.
2. Lock the lid. Select the Manual mode and cook for 4 minutes on High Pressure.
3. Once cooking is complete, do a quick pressure release. Carefully open the lid.
4. Mix in the shrimp and stir well. Replace the lid loosely and let stand for 3 to 4 minutes. Sprinkle with the salt and Old Bay. Transfer the shrimp to a large colander and drain.
5. Serve.

## Red Snapper Poached in Salsa

**Prep time: 5 minutes | Cook time: 3 to 4 minutes | Serves 2**

2 (6-ounce / 170-g) snapper fillets
1 teaspoon kosher salt
½ teaspoon freshly ground black pepper

1½ cups fresh salsa
¼ cup pale lager beer or water
½ lime
Cooked rice, for serving

1. Place the trivet inside the inner pot of your Instant Pot.
2. Sprinkle the fish with the salt and pepper. Pour the salsa and beer into the pot and top with the fish. Squeeze the fresh lime juice over the fish and salsa.
3. Lock the lid. Select the Manual mode and set the cooking time for 3 to 4 minutes on High Pressure, depending on the thickness of the fish.
4. Once the cooking is complete, use a quick pressure release. Carefully open the lid.
5. Transfer the fish to a serving plate and serve over rice.

## Steamed Fish with Tomatoes and Olives

**Prep time: 15 minutes | Cook time: 10 minutes | Serves 4**

4 white fish fillets
1 cup water
1 cup olives, pitted and chopped
1 pound (454 g) cherry tomatoes, cut into halves

1 tablespoon olive oil
½ teaspoon dried thyme
1 clove garlic, minced
Salt and ground black pepper, to taste

1. Pour the water into the Instant Pot and insert a steamer basket.
2. Add the fish fillets to the basket. Top with the olives and tomato halves. Stir in the olive oil, thyme, garlic, salt, and pepper.
3. Secure the lid. Press the Manual button on your Instant Pot and set the cooking time for 10 minutes on Low Pressure.
4. Once the timer beeps, do a natural pressure release for 10 minutes. Carefully remove the lid.
5. Serve the fish with the mix.

## Crab Bisque

**Prep time: 5 minutes | Cook time: 3 minutes | Serves 4**

4 tablespoons grass-fed butter, softened
1 pound (454 g) frozen crab meat, thawed
3 cups grass-fed bone broth
1 (14-ounce / 397-g) can sugar-free crushed tomatoes
8 ounces (227 g) full-fat cream cheese, softened
¼ cup heavy whipping cream

¼ cup chopped bell peppers
2 stalks celery, chopped
¼ small onion, thinly sliced
1 teaspoon Old Bay seasoning
½ teaspoon ground cayenne pepper
½ teaspoon kosher salt
½ teaspoon freshly ground black pepper

1. Press the Sauté button on the Instant Pot and melt the butter.
2. Add the remaining ingredients to the Instant Pot and stir to combine.
3. Secure the lid. Select the Manual mode and set the cooking time for 3 minutes at Low Pressure.
4. Once cooking is complete, do a quick pressure release. Carefully open the lid.
5. If you prefer a smoother soup, you can purée it with an immersion blender.
6. Ladle into bowls and serve hot.

## Honey Salmon

**Prep time: 10 minutes | Cook time: 0 minutes | Serves 4**

**Salmon:**
1 cup water
1 pound (454 g) salmon fillets

½ teaspoon salt
¼ teaspoon black pepper

**Sauce:**
½ cup honey
4 cloves garlic, minced
4 tablespoons soy sauce

2 tablespoons rice vinegar
1 teaspoon sesame seeds

1. Pour the water into the Instant Pot and insert a trivet.
2. Season the salmon fillets with salt and pepper to taste, then place on the trivet.

3. Secure the lid. Select the Manual mode and set the cooking time for 0 minutes at High Pressure.
4. Once cooking is complete, do a natural pressure release for 10 minutes, then release any remaining pressure. Carefully open the lid.
5. Meanwhile, whisk together all the ingredients for the sauce in a small bowl until well mixed.
6. Transfer the fillets to a plate and pour the sauce over them. Serve hot.

## Mussels in White Wine

**Prep time: 10 minutes | Cook time: 6 minutes | Serves 4**

6 tablespoons butter
4 shallots, chopped
1 cup white wine
1½ cups chicken

stock
3 pounds (1.4 kg) mussels, cleaned and debearded

1. Set your Instant Pot to Sauté and melt the butter.
2. Add the shallots and sauté for 2 minutes.
3. Pour the white wine into the pot, stir, and cook for 1 minute more.
4. Stir in the chicken stock and mussels.
5. Secure the lid. Select the Manual mode and set the cooking time for 3 minutes at High Pressure.
6. When the timer beeps, perform a quick pressure release. Carefully remove the lid.
7. Serve hot.

## Simple Crab Legs

**Prep time: 5 minutes | Cook time: 3 minutes | Serves 5**

1 cup water
2 pounds (907 g) crab legs, thawed

1. Pour the water into the Instant Pot and add a trivet. Put the crab legs on the trivet.
2. Secure the lid. Select the Manual mode and set the cooking time for 3 minutes at High Pressure.
3. Once cooking is complete, do a quick pressure release. Carefully open the lid.
4. Transfer the crab legs to a plate and serve.

## Creamy Tuna and Eggs

**Prep time: 5 minutes | Cook time: 15 minutes | Serves 4**

| | |
|---|---|
| 2 cans tuna, drained | ½ cup water |
| 2 eggs, beaten | ¾ cup milk |
| 1 can cream of celery soup | ¼ cup diced onions |
| 2 carrots, peeled and chopped | 2 tablespoons butter |
| 1 cup frozen peas | Salt and ground black pepper, to taste |

1. Combine all the ingredients in the Instant Pot and stir to mix well.
2. Secure the lid. Select the Manual mode and set the cooking time for 15 minutes at High Pressure.
3. Once cooking is complete, do a quick pressure release. Carefully open the lid.
4. Divide the mix into bowls and serve.

## Citrus Mahi Mahi

**Prep time: 5 minutes | Cook time: 4 minutes | Serves 4**

| | |
|---|---|
| ½ cup filtered water | ½ teaspoon garlic, minced |
| 3 tablespoons grass-fed butter, softened | ½ teaspoon kosher salt |
| 1 tablespoon grated ginger | ½ teaspoon freshly ground black pepper |
| ½ lime, juiced | 4 mahi mahi fillets |
| ½ lemon, juiced | Cooking spray |
| ½ teaspoon dried basil | |

1. Add the water to the Instant Pot and place the trivet inside the pot.
2. Mix together the butter, ginger, lime juice, lemon juice, basil, garlic, salt, and black pepper in a large bowl. Stir well.
3. Add the mahi mahi filets to this mixture and stir to coat. Spray an Instant Pot-friendly dish with cooking spray and place the fillets in the dish.
4. Place the dish onto the pot and wrap loosely in aluminum foil.
5. Secure the lid. Select the Manual mode and cook for 4 minutes on Low Pressure.
6. Once cook is complete, do a quick pressure release. Carefully open the lid.
7. Transfer the fillets to a serving plate and serve immediately.

## Cod with Orange Sauce

**Prep time: 10 minutes | Cook time: 7 minutes | Serves 4**

| | |
|---|---|
| 4 cod fillets, boneless | Salt and ground black pepper, to taste |
| 1 cup white wine | 4 spring onions, chopped |
| Juice from 1 orange | |
| A small grated ginger piece | |

1. Combine the wine, orange juice, and ginger in your Instant Pot and stir well.
2. Insert a steamer basket. Arrange the cod fillets on the basket. Sprinkle with the salt and pepper.
3. Secure the lid. Press the Manual button on your Instant Pot and set the cooking time for 7 minutes on High Pressure.
4. Once the timer beeps, do a quick pressure release. Carefully remove the lid.
5. Drizzle the sauce all over the fish and sprinkle with the green onions.
6. Transfer to a serving plate and serve immediately.

## Lemony Shrimp

**Prep time: 10 minutes | Cook time: 3 minutes | Serves 4 to 6**

| | |
|---|---|
| 2 tablespoons butter | 2 pounds (907 g) shrimp |
| 1 tablespoon lemon juice | Salt and ground black pepper, to taste |
| 1 tablespoon garlic, minced | 1 tablespoon parsley, for garnish |
| ½ cup chicken stock | |
| ½ cup white wine | |

1. Place the butter, lemon juice, and garlic in your Instant Pot.
2. Stir in the stock and wine.
3. Add the shrimp and sprinkle with the salt and pepper. Stir well.
4. Secure the lid. Press the Manual button on your Instant Pot and set the cooking time for 3 minutes at High Pressure.
5. Once the timer beeps, do a quick pressure release. Carefully remove the lid.
6. Serve topped with the parsley.

## Curry-Flavored Shrimp

**Prep time: 10 minutes | Cook time: 4 minutes | Serves 2 to 4**

2 cups water
1 pound (454 g) shrimp, peeled and deveined
8 ounces (227 g) unsweetened coconut milk

1 teaspoon curry powder
1 tablespoon garlic, minced
Salt and ground black pepper, to taste

1. Pour the water into the Instant Pot and insert a trivet.
2. Mix together the shrimp, coconut milk, curry powder, and garlic in a large bowl. Sprinkle with the salt and pepper.
3. Add the mixture to the pan and place the dish onto the trivet, uncovered.
4. Secure the lid. Press the Manual button on the Instant Pot and cook for 4 minutes at Low Pressure.
5. Once cooking is complete, use a quick pressure release. Carefully open the lid.
6. Stir well and serve.

## Steamed Shrimp with Asparagus

**Prep time: 10 minutes | Cook time: 2 minutes | Serves 2**

1 pound (454 g) shrimp, frozen or fresh, peeled and deveined
1 cup water
6 ounces (170 g)

asparagus
1 teaspoon olive oil
½ tablespoon Cajun seasoning (or your choice of seasoning)

1. Pour the water into the Instant pot and place the trivet inside the pot.
2. Place the asparagus onto the trivet.
3. Arrange the shrimp on the asparagus and drizzle the olive oil over the top. Season with Cajun seasoning.
4. Press the Steam button on the Instant pot and cook for 2 minutes at Low Pressure.
5. Once the timer beeps, do a quick pressure release. Carefully remove the lid.
6. Transfer to a serving plate and serve immediately.

## Shrimp Spaghetti with Parmesan

**Prep time: 5 minutes | Cook time: 10 minutes | Serves 4**

6 tablespoons butter, divided
12 ounces (340 g) small shrimp, peeled and deveined
½ teaspoon salt
4 cups chicken broth
1 pound (454 g)

spaghetti
1 cup grated Parmesan cheese
1 cup heavy whipping cream
1 teaspoon lemon pepper

1. Set your Instant Pot to Sauté and add 2 tablespoons of butter.
2. Add the shrimp and salt to the Instant Pot and sauté for 4 minutes, or until the flesh is pink and opaque. Remove the shrimp and set aside.
3. Add the broth and scrape up any bits on the bottom of the pot.
4. Break the spaghetti in half and add to the pot. Place the remaining 4 tablespoons of butter on top.
5. Secure the lid. Press the Manual button on the Instant Pot and cook for 5 minutes on High Pressure.
6. Once the timer goes off, use a quick pressure release. Carefully open the lid.
7. Fold in the cooked shrimp, Parmesan, cream, and lemon pepper. Stir until thoroughly combined.
8. Transfer to a serving plate and serve hot.

## Chili-Lemon Sockeye Salmon

**Prep time: 5 minutes | Cook time: 5 minutes | Serves 4**

4 wild sockeye
salmon fillets
¼ cup lemon juice
2 tablespoons
assorted chili pepper
seasoning
Salt and ground
black pepper, to taste
1 cup water

1. Drizzle the salmon fillets with lemon juice. Season with the chili pepper seasoning, salt, and pepper.
2. Pour the water into the Instant Pot and add a steamer basket. Put the salmon fillets in the steamer basket.
3. Secure the lid. Select the Manual mode and set the cooking time for 5 minutes at High Pressure.
4. Once cooking is complete, do a quick pressure release. Carefully open the lid.
5. Remove from the Instant Pot and serve.

## Lemon Octopus

**Prep time: 10 minutes | Cook time: 15 to 20 minutes | Serves 6**

1 cup water
3 tablespoons freshly
squeezed lemon juice
2½ pounds (1.1
kg) whole octopus,
cleaned and sliced
Salt and ground
black pepper, to taste

1. Pour the water and lemon juice into the Instant Pot.
2. Add the octopus, salt, and pepper and stir to mix well.
3. Secure the lid. Select the Manual mode and set the cooking time for 15 minutes at High Pressure.
4. Once cooking is complete, do a quick pressure release. Carefully open the lid.
5. If the octopus are not tender enough, return to the pot and cook for another 5 minutes.
6. Serve warm.

## Simple Scallops

**Prep time: 10 minutes | Cook time: 6 minutes | Serves 2**

1 cup water
1 pound (454 g)
sea scallops, shells
removed
1 tablespoon olive oil
½ cup soy sauce
3 tablespoons maple
syrup
½ teaspoon garlic
powder
½ teaspoon ground
ginger
½ teaspoon salt

1. Pour the water into the Instant Pot and insert a trivet.
2. Toss the scallops, olive oil, soy sauce, maple syrup, garlic powder, ginger, and salt in a baking pan until well coated. Place the pan on the trivet.
3. Lock the lid. Select the Steam mode and set the cooking time for 6 minutes at High Pressure.
4. Once cooking is complete, do a quick pressure release. Carefully open the lid.
5. Allow to cool for 5 minutes in the pan before removing and serving.

## Huli Huli Chicken

**Prep time: 5 minutes | Cook time: 10 minutes | Serves 8**

1 cup crushed pineapple, drained
$1/_3$ cup reduced-sodium soy sauce
¾ cup ketchup
3 tablespoons lime juice
3 tablespoons packed brown sugar
1 garlic clove, minced
8 boneless, skinless chicken thighs, about 2 pounds (907 g)
Hot cooked rice, for serving

1. Mix together the pineapple, soy sauce, ketchup, lime juice, sugar, and clove in a mixing bowl.
2. Add the chicken to your Instant Pot and place the mixture on top.
3. Secure the lid. Press the Manual button on the Instant Pot and set the cooking time for 10 minutes at High Pressure.
4. Once cooking is complete, use a natural pressure release for 5 minutes and then release any remaining pressure. Carefully open the lid.
5. Serve with the cooked rice.

## Keto Bruschetta Chicken

**Prep time: 5 minutes | Cook time: 20 minutes | Serves 2**

½ cup filtered water
2 boneless, skinless chicken breasts
1 (14-ounce / 397-g) can sugar-free or low-sugar crushed tomatoes
¼ teaspoon dried basil
½ cup shredded full-fat Cheddar cheese
¼ cup heavy whipping cream

1. Add the filtered water, chicken breasts, tomatoes, and basil to your Instant Pot.
2. Lock the lid. Press the Manual button and set the cooking time for 20 minutes on High Pressure.
3. Once cooking is complete, use a quick pressure release. Carefully open the lid.
4. Fold in the cheese and cream and stir until the cheese is melted.
5. Serve immediately.

## Orange Chicken Breasts

**Prep time: 5 minutes | Cook time: 18 minutes | Serves 4**

4 chicken breasts
¾ cup orange marmalade
¾ cup barbecue sauce
¼ cup water
2 tablespoons soy sauce
1 tablespoon cornstarch, mixed with 2 tablespoons water
2 tablespoons green onions, chopped

1. Combine all the ingredients except the cornstarch mixture and green onions in the Instant Pot.
2. Secure the lid. Select the Poultry mode and set the cooking time for 15 minutes at High Pressure.
3. Once cooking is complete, do a quick pressure release. Carefully open the lid.
4. Set your Instant Pot to Sauté and stir in the cornstarch mixture. Simmer for a few minutes until the sauce is thickened.
5. Add the green onions and stir well. Serve immediately.

## Garlic Chicken

**Prep time: 10 minutes | Cook time: 20 minutes | Serves 4**

2 chicken breasts, skinless, boneless and halved
1 cup tomato sauce
¼ cup sweet chili sauce
¼ cup chicken stock
4 garlic cloves, minced
1 tablespoon chopped basil

1. Combine all the ingredients in the Instant Pot.
2. Secure the lid. Select the Poultry mode and set the cooking time for 20 minutes at High Pressure.
3. Once cooking is complete, do a natural pressure release for 10 minutes, then release any remaining pressure. Carefully open the lid.
4. Divide the chicken breasts among four plates and serve.

## Chicken with 40 Garlic Cloves

**Prep time: 5 minutes | Cook time: 20 minutes | Serves 6**

| | |
|---|---|
| 1 tablespoon butter | Salt and pepper, to taste |
| 1 tablespoon olive oil | 40 cloves of garlic, peeled and sliced |
| 2 chicken breasts, bone and skin not removed | 2 sprigs of thyme |
| 4 chicken thighs, bone and skin not removed | ¼ cup chicken broth |
| | ¼ cup dry white wine |
| | Parsley, for garnish |

1. Set your Instant Pot to Sauté. Add the butter and oil.
2. Fold in the chicken pieces and stir well. Sprinkle with the salt and pepper.
3. Mix in the garlic cloves and sauté for an additional 5 minutes until fragrant.
4. Add the thyme, chicken broth, and white wine. Stir well.
5. Secure the lid. Select the Manual mode and set the cooking time for 15 minutes on High Pressure.
6. Once cooking is complete, use a quick pressure release. Carefully open the lid.
7. Transfer to a serving dish and serve garnished with parsley.

## Spicy Chicken and Smoked Sausage

**Prep time: 35 minutes | Cook time: 15 minutes | Serves 11**

| | |
|---|---|
| 1 (6-ounce / 170-g) can tomato paste | 1½ teaspoons dried oregano |
| 1 (14½-ounce / 411-g) can diced tomatoes, undrained | ½ teaspoon hot pepper sauce |
| 1 (14½-ounce / 411-g) can beef broth or chicken broth | 1¼ teaspoons salt |
| 2 medium green peppers, chopped | ½ teaspoon cayenne pepper |
| 1 medium onion, chopped | 1 pound (454 g) smoked sausage, halved and cut into ¼-inch slices |
| 5 garlic cloves, minced | 1 pound (454 g) boneless, skinless chicken breasts, cut into 1-inch cubes |
| 3 celery ribs, chopped | ½ pound (227 g) uncooked shrimp, peeled and deveined |
| 3 teaspoons dried parsley flakes | Hot cooked rice, for serving |
| 2 teaspoons dried basil | |

1. Mix together the tomato paste, tomatoes, and broth in your Instant Pot. Stir in the green peppers, onion, garlic, celery, and seasonings. Fold in the sausage and chicken.
2. Secure the lid. Press the Manual button and set the cooking time for 8 minutes on High Pressure.
3. Once the timer goes off, do a quick pressure release. Carefully open the lid.
4. Set the Instant Pot to sauté. Add the shrimp and stir well. Cook for another 5 minutes, or until the shrimp turn pink, stirring occasionally.
5. Serve over the cooked rice.

## Lemony Chicken With Potatoes

**Prep time: 5 minutes | Cook time: 21 minutes | Serves 4**

| | |
|---|---|
| 2 pounds (907 g) chicken thighs | ¾ cup low-sodium chicken broth |
| 1 teaspoon fine sea salt | 2 tablespoons Italian seasoning |
| ½ teaspoon ground black pepper | 2 to 3 tablespoons Dijon mustard |
| 2 tablespoons olive oil | 2 to 3 pounds (907 to 1361 g) red potatoes, quartered |
| ¼ cup freshly squeezed lemon juice | |

1. Sprinkle the chicken with the salt and pepper.
2. Add the oil to your Instant Pot. Select the Sauté mode. Add the chicken and sauté for 3 minutes until browned on both sides.
3. Meanwhile, make the sauce by stirring together the lemon juice, chicken broth, Italian seasoning, and mustard in a medium mixing bowl.
4. Drizzle the sauce over the chicken. Fold in the potatoes.
5. Secure the lid. Press the Manual button on the Instant Pot and cook for 15 minutes on High Pressure.
6. Once cooking is complete, do a quick pressure release. Carefully remove the lid.
7. Transfer the chicken to a serving dish and serve immediately.

## Indian Butter Chicken

**Prep time: 10 minutes | Cook time: 15 minutes | Serves 4**

3 tablespoons butter or ghee, at room temperature, divided
1 medium yellow onion, halved and sliced through the root end
1 (10-ounce / 284-g) can Ro-Tel tomatoes with green chilies, with juice
2 tablespoons mild

Indian curry paste
1½ pounds (680 g) boneless, skinless chicken thighs, fat trimmed, cut into 2- to 3-inch pieces
2 tablespoons all-purpose flour
Salt and freshly ground black pepper, to taste

1. Add 1 tablespoon of the butter in the Instant Pot and select the Sauté mode. Add the onion and sauté for 6 minutes until browned.
2. Stir in the tomatoes and scrape any browned bits from the pot. Add the curry paste and stir well. Fold in the chicken and stir to coat.
3. Secure the lid. Press the Manual button on the Instant Pot and cook for 8 minutes on High Pressure.
4. Once cooking is complete, use a quick pressure release.
5. Combine the remaining 2 tablespoons of butter and the flour in a small bowl and stir until smooth.
6. Select the Sauté mode. Add the flour mixture to the chicken in two additions, stirring between additions. Sauté for 1 minute, or until the sauce is thickened.
7. Sprinkle with the salt and pepper and serve.

## BBQ Chicken, Sausage, and Veggies

**Prep time: 10 minutes | Cook time: 25 minutes | Serves 8**

4 chicken drumsticks, skin removed
4 bone-in chicken thighs, skin removed
1 large sweet red pepper, cut into 1-inch pieces
1 medium onion,

chopped
1 cup chicken broth
1 (12-ounce / 340-g) package smoked sausage links, cut into 1-inch pieces
1 cup barbecue sauce

1. Place the chicken pieces, sausage, pepper, onion, and broth in the Instant Pot and drizzle with the barbecue sauce.
2. Secure the lid. Select the Manual mode and set the cooking time for 12 minutes on High Pressure.
3. Once the timer goes off, use a quick pressure release. Carefully open the lid.
4. Remove the chicken, sausage and veggies from the Instant Pot and keep warm.
5. Set the Instant Pot to Sauté and bring the liquid to a boil. Let simmer for 12 to 15 minutes, or until the sauce is thickened, stirring frequently.
6. Serve the chicken, sausage and veggies with the sauce.

## Cashew Chicken

**Prep time: 3 minutes | Cook time: 15 minutes | Serves 6**

2 pounds (907 g) chicken thighs, bones, and skin removed
¼ cup soy sauce
¼ teaspoon black pepper
2 tablespoons ketchup
2 tablespoons rice vinegar
1 clove of garlic, minced
1 tablespoon brown

sugar
1 teaspoon grated ginger
1 tablespoon cornstarch + 2 tablespoons water
$^1/_3$ cup cashew nuts, toasted
2 tablespoons sesame seeds, toasted
¼ cup green onions, chopped

1. Add all the ingredients except for the cashew nuts, sesame seeds, cornstarch slurry, and green onions to the Instant Pot and stir to combine.
2. Secure the lid. Select the Manual mode and cook for 15 minutes on High Pressure.
3. Once cooking is complete, use a quick pressure release. Carefully open the lid.
4. Select the Sauté mode and stir in the cornstarch slurry. Let simmer until the sauce is thickened.
5. Stir in the cashew nuts, sesame seeds, and green onions.
6. Transfer to a serving dish and serve immediately.

## Cheesy Black Bean Chicken

**Prep time: 10 minutes | Cook time: 8 minutes | Serves 8**

1½ pounds (680 g) boneless, skinless chicken breasts
1 medium green pepper, chopped
1 medium sweet red pepper, chopped
2 (16-ounce /454-g)

jars black bean and corn salsa
1 (12-ounce / 340-g) package tortilla chips
2 cups shredded Mexican cheese blend

1. Add the chicken, peppers, and salsa to your Instant Pot.
2. Secure the lid. Press the Manual button on the Instant Pot and set the cooking time for 8 minutes on High Pressure.
3. Once cooking is complete, use a natural pressure release for 7 minutes and then release any remaining pressure. Carefully open the lid.
4. Remove the chicken from the pot to a plate and shred with two forks.
5. Transfer the chicken back to the Instant Pot and stir to combine.
6. Serve the chicken over chips with a slotted spoon. Scatter the cheese on top.

## Chipotle Chicken Fajita

**Prep time: 15 minutes | Cook time: 10 minutes | Serves 2**

1 tablespoon oil
½ green bell pepper, sliced
¼ red onion, sliced
2 skinless, boneless chicken breasts
½ cup water
2 canned chipotle chiles in adobo sauce, deseeded and

minced
Kosher salt, to taste
3 tablespoons mayonnaise
¼ cup sour cream
½ tablespoon freshly squeezed lime juice
Freshly ground black pepper, to taste

1. Set your Instant Pot to Sauté and heat the oil until it shimmers.
2. Add the bell pepper and onion and sauté for 3 to 4 minutes until tender.
3. Remove from the Instant Pot to a small bowl and set aside to cool.
4. Add the chicken breasts, water, and a few teaspoons of adobo sauce to the pot and season with salt to taste.

5. Lock the lid. Select the Poultry mode and set the cooking time for 6 minutes at High Pressure.
6. Once cooking is complete, do a natural pressure release for 5 minutes, then release any remaining pressure. Carefully open the lid.
7. Remove the chicken from the pot to a cutting board and allow to cool for 10 minutes. Slice the chicken breasts into cubes and place in a medium bowl.
8. Add the cooked bell pepper and onion, mayo, sour cream, chipotle chiles, lime juice, salt, and pepper to the bowl of chicken and toss to coat. Serve immediately.

## Chicken Salad with Cranberries

**Prep time: 10 minutes | Cook time: 6 to 10 minutes | Serves 2**

1 pound (454 g) skinless, boneless chicken breasts
½ cup water
2 teaspoons kosher salt, plus more for seasoning
½ cup mayonnaise
1 celery stalk, diced
2 tablespoons diced red onion

½ cup chopped dried cranberries
¼ cup chopped walnuts
1 tablespoon freshly squeezed lime juice
¼ shredded unpeeled organic green apple
Freshly ground black pepper, to taste

1. Add the chicken, water, and 2 teaspoons of salt to your Instant Pot.
2. Lock the lid. Press the Poultry button on the Instant Pot and cook for 6 minutes on High Pressure.
3. Once cooking is complete, use a natural pressure release for 5 minutes and then release any remaining pressure. Carefully open the lid.
4. Remove the chicken from the Instant Pot to a cutting board and let sit for 5 to 10 minutes.
5. Shred the meat, transfer to a bowl, and add ¼ cup of the cooking liquid.
6. Mix in the mayonnaise and stir until well coated. Add the celery, onion, cranberries, walnuts, lime juice, and apple. Sprinkle with the salt and pepper.
7. Serve immediately.

## Chicken and Broccoli Rice

**Prep time: 5 minutes | Cook time: 10 minutes | Serves 4**

Cooking spray
2 boneless, skinless chicken breasts, cut into 1-inch pieces
4 cups broccoli florets
4 cups low-sodium chicken broth
1 cup long-grain white rice
½ teaspoon fine sea salt
¼ teaspoon ground black pepper
1½ cups shredded Cheddar cheese

1. Spitz the inner pot of your Instant Pot with cooking spray. Add the chicken, broccoli, broth, rice, salt, and pepper.
2. Secure the lid. Press the Manual button and set the cooking time for 10 minutes on High Pressure.
3. Once cooking is complete, do a quick pressure release. Carefully open the lid.
4. Add the cheese and stir until melted.
5. Serve immediately.

## Chili Chicken Zoodles

**Prep time: 10 minutes | Cook time: 20 minutes | Serves 4**

2 chicken breasts, skinless, boneless and halved
1½ cups chicken stock
3 celery stalks, chopped
1 tablespoon tomato sauce
1 teaspoon chili powder
A pinch of salt and black pepper
2 zucchinis, spiralized
1 tablespoon chopped cilantro

1. Mix together all the ingredients except the zucchini noodles and cilantro in the Instant Pot.
2. Secure the lid. Select the Manual mode and set the cooking time for 15 minutes at High Pressure.
3. Once cooking is complete, do a natural pressure release for 10 minutes, then release any remaining pressure. Carefully open the lid.
4. Set your Instant Pot to Sauté and add the zucchini noodles. Cook for about 5 minutes, stirring often, or until softened.
5. Sprinkle the cilantro on top for garnish before serving.

## Sweet and Sour Chicken

**Prep time: 5 minutes | Cook time: 20 minutes | Serves 8**

1 tablespoon olive oil
4 cloves garlic, minced
1 onion, chopped
2 pounds (907 g) chicken meat
1 green bell pepper, julienned
½ cup molasses
½ cup ketchup
¼ cup soy sauce
1 tablespoon cornstarch, mixed with 2 tablespoons water

1. Set your Instant Pot to Sauté and heat the olive oil.
2. Add the garlic, onion, and chicken and stir-fry for about 5 minutes until lightly golden.
3. Stir in the bell pepper, molasses, ketchup, and soy sauce.
4. Secure the lid. Select the Poultry mode and set the cooking time for 15 minutes at High Pressure.
5. Once cooking is complete, do a quick pressure release. Carefully open the lid.
6. Set your Instant Pot to Sauté again and whisk in the cornstarch mixture until thickened.
7. Allow to cool for 5 minutes before serving.

## BBQ Chicken and Potatoes

**Prep time: 5 minutes | Cook time: 10 minutes | Serves 8**

2 pounds (907 g) chicken
3 large potatoes, peeled and chopped
1 large onion, sliced
1 cup BBQ sauce
½ cup water
1 tablespoon minced garlic
1 tablespoon Italian seasoning

1. Combine all the ingredients in the Instant Pot.
2. Secure the lid. Select the Poultry mode and set the cooking time for 10 minutes at High Pressure.
3. Once cooking is complete, do a quick pressure release. Carefully open the lid.
4. Serve warm.

## Chicken Verde with Green Chile

**Prep time: 5 minutes | Cook time: 15 minutes | Serves 4**

3 pounds (1.4 kg) bone-in, skin-on chicken drumsticks and/or thighs
1 (27-ounce / 765-g) can roasted poblano peppers, drained
1 (15-ounce / 425-g) jar salsa verde (green chile salsa)
1 (7-ounce / 198-g) jar chopped green chiles, drained
1 onion, chopped
1 tablespoon chopped jalapeño (optional)
1 tablespoon ground cumin
4 teaspoons minced garlic
1 teaspoon fine sea salt

1. Mix together all the ingredients in your Instant Pot and stir to combine.
2. Secure the lid. Press the Manual button and set the cooking time for 15 minutes on High Pressure.
3. Once the timer goes off, use a quick pressure release. Carefully open the lid.
4. Remove the chicken from the Instant Pot to a plate with tongs. Let cool for 5 minutes.
5. Remove the bones and skin and discard. Shred the chicken with two forks.
6. Transfer the chicken back to the sauce and stir to combine.
7. Serve immediately.

## Asian Honey Garlic Chicken

**Prep time: 5 minutes | Cook time: 15 minutes | Serves 6**

1½ pounds (680 g) chicken breasts, cut into cubes
3 cloves of garlic, minced
6 tablespoons honey
2 tablespoons online powder
1½ tablespoons soy sauce
½ tablespoon sriracha sauce
1 cup water
1 tablespoon cornstarch + 2 tablespoons water
1 tablespoon sesame oil
Green onions, chopped

1. Add all the ingredients except the cornstarch slurry, sesame oil, and green onions to the Instant Pot and stir to combine.

2. Secure the lid. Select the Poultry mode and cook for 15 minutes on High Pressure.
3. Once the timer goes off, use a quick pressure release. Carefully open the lid.
4. Select the Sauté mode. Fold in the cornstarch slurry. Stir well.
5. Let simmer until the sauce is thickened.
6. Mix in the sesame oil and green onions and stir to combine.
7. Serve immediately.

## Chicken Lo Mein

**Prep time: 10 minutes | Cook time: 10 minutes | Serves 4**

1 tablespoon toasted sesame oil
1 garlic clove, minced
1½ pounds (680 g) boneless, skinless chicken breast, cut into bite-size pieces
8 ounces (227 g) dried linguine, broken in half
1 cup broccoli florets
1 carrot, peeled and thinly sliced
1 cup snow peas

**Sauce:**
1½ cups low-sodium chicken broth
1 tablespoon fish sauce
1 tablespoon soy sauce
1 tablespoon Shaoxing rice wine
1 tablespoon brown sugar
1 teaspoon grated fresh ginger

1. Press the Sauté button on the Instant Pot and heat the sesame oil until shimmering.
2. Add the garlic and chicken and sauté for about 5 minutes, stirring occasionally, or until the garlic is lightly browned.
3. Fan the noodles across the bottom of the Instant Pot. Top with the broccoli florets, carrot, finished by snow peas.
4. Whisk together all the ingredients for the sauce in a medium bowl until the sugar is dissolved. Pour the sauce over the top of the vegetables.
5. Secure the lid. Select the Manual mode and set the cooking time for 5 minutes at High Pressure.
6. Once cooking is complete, do a quick pressure release. Carefully open the lid.
7. Stir the noodles, breaking up any clumps, or until the liquid has absorbed. Serve warm.

## Crack Chicken with Bacon

**Prep time: 5 minutes | Cook time: 15 minutes | Serves 2**

| | |
|---|---|
| ½ cup grass-fed bone broth | ¼ cup tablespoons keto-friendly ranch dressing |
| ½ pound (227 g) boneless, skinless chicken breasts | 3 slices bacon, cooked, chopped into small pieces |
| 2 ounces (57 g) cream cheese, softened | ½ cup shredded full-fat Cheddar cheese |

1. Add the bone broth, chicken, cream cheese, and ranch dressing to your Instant Pot and stir to combine.
2. Secure the lid. Press the Manual button and set the cooking time for 15 minutes on High Pressure.
3. When the timer goes off, do a quick pressure release. Carefully open the lid.
4. Add the bacon and cheese and stir until the cheese has melted.
5. Serve.

## Browned Chicken with Veggies

**Prep time: 10 minutes | Cook time: 25 minutes | Serves 4**

| | |
|---|---|
| 2 tablespoons olive oil | bell peppers |
| 1 yellow onion, chopped | 1 cup cubed tomato |
| 2 chicken breasts, skinless, boneless and cubed | 1 cup chicken stock |
| | 1 teaspoon Creole seasoning |
| 1 cup cubed mixed | A pinch of cayenne pepper |

1. Set your Instant Pot to Sauté and heat the olive oil until hot.
2. Add the onion and chicken cubes and brown for 5 minutes. Stir in the remaining ingredients.
3. Secure the lid. Select the poultry mode and set the cooking time for 20 minutes at High Pressure.
4. Once cooking is complete, do a natural pressure release for 10 minutes, then release any remaining pressure. Carefully open the lid.
5. Serve warm.

## Authentic Belizean Stewed Chicken

**Prep time: 5 minutes | Cook time: 20 minutes | Serves 8**

| | |
|---|---|
| 1 tablespoon coconut oil | 2 tablespoons achiote seasoning |
| 3 cloves garlic, minced | 1 tablespoon granulated sugar |
| 1 onion, sliced | 1 teaspoon dried oregano |
| 4 whole chicken legs | 1 teaspoon ground cumin |
| 2 cups chicken stock | Salt and pepper, to taste |
| 3 tablespoons Worcestershire sauce | |
| 2 tablespoons white vinegar | |

1. Set your Instant Pot to Sauté and melt the coconut oil.
2. Add the garlic, onion, and chicken legs and keep stirring until the chicken legs are golden brown.
3. Add the remaining ingredients to the Instant Pot and stir to combine.
4. Secure the lid. Select the Poultry mode and set the cooking time for 15 minutes at High Pressure.
5. Once cooking is complete, do a quick pressure release. Carefully open the lid.
6. Divide the chicken legs among plates and serve.

## Simple Shredded Chicken

**Prep time: 3 minutes | Cook time: 30 minutes | Serves 8**

| | |
|---|---|
| 4 pounds (1.8 kg) chicken breasts | Salt and pepper, to taste |
| ½ cup water | |

1. Combine all the ingredients in the Instant Pot.
2. Secure the lid. Select the Poultry mode and set the cooking time for 30 minutes at High Pressure.
3. Once cooking is complete, do a natural pressure release for 10 minutes, then release any remaining pressure. Carefully open the lid.
4. Transfer the chicken breasts to a plate and shred them with two forks. Serve warm.

## Citrusy Chicken Tacos

**Prep time: 5 minutes | Cook time: 20 minutes | Serves 12**

¼ cup olive oil
12 chicken breasts, skin and bones removed
8 cloves of garlic, minced
²/₃ cup orange juice, freshly squeezed
²/₃ cup lime juice, freshly squeezed
2 tablespoons ground cumin
1 tablespoon dried oregano
1 tablespoon orange peel
Salt and pepper, to taste
¼ cup cilantro, chopped

1. Set your Instant Pot to Sauté. Add and heat the oil.
2. Add the chicken breasts and garlic. Cook until the chicken pieces are lightly browned.
3. Add the orange juice, lime juice, cumin, oregano, orange peel, salt, and pepper. Stir well.
4. Secure the lid. Select the Poultry mode and cook for 15 minutes on High Pressure.
5. Once cooking is complete, do a quick pressure release. Carefully remove the lid.
6. Serve garnished with the cilantro.

## Turkey Soup with Carrots and Orzo

**Prep time: 10 minutes | Cook time: 10 minutes | Serves 2**

2 teaspoons oil
1 small onion, diced
1 celery stalk, diced
2 carrots, diced
2 garlic cloves, minced
½ pound (227 g) chopped turkey breast tenderloin
3 cups low-sodium turkey stock, divided
¹/₃ cup orzo
1 thyme sprig or
¼ teaspoon dried thyme
1 bay leaf
Kosher salt, to taste
Freshly ground black pepper, to taste
2 cups chopped kale
1 tablespoon chopped fresh parsley
1 tablespoon freshly squeezed lemon juice

1. Press the Sauté button on the Instant Pot and heat the oil.

2. Add the onion, celery, and carrots and sauté for 3 minutes until softened.
3. Stir in the garlic and cook for 1 minute. Add the turkey, 2 cups of turkey stock, orzo, thyme sprig, and bay leaf. Sprinkle with the salt and black pepper and stir well.
4. Secure the lid. Select the Manual mode and set the cooking time for 6 minutes at High Pressure.
5. Once cooking is complete, do a natural pressure release for 4 minutes, then release any remaining pressure. Carefully open the lid.
6. Discard the thyme sprig and bay leaf. Set your Instant Pot to Sauté. Add the remaining 1 cup of turkey stock, kale, parsley, and lemon juice and stir to combine. Taste and season with salt and black pepper to taste.
7. Let the mixture simmer for 2 minutes until heated through. Serve warm.

## Chicken and Peas Casserole with Cheese

**Prep time: 10 minutes | Cook time: 30 minutes | Serves 4**

2 pounds (907 g) chicken breast, skinless, boneless and cubed
1 cup veggie stock
1 cup peas
1 tablespoon Italian seasoning
1 tablespoon sweet paprika
A pinch of salt and black pepper
1 cup coconut cream
1 cup shredded Cheddar cheese

1. Stir together the chicken cubes, veggie stock, peas, Italian seasoning, paprika, salt, and pepper in the Instant Pot. Pour the coconut cream over top.
2. Secure the lid. Select the Poultry mode and set the cooking time for 20 minutes at High Pressure.
3. Once cooking is complete, do a quick pressure release. Remove the lid.
4. Scatter the shredded cheese all over. Put the lid back on and cook on High Pressure for an additional 10 minutes.
5. Once cooking is complete, do a quick pressure release. Carefully open the lid.
6. Serve warm.

## Paprika Chicken with Cucumber Salad

**Prep time: 10 minutes | Cook time: 20 minutes | Serves 4**

1 tablespoon olive oil
1 yellow onion, chopped
2 chicken breasts, skinless, boneless and halved

1 cup chicken stock
1 tablespoon sweet paprika
½ teaspoon cinnamon powder

**Salad:**

2 cucumbers, sliced
1 tomato, cubed
1 avocado, peeled,

pitted, and cubed
1 tablespoon chopped cilantro

1. Press the Sauté button on the Instant Pot and heat the olive oil until it shimmers.
2. Add the onion and chicken breasts and sauté for 5 minutes, stirring occasionally, or until the onion is translucent. Stir in the chicken stock, paprika, and cinnamon powder.
3. Secure the lid. Select the Manual mode and set the cooking time for 15 minutes at High Pressure.
4. Meanwhile, toss all the ingredients for the salad in a bowl. Set aside.
5. Once cooking is complete, do a natural pressure release for 10 minutes, then release any remaining pressure. Carefully open the lid.
6. Divide the chicken breasts between four plates and serve with the salad on the side.

## Mongolian Chicken

**Prep time: 5 minutes | Cook time: 20 minutes | Serves 6**

2 tablespoons olive oil
10 cloves garlic, minced
1 onion, minced
4 large boneless, skinless chicken breasts, cut into cubes
1 cup water
1 cup soy sauce
1 cup brown sugar

1 cup chopped carrots
1 tablespoon garlic powder
1 tablespoon grated ginger
1 teaspoons red pepper flakes
1 tablespoon cornstarch, mixed with 2 tablespoons water

1. Set your Instant Pot to Sauté and heat the olive oil.
2. Add the garlic and onion and sauté for about 3 minutes until fragrant.
3. Add the chicken cubes and brown each side for 3 minutes. Add the remaining ingredients except the cornstarch mixture to the Instant Pot and stir well.
4. Secure the lid. Select the Poultry mode and set the cooking time for 15 minutes at High Pressure.
5. Once cooking is complete, do a natural pressure release for 10 minutes, then release any remaining pressure. Carefully open the lid.
6. Set your Instant Pot to Sauté again and whisk in the cornstarch mixture until the sauce thickens.
7. Serve warm.

## Honey-Glazed Chicken with Sesame

**Prep time: 5 minutes | Cook time: 25 minutes | Serves 6**

1 tablespoon olive oil
2 cloves garlic, minced
½ cup diced onions
4 large boneless, skinless chicken breasts
Salt and pepper, to taste
½ cup soy sauce

½ cup honey
¼ cup ketchup
2 teaspoons sesame oil
¼ teaspoon red pepper flakes
2 green onions, chopped
1 tablespoon sesame seeds, toasted

1. Press the Sauté button on the Instant Pot and heat the olive oil.
2. Add the garlic and onions and sauté for about 3 minutes until fragrant.
3. Add the chicken breasts and sprinkle with the salt and pepper. Brown each side for 3 minutes.
4. Stir in the soy sauce, honey, ketchup, sesame oil, and red pepper flakes.
5. Secure the lid. Select the Poultry mode and set the cooking time for 20 minutes at High Pressure.
6. Once cooking is complete, do a natural pressure release for 10 minutes, then release any remaining pressure. Carefully open the lid.
7. Sprinkle the onions and sesame seeds on top for garnish before serving.

## Spicy Mexican Chicken

**Prep time: 5 minutes | Cook time: 17 minutes | Serves 4**

2 tablespoons avocado oil
½ cup water
1 pound (454 g) ground chicken
1 (14-ounce / 397-g) can low-sugar fire roasted tomatoes
½ jalapeño, finely chopped
¼ poblano chili pepper, finely chopped
½ teaspoon crushed red pepper
½ teaspoon coriander
½ teaspoon chili powder
½ teaspoon curry powder
½ teaspoon kosher salt
½ teaspoon freshly ground black pepper

1. Press the Sauté button on the Instant Pot and heat the avocado oil.
2. Pour the water into the Instant Pot and stir in the remaining ingredients.
3. Secure the lid. Select the Manual mode and set the cooking time for 17 minutes at High Pressure.
4. Once cooking is complete, do a quick pressure release. Carefully open the lid.
5. Let the chicken cool for 5 minutes and serve.

## Butter Chicken (Murgh Makhani)

**Prep time: 3 minutes | Cook time: 20 minutes | Serves 4**

1 pound (454 g) chicken meat
1 can crushed tomatoes
6 cloves garlic
2 teaspoons grated ginger
1 teaspoon garam masala
1 teaspoon turmeric
1 teaspoon paprika
1 teaspoon cumin
½ teaspoon cayenne pepper

1. Combine all the ingredients in the Instant Pot.
2. Lock the lid. Select the Poultry mode and set the cooking time for 20 minutes at High Pressure.
3. Once cooking is complete, do a natural pressure release for 10 minutes, then release any remaining pressure. Carefully open the lid.
4. Serve warm.

## Creamy Chicken with Cilantro

**Prep time: 5 minutes | Cook time: 25 minutes | Serves 4**

2 chicken breasts, skinless, boneless and halved
1 cup tomato sauce
1 cup plain Greek yogurt
¾ cup coconut cream
¼ cup chopped cilantro
2 teaspoons garam masala
2 teaspoons ground cumin
A pinch of salt and black pepper

1. Thoroughly combine all the ingredients in the Instant Pot.
2. Lock the lid. Select the Poultry mode and set the cooking time for 25 minutes at High Pressure.
3. Once cooking is complete, do a natural pressure release for 5 minutes, then release any remaining pressure. Carefully open the lid.
4. Transfer the chicken breasts to a plate and serve.

## Moringa Chicken Soup

**Prep time: 3 minutes | Cook time: 18 minutes | Serves 8**

1½ pounds (680 g) chicken breasts
5 cups water
1 cup chopped tomatoes
2 cloves garlic, minced
1 onion, chopped
1 thumb-size ginger
Salt and pepper, to taste
2 cups moringa leaves or kale leaves

1. Combine all the ingredients except the moringa leaves in the Instant Pot.
2. Secure the lid. Select the Poultry mode and set the cooking time for 15 minutes at High Pressure.
3. Once cooking is complete, do a natural pressure release for 10 minutes, then release any remaining pressure. Carefully open the lid.
4. Set your Instant Pot to Sauté and stir in the moringa leaves. Allow to simmer for 3 minutes until softened.
5. Divide into bowls and serve warm.

## Chicken with White Wine Mushroom Sauce

**Prep time: 5 minutes | Cook time: 22 minutes | Serves 12**

2 tablespoons vegetable oil
4 cloves garlic, minced
1 onion, chopped
6 chicken breasts, halved
1¼ pounds (567 g) cremini mushrooms, sliced
1½ cups dry white wine
1 cup chicken broth
1 tablespoon lemon juice, freshly squeezed
1 tablespoon thyme
2 bay leaves
Salt and pepper, to taste
2 tablespoons cornstarch, mixed with 2 tablespoons water

1. Set your Instant Pot to Sauté and heat the vegetable oil.
2. Add the garlic, onion, and chicken and brown for about 5 minutes.
3. Fold in the mushrooms, white wine, chicken broth, lemon juice, thyme, bay leaves, salt, and pepper and stir to incorporate.
4. Secure the lid. Select the Poultry mode and set the cooking time for 15 minutes at High Pressure.
5. Once cooking is complete, do a quick pressure release. Carefully open the lid.
6. Set your Instant Pot to Sauté again and stir in the cornstarch mixture. Let simmer for a few minutes until the sauce is thickened.
7. Allow to cool for 5 minutes before serving.

## Turkey and Mushrooms Meatballs

**Prep time: 10 minutes | Cook time: 30 minutes | Serves 4**

1 pound (454 g) ground turkey meat
10 white mushrooms, sliced
½ cup almond meal
¼ cup grated Parmesan cheese
¼ cup parsley, chopped
1 egg, whisked
1 red onion, chopped
4 garlic cloves, minced
A pinch of salt and black pepper
2 tablespoons olive oil
1½ cups tomato sauce

1. Mix together all the ingredients except the oil and sauce in a large bowl and stir until well combined. Shape the mixture into medium meatballs with your hands.
2. Press the Sauté button on the Instant Pot and heat the olive oil.
3. Add the meatballs and brown each side for 2 minutes. Pour in the tomato sauce.
4. Secure the lid. Select the Poultry mode and set the cooking time for 25 minutes at High Pressure.
5. Once cooking is complete, do a natural pressure release for 10 minutes, then release any remaining pressure. Carefully open the lid.
6. Serve warm.

## Turkey Breast with Cauliflower Sauté

**Prep time: 10 minutes | Cook time: 35 minutes | Serves 4**

2 tablespoons olive oil
2 garlic cloves, minced
1 yellow onion, chopped
1 cup cauliflower florets
A pinch of dried rosemary
A pinch of salt and black pepper
1 cup chicken stock
2 pounds (907 g) turkey breast, skinless, boneless and sliced

1. Press the Sauté button on the Instant Pot and heat the olive oil.
2. Add the garlic, onion, cauliflower, rosemary, salt, and pepper to the Instant Pot, toss and sauté for 10 minutes, stirring occasionally. Stir in the chicken stock and turkey.
3. Secure the lid. Select the Manual mode and set the cooking time for 25 minutes at High Pressure.
4. Once cooking is complete, do a natural pressure release for 10 minutes, then release any remaining pressure. Carefully open the lid.
5. Divide the mixture among four plates and serve.

## Instant Pot Whole Chicken

**Prep time: 5 minutes | Cook time: 25 minutes | Serves 6**

4 tablespoons grass-fed butter, softened
1 teaspoon dried cilantro
1 teaspoon dried basil
½ teaspoon kosher
salt
½ teaspoon freshly ground black pepper
½ cup grass-fed bone broth
1 whole chicken

1. Stir together the softened butter, cilantro, basil, salt, and pepper in a large bowl until combined.
2. Pour the bone broth into the Instant Pot. Place the chicken in the Instant Pot with the breast facing down and lightly baste with the butter mixture.
3. Secure the lid. Select the Meat/Stew mode and set the cooking time for 25 minutes at High Pressure.
4. Once cooking is complete, do a natural pressure release for 15 minutes, then release any remaining pressure. Carefully open the lid.
5. Remove the chicken from the Instant Pot and serve.

## Paprika Chicken

**Prep time: 5 minutes | Cook time: 40 minutes | Serves 6**

1¾ tablespoons olive oil
1½ teaspoons salt
½ teaspoon pepper
1 teaspoon minced
garlic
1 teaspoon paprika
1 whole chicken
1 cup chicken broth

1. Stir together the olive oil, salt, pepper, garlic, and paprika in a small bowl. Rub the mixture all over the chicken until evenly coated.
2. Pour the chicken broth into the Instant Pot and add the coated chicken.
3. Secure the lid. Select the Poultry mode and set the cooking time for 40 minutes at High Pressure.
4. Once cooking is complete, do a natural pressure release for 15 minutes, then release any remaining pressure. Carefully open the lid.
5. Serve warm.

## Chicken Cacciatore

**Prep time: 15 minutes | Cook time: 15 minutes | Serves 6**

1 broiler/fryer chicken (3 to 4 pounds / 1.4 to 1.8 kg), cut up and skin removed
1 (4-ounce / 113-g) can mushroom stems and pieces, drained
1 (14½-ounce / 411-g) can diced tomatoes, undrained
1 (8-ounce / 227-g) can tomato sauce
¼ cup white wine or water
2 medium onions, thinly sliced
2 garlic cloves, minced
1 bay leaf
1 to 2 teaspoon dried oregano
½ teaspoon dried basil
1 teaspoon salt
¼ teaspoon pepper

1. Combine all the ingredients in the Instant Pot.
2. Secure the lid. Select the Poultry mode and set the cooking time for 15 minutes at High Pressure.
3. Once cooking is complete, do a natural pressure release for 10 minutes, then release any remaining pressure. Carefully open the lid.
4. Discard the bay leaf and serve on a plate.

## Pomegranate Glazed Turkey

**Prep time: 10 minutes | Cook time: 30 minutes | Serves 4**

1 tablespoon olive oil
1 big turkey breast, skinless, boneless and sliced
1 cup chicken stock
1 cup pomegranate seeds
1 tablespoon sweet paprika
1 tablespoon chopped cilantro
A pinch of salt and black pepper

1. Press the Sauté button on the Instant Pot and heat the olive oil.
2. Add the turkey slices and brown for about 5 minutes. Add the remaining ingredients to the Instant Pot and stir well.
3. Secure the lid. Select the Poultry mode and set the cooking time for 25 minutes at High Pressure.
4. Once cooking is complete, do a natural pressure release for 10 minutes, then release any remaining pressure. Carefully open the lid.
5. Cool for 5 minutes and serve warm.

## Garlic Lime Turkey Wings

**Prep time: 10 minutes | Cook time: 30 minutes | Serves 4**

1 tablespoon avocado oil
1 yellow onion, chopped
2 turkey wings, halved
4 garlic cloves, minced
1 cup chicken stock
2 tablespoons lime juice
1 tablespoon grated lime zest
A pinch of salt and black pepper

1. Press the Sauté button on the Instant Pot and heat the avocado oil.
2. Add the onion and sauté for 2 minutes until softened.
3. Add the remaining ingredients to the Instant Pot and mix well.
4. Secure the lid. Select the Manual mode and set the cooking time for 28 minutes at High Pressure.
5. Once cooking is complete, do a natural pressure release for 10 minutes, then release any remaining pressure. Carefully open the lid.
6. Let the turkey wings cool for 5 minutes before serving.

## Chicken Pasta Puttanesca

**Prep time: 10 minutes | Cook time: 9 minutes | Serves 4**

2 (6- to 7-ounce / 170- to 198-g) boneless, skinless chicken breasts
Salt and freshly ground black pepper, to taste
2 tablespoons olive oil
12 ounces (340 g) dry penne pasta
1 (14.5-ounce / 411-g) can diced tomatoes with Italian
herbs, with juices
2½ cups store-bought chicken or vegetable broth, or homemade
4 oil-packed rolled anchovies with capers, plus 1 tablespoon oil from the jar
½ cup oil-cured black or Kalamata olives
Pinch of red pepper flakes

1. Using paper towels, pat the chicken dry. Sprinkle with the salt and pepper.
2. Press the Sauté button on your Instant Pot. Add and heat the oil.
3. Add the chicken and cook for 3 minutes, or until the chicken is nicely browned on one side.
4. Stir in the penne, tomatoes, broth, anchovies and oil, olives, red pepper flakes, and pepper. Place the chicken on top.
5. Secure the lid. Select the Manual mode and set the cooking time for 6 minutes on Low Pressure.
6. When the timer beeps, do a quick pressure release. Carefully open the lid.
7. Remove the chicken from the Instant Pot to a cutting board and cut into bite-size pieces. Transfer the chicken back to the pot and stir until well mixed.
8. Lock the lid and let sit for 5 minutes, or until the liquid is thickened.
9. Serve immediately.

## Balsamic Caramelized Onion Turkey

**Prep time: 10 minutes | Cook time: 30 minutes | Serves 4**

1 tablespoon olive oil
2 cups red onions, sliced
2 tablespoons balsamic vinegar
2½ pounds (1.1 kg) turkey breast,
skinless, boneless and sliced
1 cup chicken stock
2 tablespoons chopped cilantro
A pinch of salt and black pepper

1. Press the Sauté button on the Instant Pot and heat the olive oil.
2. Add the onions and balsamic vinegar and sauté for 5 minutes. Stir in the turkey and cook for another 5 minutes until browned. Add the remaining ingredients to the Instant Pot.
3. Secure the lid. Select the Poultry mode and set the cooking time for 20 minutes at High Pressure.
4. Once cooking is complete, do a natural pressure release for 10 minutes, then release any remaining pressure. Carefully open the lid.
5. Divide the mix between four plates and serve warm.

## Seared Duck with Chives

**Prep time: 10 minutes | Cook time: 20 minutes | Serves 4**

1 tablespoon avocado oil
2 duck breasts, boneless, skin scored and halved
1 yellow onion, chopped
1 cup chicken stock
2 teaspoons dried thyme
A pinch of salt and black pepper
1 tablespoon chopped chives

1. Press the Sauté button on the Instant Pot and heat the avocado oil.
2. Add the halved duck breasts, skin-side down, and sear for 2 minutes until lightly browned.
3. Add the remaining ingredients except the chives to the Instant Pot.
4. Secure the lid. Select the Poultry mode and set the cooking time for 18 minutes at High Pressure.
5. Once cooking is complete, do a natural pressure release for 10 minutes, then release any remaining pressure. Carefully open the lid.
6. Serve the duck breasts with the chives sprinkled on top.

# Chapter 9 Pork

## Pork Chops with Sauerkraut

**Prep time: 15 minutes | Cook time: 30 minutes | Serves 4**

2 tablespoons olive oil
4 (1-inch-thick) bone-in pork loin chops
1 teaspoon sea salt
½ teaspoon ground black pepper
4 slices bacon, diced
3 large carrots, peeled and sliced
1 large onion, peeled and diced
1 stalk celery, finely chopped
1 clove garlic, peeled
and minced
1 (12-ounce / 340-g) bottle lager
2 medium red apples, peeled, cored, and quartered
4 medium red potatoes, peeled and quartered
1 (1-pound / 454-g) bag high-quality sauerkraut, rinsed and drained
1 tablespoon caraway seeds

1. Set your Instant Pot to Sauté. Add and heat the olive oil.
2. Sprinkle the pork chops with the salt and pepper. Working in batches, sear the pork chops for 1 to 2 minutes on each side. Set aside.
3. Add the bacon, carrots, onion, and celery to the Instant Pot. Sauté for 3 to 5 minutes, or until the onions are translucent.
4. Fold in the garlic and cook for an additional 1 minute. Pour in the beer and deglaze the bottom of the pot by scraping out any browned bits from the pot. Let simmer uncovered for 5 minutes.
5. Mix in the apples, potatoes, and sauerkraut. Sprinkle the caraway seeds on top. Slightly prop pork chops up against the sides of the pot to avoid crowding the pork.
6. Secure the lid. Select the Manual function and cook for 15 minutes on High Pressure.
7. Once the timer goes off, do a natural pressure release for 5 minutes and release any remaining pressure. Carefully remove the lid.
8. Transfer to a serving plate and serve immediately.

## Vinegary Pork Chops with Figs and Pears

**Prep time: 10 minutes | Cook time: 10 minutes | Serves 2**

2 (1-inch-thick) bone-in pork chops
1 teaspoon sea salt
1 teaspoon ground black pepper
¼ cup chicken broth
¼ cup balsamic vinegar
1 tablespoon dried mint

2 tablespoons avocado oil
5 dried figs, stems removed and halved
3 pears, peeled, cored, and diced large
1 medium sweet onion, peeled and sliced

1. Pat the pork chops dry with a paper towel and sprinkle both sides generously with the salt and pepper. Set aside.
2. Stir together the broth, vinegar, and mint in a small bowl. Set aside.
3. Set the Instant Pot to Sauté. Add and heat the oil. Sear the pork chops for 5 minutes on each side and transfer to a plate.
4. Pour in the broth mixture and deglaze the Instant Pot, scraping any browned bits from the pot.
5. Add the onions to the pot and scatter the figs and pears on top. Return the pork chops to the pot.
6. Secure the lid. Select the Steam function and cook for 3 minutes on High Pressure.
7. Once the timer goes off, do a natural pressure release for 10 minutes and then release any remaining pressure. Carefully open the lid.
8. Transfer to a serving dish with a slotted spoon. Serve immediately.

## Pork Chops with Bell Peppers

**Prep time: 10 minutes | Cook time: 35 minutes | Serves 4**

2 tablespoons olive oil
4 pork chops
1 red onion, chopped
3 garlic cloves, minced
1 red bell pepper, roughly chopped

1 green bell pepper, roughly chopped
2 cups beef stock
A pinch of salt and black pepper
1 tablespoon parsley, chopped

1. Press the Sauté on your Instant Pot. Add and heat the oil. Brown the pork chops for 2 minutes.
2. Fold in the onion and garlic and brown for an additional 3 minutes.
3. Stir in the bell peppers, stock, salt, and pepper.
4. Lock the lid. Select the Manual mode and cook for 30 minutes on High Pressure.
5. Once cooking is complete, use a natural pressure release for 10 minutes and then release any remaining pressure. Carefully open the lid.
6. Divide the mix among the plates and serve topped with the parsley.

## Honey Barbecue Baby Back Ribs

**Prep time: 10 minutes | Cook time: 25 minutes | Serves 4**

2 racks baby back ribs (3 pounds / 1.4 kg; about 4 ribs each), cut into 5- to 6-inch portions
2 tablespoons chili powder
2 tablespoons

toasted sesame oil
3 tablespoons grainy mustard
1 tablespoon red wine vinegar
1 cup ketchup
$1/3$ cup honey
½ cup chicken broth

1. Rub the ribs all over with the chili powder.
2. Mix together the remaining ingredients in your Instant Pot and stir until the honey has dissolved.
3. Dip the ribs in the sauce to coat. Using tongs, arrange the ribs standing upright against the sides of the pot.
4. Secure the lid. Select the Manual function and cook for 25 minutes on High Pressure.
5. Preheat the broiler and adjust an oven rack so that it is 4 inches below the broiler element. Line a baking sheet with aluminum foil.
6. When the timer beeps, use a natural pressure release for 15 minutes and then release any remaining pressure. Carefully open the lid.
7. Transfer the ribs with tongs to the prepared baking sheet, meaty side up.
8. Stir the cooking liquid and pour over the ribs with a spoon. Broil the ribs for 5 minutes until browned in places.
9. Transfer the ribs to a serving plate and serve warm.

## Cinnamon and Orange Pork

**Prep time: 10 minutes | Cook time: 35 minutes | Serves 4**

4 pork chops
1 tablespoon cinnamon powder
3 garlic cloves, minced
½ cup beef stock
Juice of 1 orange
1 tablespoon grated ginger
1 teaspoon dried rosemary
A pinch of salt and black pepper

1. Stir together all the ingredients in your Instant Pot.
2. Secure the lid. Press the Manual button on the Instant Pot and set the cooking time for 35 minutes on High Pressure.
3. Once cooking is complete, perform a natural pressure release for 10 minutes and then release any remaining pressure. Carefully open the lid.
4. Divide the mix among the plates and serve immediately.

## Pork Shoulder and Celery

**Prep time: 10 minutes | Cook time: 30 minutes | Serves 4**

2 tablespoons avocado oil
4 garlic cloves, minced
2 pounds (907 g) pork shoulder, boneless and cubed
1½ cups beef stock
2 celery stalks, chopped
2 tablespoons chili powder
1 tablespoon chopped sage
A pinch of salt and black pepper

1. Press the Sauté button on the Instant Pot and heat the avocado oil.
2. Add the garlic and sauté for 2 minutes until fragrant.
3. Stir in the pork and brown for another 3 minutes.
4. Add the remaining ingredients to the Instant Pot and mix well.
5. Secure the lid. Select the Manual mode and set the cooking time for 25 minutes at High Pressure.
6. Once cooking is complete, do a natural pressure release for 10 minutes, then release any remaining pressure. Carefully open the lid.
7. Serve warm.

## Pork with Cherry Sauce

**Prep time: 5 minutes | Cook time: 25 minutes | Serves 4**

4 pork chops
A pinch of salt and black pepper
1 cup beef stock
1 cup cherries, pitted
1 tablespoon
chopped parsley
1 tablespoon balsamic vinegar
1 tablespoon avocado oil

1. Press the Sauté button on the Instant Pot. Add and heat the oil.
2. Brown the pork chops for 2 minutes per side.
3. Stir in the remaining the ingredients. Secure the lid. Press the Manual button and cook for 20 minutes on High Pressure.
4. When the timer goes off, perform a natural pressure release for 5 minutes and then release any remaining pressure. Carefully open the lid.
5. Divide the mix among the plates and serve immediately.

## Jamaican Pork Roast

**Prep time: 10 minutes | Cook time: 55 minutes | Serves 6**

¼ cup Jamaican jerk spice blend
¾ tablespoon olive oil
2 pounds (907 g) pork shoulder
¼ cup beef broth

1. Rub the jerk spice blend and olive oil all over the pork shoulder and set aside to marinate for 10 minutes.
2. When ready, press the Sauté button on the Instant Pot and add the pork.
3. Sear for 4 minutes. Flip the pork and cook for 4 minutes.
4. Pour the beef broth into the Instant Pot.
5. Secure the lid. Select the Manual mode and set the cooking time for 45 minutes at High Pressure.
6. Once cooking is complete, do a natural pressure release for 10 minutes, then release any remaining pressure. Carefully open the lid.
7. Serve hot.

## Cocoa and Chili Pork

**Prep time: 10 minutes | Cook time: 30 minutes | Serves 4**

4 pork chops
2 tablespoons hot sauce
2 tablespoons cocoa powder
2 teaspoons chili powder

1 cup beef stock
¼ teaspoon ground cumin
1 tablespoon chopped parsley
A pinch of salt and black pepper

1. Stir together all the ingredients in your Instant Pot.
2. Secure the lid. Press the Manual button on the Instant Pot and set the cooking time for 30 minutes on High Pressure.
3. Once cooking is complete, perform a natural pressure release for 10 minutes and then release any remaining pressure. Carefully open the lid.
4. Divide the mix among the plates and serve with a side salad.

## Maple-Glazed Spareribs

**Prep time: 40 minutes | Cook time: 30 minutes | Serves 6**

2 racks (about 3 pounds / 1.4 kg) baby back pork ribs, cut into 2-rib sections
1 teaspoon instant coffee crystals
1 teaspoon sea salt
½ teaspoon ground cumin
½ teaspoon chili powder
½ teaspoon ground mustard
½ teaspoon cayenne pepper
½ teaspoon onion

powder
½ teaspoon garlic powder
¼ teaspoon ground coriander
¼ cup soy sauce
¼ cup pure maple syrup
2 tablespoons tomato paste
1 tablespoon apple cider vinegar
1 tablespoon olive oil
1 medium onion, peeled and large diced

1. Mix together the coffee, salt, cumin, chili powder, mustard, cayenne pepper, onion powder, garlic powder, and coriander in a mixing bowl. Rub the mixture into the rib sections with your hands. Refrigerate for at least 30 minutes, covered. Set aside.

2. Stir together the soy sauce, maple syrup, tomato paste, and apple cider vinegar in a small mixing bowl.
3. Set your Instant Pot to Sauté and heat the olive oil. Add the onions and sauté for 3 to 5 minutes until translucent.
4. Stir in the soy sauce mixture. Add a few ribs at a time with tongs and gently stir to coat. Arrange the ribs standing upright, meat-side outward. Secure the lid.
5. Select the Manual function and cook for 25 minutes on High Pressure.
6. Once cooking is complete, use a natural pressure release for 10 minutes and then release any remaining pressure. Carefully open the lid.
7. Transfer the ribs to a serving plate and serve warm.

## Pork Tenderloin with Cherry and Rosemary

**Prep time: 5 minutes | Cook time: 25 minutes | Serves 6**

2 tablespoons avocado oil
2 (3-pound / 1.4 kg) pork tenderloins, halved
½ cup balsamic vinegar
¼ cup cherry preserves

¼ cup finely chopped fresh rosemary
¼ cup olive oil
½ teaspoon sea salt
¼ teaspoon ground black pepper
4 garlic cloves, minced

1. Set your Instant Pot to Sauté. Add and heat the oil. Add the pork and brown for about 2 minutes on each side.
2. Stir together the remaining ingredients in a small bowl and pour over the pork. Secure the lid.
3. Select the Manual function and cook for 20 minutes on High Pressure.
4. Once cooking is complete, use a natural pressure release for 5 minutes and then release any remaining pressure. Carefully open the lid.
5. Remove the tenderloin from the Instant Pot to a cutting board. Let stand for 5 minutes.
6. Cut into medallions before serving.

## Paprika Pork and Brussels Sprouts

**Prep time: 10 minutes | Cook time: 30 minutes | Serves 4**

2 tablespoons olive oil
2 pounds (907 g) pork shoulder, cubed
2 cups Brussels sprouts, trimmed and halved
1½ cups beef stock
1 tablespoon sweet paprika
1 tablespoon chopped parsley

1. Press the Sauté button on the Instant Pot and heat the olive oil.
2. Add the pork and brown for 5 minutes. Stir in the remaining ingredients.
3. Secure the lid. Select the Manual mode and set the cooking time for 25 minutes at High Pressure.
4. Once cooking is complete, do a natural pressure release for 10 minutes, then release any remaining pressure. Carefully open the lid.
5. Divide the mix between plates and serve warm.

## Pork Tenderloin in Salsa

**Prep time: 20 minutes | Cook time: 15 minutes | Serves 8**

2 teaspoons grapeseed oil
3 pounds (1.4 kg) pork tenderloin, cut into slices
1 teaspoon granulated garlic
½ teaspoon dried marjoram
½ teaspoon dried thyme
1 teaspoon paprika
1 teaspoon ground cumin
Sea salt and ground black pepper, to taste
1 cup water
1 avocado, pitted, peeled, and sliced

**Salsa:**
1 cup puréed tomatoes
1 teaspoon granulated garlic
2 bell peppers, deveined and chopped
1 cup chopped onion
2 tablespoons minced fresh cilantro
3 teaspoons lime juice
1 minced jalapeño, chopped
Avocado slices, for serving

1. Press the Sauté button on your Instant Pot. Add and hear the oil. Sear the pork until nicely browned on all sides.

2. Stir in the garlic, seasonings, and water.
3. Lock the lid. Select the Manual mode and set the cooking time for 12 minutes at High Pressure.
4. Once the timer beeps, use a natural pressure release for 10 minutes. Carefully open the lid.
5. Remove the tenderloin. Shred with two forks and reserve.
6. Meanwhile, stir together all the ingredients for the salsa in a mixing bowl.
7. Spoon the salsa over the prepared pork.
8. Divide the pork among bowls and serve garnished with the avocado slices.

## Carolina-Style Pork Barbecue

**Prep time: 10 minutes | Cook time: 40 minutes | Serves 4 to 6**

1 (4-pound / 1.8-kg) boneless pork shoulder or pork butt roast
3 tablespoons packed brown sugar
1½ teaspoons
smoked paprika
1 tablespoon seasoning salt
1 cup ketchup
½ cup water
½ cup cider vinegar

1. On a clean work surface, trim any excess fat off the outside of the pork shoulder, then cut the pork into four large pieces.
2. Mix together the brown sugar, paprika, and seasoning salt in a small bowl. Rub this mixture all over the pork pieces.
3. Place the ketchup, water, and vinegar into the Instant Pot and stir well. Add the pork pieces to the pot, turning to coat.
4. Secure the lid. Select the Manual mode and set the cooking time for 40 minutes at High Pressure.
5. Once cooking is complete, do a natural pressure release for 5 minutes, then release any remaining pressure. Carefully open the lid.
6. Remove the pork pieces from the pot to a cutting board. Using two forks to shred them and discard any large chunks of fat.
7. Spoon the sauce over the pork and serve immediately.

## Pork Cutlets with Creamy Mustard Sauce

**Prep time: 20 minutes | Cook time: 13 minutes | Serves 6**

| | |
|---|---|
| 6 pork cutlets | 2 tablespoons olive |
| ½ teaspoon dried | oil |
| rosemary | ½ cup water |
| ½ teaspoon dried | ½ cup vegetable |
| marjoram | broth |
| ¼ teaspoon paprika | 1 tablespoon butter |
| ¼ teaspoon cayenne | 1 cup heavy cream |
| pepper | 1 tablespoon yellow |
| Kosher salt and | mustard |
| ground black pepper, | ½ cup shredded |
| to taste | Cheddar cheese |

1. Sprinkle both sides of the pork cutlets with rosemary, marjoram, paprika, cayenne pepper, salt, and black pepper.
2. Press the Sauté button on the Instant Pot and heat the olive oil until sizzling.
3. Add the pork cutlets and sear both sides for about 3 minutes until lightly browned.
4. Pour in the water and vegetable broth.
5. Secure the lid. Select the Manual mode and set the cooking time for 8 minutes at High Pressure.
6. When the timer beeps, perform a quick pressure release. Carefully open the lid. Transfer the pork cutlets to a plate and set aside.
7. Press the Sauté button again and melt the butter.
8. Stir in the heavy cream, mustard, and cheese and cook for another 2 minutes until heated through.
9. Add the pork cutlets to the sauce, turning to coat.
10. Remove from the Instant Pot and serve.

## Pork, Green Beans, and Corn

**Prep time: 10 minutes | Cook time: 35 minutes | Serves 4**

| | |
|---|---|
| 2 pounds (907 | 2 garlic cloves, |
| g) pork shoulder, | minced |
| boneless and cubed | 1 teaspoon ground |
| 1 cup green beans, | cumin |
| trimmed and halved | A pinch of salt and |
| 1 cup corn | black pepper |
| 1 cup beef stock | |

1. Combine all the ingredients in the Instant Pot.
2. Secure the lid. Select the Manual mode and set the cooking time for 35 minutes at High Pressure.
3. Once cooking is complete, do a natural pressure release for 10 minutes, then release any remaining pressure. Carefully open the lid.
4. Divide the mix among four plates and serve.

## Curry Pork Steak

**Prep time: 15 minutes | Cook time: 15 minutes | Serves 6**

| | |
|---|---|
| 1 teaspoon cumin | coconut cream |
| seeds | 2 tablespoons |
| 1 teaspoon fennel | balsamic vinegar |
| seeds | 2 tablespoons |
| ½ teaspoon mustard | chopped scallions |
| seeds | 2 cloves garlic, finely |
| 2 chili peppers, | minced |
| deseeded and | 1 teaspoon curry |
| minced | powder |
| 1 teaspoon mixed | 1 teaspoon grated |
| peppercorns | fresh ginger |
| ½ teaspoon ground | ¼ teaspoon crushed |
| bay leaf | red pepper flakes |
| 1 tablespoon sesame | ¼ teaspoon ground |
| oil | black pepper |
| 1½ pounds (680 g) | 1 cup vegetable |
| pork steak, sliced | broth |
| 1 cup chicken broth | Sea salt, to taste |
| 3 tablespoons | |

1. Heat a skillet over medium-high heat and roast the cumin seeds, fennel seeds, mustard seeds, peppers, peppercorns, and ground bay leaf and until aromatic.
2. Set the Instant Pot to Sauté. Add and heat the sesame oil until sizzling. Sear the pork steak until nicely browned.
3. Stir in the roasted seasonings and the remaining ingredients.
4. Lock the lid. Select the Manual mode and set the cooking time for 8 minutes at High Pressure.
5. When the timer beeps, do a quick pressure release. Carefully open the lid.
6. Divide the mix among bowls and serve immediately.

## Pork Chops with Brussels Sprouts

**Prep time: 10 minutes | Cook time: 30 minutes | Serves 4**

| | |
|---|---|
| 1½ pound (680 g) pork chops | seasoning |
| 1 pound (454 g) Brussels sprouts, trimmed and halved | 1 cup beef stock |
| | A pinch of salt and black pepper |
| 2 tablespoons Cajun | 1 tablespoon parsley, chopped |

1. Stir together all the ingredients in your Instant Pot.
2. Secure the lid. Press the Manual button on the Instant Pot and set the cooking time for 30 minutes on High Pressure.
3. Once cooking is complete, perform a natural pressure release for 10 minutes and then release any remaining pressure. Carefully open the lid.
4. Divide the mix among the plates and serve immediately.

## Balsamic Pork with Asparagus

**Prep time: 10 minutes | Cook time: 30 minutes | Serves 4**

| | |
|---|---|
| 1 tablespoon olive oil | 1 teaspoon smoked paprika |
| 4 garlic cloves, minced | A pinch of salt and black pepper |
| 1 yellow onion, chopped | 1 bunch asparagus, trimmed |
| 2 pounds (907 g) pork roast | 2 tablespoons balsamic vinegar |
| 1 cup beef stock | 1 teaspoon chopped chives |
| 1 tablespoon chopped basil | |

1. Press the Sauté button on the Instant Pot and heat the olive oil.
2. Add the garlic and onion and sauté for 2 minutes until fragrant.
3. Add the pork and brown for an additional 5 minutes.
4. Fold in the beef stock, basil, paprika, salt, and pepper and stir to combine.
5. Secure the lid. Select the Manual mode and set the cooking time for 20 minutes at High Pressure.
6. Once cooking is complete, do a natural pressure release for 10 minutes, then release any remaining pressure. Carefully open the lid.

7. Press the Sauté button again and stir in the asparagus, vinegar, and chives. Cook for an additional 7 minutes until the asparagus is tender.
8. Divide the mix among four plates and serve.

## Dublin Coddle

**Prep time: 8 minutes | Cook time: 25 minutes | Serves 2**

| | |
|---|---|
| 1 teaspoon oil | Kosher salt and freshly ground black pepper, to taste |
| ½ pound (227 g) fully cooked kielbasa sausage, cut into 2-inch pieces | 2 carrots, peeled and chopped |
| ½ pound (227 g) uncooked thick-cut bacon, chopped | 2 medium potatoes, quartered and thickly sliced |
| 1 onion, chopped | 1 cup apple cider |
| 2 garlic cloves, minced | 1 teaspoon ham bouillon powder |
| ½ teaspoon dried tarragon | ¼ cup chopped fresh parsley, for garnish |
| 1 bay leaf | |

1. Set your Instant Pot to Sauté and heat the oil until sizzling.
2. Add the sausage and bacon and sauté for 3 to 5 minutes, or until crisp and browned. Remove from the pot to a plate and set aside.
3. Add the onion to the rendered bacon fat in the Instant Pot and cook for 3 to 4 minutes until tender. Stir in the garlic, tarragon, and bay leaf and sauté for 1 minute more. Sprinkle with the salt and pepper.
4. Fold in the carrots and potatoes. Return the sausage and bacon to the Instant Pot and add the apple cider and ham bouillon powder. Stir well.
5. Lock the lid. Select the Manual mode and set the cooking time for 12 minutes at High Pressure.
6. Once cooking is complete, do a natural pressure release for 5 minutes, then release any remaining pressure. Carefully open the lid.
7. Discard the bay leaf. Add more salt and pepper, if desired. Sprinkle the parsley on top for garnish before serving.

## Pork Roast with Sweet Potatoes

**Prep time: 10 minutes | Cook time: 40 minutes | Serves 4**

1 tablespoon olive oil
2 red onions, chopped
2 pounds (907 g) pork shoulder, sliced
2 sweet potatoes, peeled and cubed
1 cup beef stock
1 teaspoon chili powder
½ teaspoon chopped rosemary
A pinch of salt and black pepper
1 cup coconut cream
1 tablespoon chopped parsley

1. Press the Sauté button on the Instant Pot and heat the olive oil.
2. Add the onions and pork and brown for 5 minutes.
3. Stir in the sweet potatoes, beef stock, chili powder, rosemary, salt, and black pepper.
4. Secure the lid. Select the Manual mode and set the cooking time for 25 minutes at High Pressure.
5. Once cooking is complete, do a natural pressure release for 10 minutes, then release any remaining pressure. Carefully open the lid.
6. Press the Sauté button again and add the coconut cream, toss, and cook for an additional 10 minutes.
7. Serve with the parsley sprinkled on top.

## Pork Sausages with Peperonata

**Prep time: 15 minutes | Cook time: 12 minutes | Serves 4**

1 teaspoon olive oil
8 pork sausages, casing removed
1 jalapeño pepper, deseeded and sliced
1 green bell pepper, deseeded and sliced
1 red bell pepper, deseeded and sliced
1 cup roasted vegetable broth
1 red onion, chopped
2 Roma tomatoes, puréed
2 garlic cloves, minced
1 tablespoon Italian seasoning
2 tablespoons fresh Italian parsley
2 tablespoons ripe olives, pitted and sliced

1. Set your Instant Pot to Sauté and heat the olive oil until sizzling.
2. Add the sausages to the hot oil and sear until no longer pink in center.
3. Add the remaining ingredients except the parsley and olives to the Instant Pot and stir to mix well.
4. Lock the lid. Select the Manual mode and set the cooking time for 8 minutes at High Pressure.
5. Once cooking is complete, do a quick pressure release. Carefully open the lid.
6. Sprinkle the parsley and olives on top for garnish and serve.

## Cheesy Pork and Broccoli

**Prep time: 10 minutes | Cook time: 30 minutes | Serves 4**

1 tablespoon olive oil
1½ pounds (680 g) pork stew meat, cubed
2 cups broccoli florets
1½ cups beef stock
¼ cup tomato purée
1 tablespoon grated ginger
A pinch of salt and black pepper
¾ cup grated Parmesan cheese
1 tablespoon chopped basil

1. Press the Sauté button on the Instant Pot and heat the olive oil.
2. Add the pork and brown for 5 minutes.
3. Stir in the broccoli, beef stock, tomato purée, ginger, salt, and pepper.
4. Secure the lid. Select the Manual mode and set the cooking time for 25 minutes at High Pressure.
5. Once cooking is complete, do a natural pressure release for 5 minutes, then release any remaining pressure. Carefully open the lid.
6. Scatter the grated cheese and basil all over. Lock the lid and allow to sit for 5 minutes.
7. Divide the mix among four plates and serve.

## Chili Pork Roast and Tomatoes

**Prep time: 10 minutes | Cook time: 35 minutes | Serves 4**

1 tablespoon olive oil
4 garlic cloves, minced
1 yellow onion, chopped
1½ pounds (680 g) pork roast
12 ounces (340 g) tomatoes, crushed
1 cup beef stock
2 tablespoons chili powder
1 tablespoon apple cider vinegar
1 teaspoon dried oregano
A pinch of salt and black pepper

1. Press the Sauté button on the Instant Pot and heat the olive oil.
2. Add the garlic and onion and sauté for 5 minutes, stirring occasionally.
3. Add the remaining ingredients to the Instant Pot and stir.
4. Secure the lid. Select the Manual mode and set the cooking time for 30 minutes at High Pressure.
5. Once cooking is complete, do a natural pressure release for 10 minutes, then release any remaining pressure. Carefully open the lid.
6. Serve hot.

## Dill Pork, Spinach and Tomatoes

**Prep time: 10 minutes | Cook time: 25 minutes | Serves 4**

2 tablespoons olive oil
½ cup chopped yellow onion
1½ pounds (680 g) pork stew meat, cubed
2 cups baby spinach
2 tomatoes, cubed
1½ cups beef stock
1 tablespoon chopped dill
1 teaspoon hot paprika
1 teaspoon dried cumin
A pinch of salt and black pepper

1. Press the Sauté button on the Instant Pot and heat the olive oil.
2. Add the onion and pork and brown for 3 minutes.
3. Add the remaining ingredients to the Instant Pot and stir well.
4. Secure the lid. Select the Manual mode and set the cooking time for 20 minutes at High Pressure.

5. Once cooking is complete, do a natural pressure release for 10 minutes, then release any remaining pressure. Carefully open the lid.
6. Serve hot.

## Nutmeg Pork

**Prep time: 10 minutes | Cook time: 30 minutes | Serves 4**

2 tablespoons olive oil
2 garlic cloves, minced
1½ pounds (680 g) pork meat, cubed
1 cup beef stock
2 tablespoons
chopped parsley
2 teaspoons ground nutmeg
½ teaspoon sweet paprika
A pinch of salt and black pepper

1. Press the Sauté button on the Instant Pot and heat the olive oil.
2. Add the garlic and pork and brown for 5 minutes, stirring occasionally.
3. Fold in the remaining ingredients and stir well.
4. Secure the lid. Select the Manual mode and set the cooking time for 25 minutes at High Pressure.
5. Once cooking is complete, do a natural pressure release for 10 minutes, then release any remaining pressure. Carefully open the lid.
6. Serve hot.

## Pork Meatloaf

**Prep time: 10 minutes | Cook time: 30 minutes | Serves 4**

| | |
|---|---|
| 2 pounds (907 g) ground pork meat | 1 tablespoon chopped parsley |
| ½ cup tomato sauce | 1 tablespoon chopped chives |
| ½ cup almond meal | A pinch of salt and black pepper |
| ½ cup coconut milk | 2 cups water |
| 2 eggs, whisked | |
| 1 yellow onion, minced | |

1. Stir together all the ingredients except the water in a large mixing bowl until well incorporated.
2. Form the mixture into a meatloaf and transfer to a loaf pan that fits the Instant Pot.
3. Pour the water into the Instant Pot and insert a steamer basket. Place the loaf pan in the basket.
4. Lock the lid. Select the Manual mode and set the cooking time for 30 minutes at High Pressure.
5. Once cooking is complete, do a natural pressure release for 10 minutes, then release any remaining pressure. Carefully open the lid.
6. Allow to cool for 5 minutes before slicing and serving.

## Pork Chops in Mushroom Sauce

**Prep time: 10 minutes | Cook time: 15 minutes | Serves 2**

| | |
|---|---|
| 1 tablespoon oil | minced |
| 2 bone-in, medium-cut pork chops | ½ small onion, sliced |
| Kosher salt and freshly ground black pepper, to taste | Splash of dry white wine |
| 4 ounces (113 g) cremini mushrooms, sliced | 1 cup chicken stock |
| 2 garlic cloves, | 1 tablespoon cornstarch |
| | 1 tablespoon butter |
| | ¾ cup sour cream |

1. Set your Instant Pot to Sauté. Add and heat the oil.
2. Sprinkle the pork chops generously with the salt and pepper. Sear the pork chops on both sides and transfer to a plate.
3. Add the mushrooms, garlic, and onion and sauté for 3 minutes until soft. Add the white wine and deglaze the pot by scraping up any browned bits on the bottom with a wooden spoon.
4. Stir in the stock. Add the seared pork chops to the pot.
5. Lock the lid. Select the Manual mode and cook for 8 minutes on High Pressure.
6. Once cooking is complete, do a natural pressure release for about 10 minutes. Carefully open the lid.
7. Select the Sauté mode.
8. Transfer the pork chops to a plate. Remove 1 tablespoon of the cooking liquid from the pot and pour in a small bowl with the cornstarch. Stir well and transfer the mixture back to the pot.
9. Mix in the butter and sour cream and stir until mixed. Let simmer for 4 to 5 minutes until thickened. Sprinkle with the salt and pepper if necessary.
10. Transfer to a serving plate and serve.

## Chese Meatballs and Spaghetti

**Prep time: 5 minutes | Cook time: 10 minutes | Serves 6**

| | |
|---|---|
| 1 pound (454 g) frozen meatballs | jar pasta sauce |
| 1 pound (454 g) dried spaghetti | 3 cups water |
| 2 tablespoons olive oil | 1 cup shredded Cheddar or Mozzarella cheese |
| 1 (24-ounce / 680-g) | Fresh basil, for garnish (optional) |

1. Place the meatballs into the Instant Pot and top with the spaghetti, fanning the noodles out.
2. Drizzle with the olive oil and pour the sauce over top. Pour the water into the Instant Pot.
3. Secure the lid. Select the Manual mode and set the cooking time for 10 minutes at High Pressure.
4. Once cooking is complete, do a quick pressure release. Carefully open the lid.
5. Add the cheese and stir well. Serve garnished with the basil, if desired.

# Chapter 10 Beef

## Thai Coconut Beef with Snap Peas

**Prep time: 30 minutes | Cook time: 40 minutes | Serves 10**

1 (3-pound / 1.4-kg) boneless beef chuck roast, halved
1 teaspoon salt
1 teaspoon ground black pepper
2 tablespoons canola oil
1 (14-ounce / 397-g) can coconut milk
½ cup creamy peanut butter
¼ cup red curry paste
2 tablespoons honey
¾ cup beef stock
2 tablespoons soy sauce
2 teaspoons minced fresh ginger root
1 large sweet red pepper, sliced
½ pound (227 g) fresh sugar snap peas, trimmed
¼ cup minced fresh cilantro

1. Sprinkle the beef with salt and pepper on a clean work surface. Select the Sauté setting of the Instant Pot. Add the canola oil and heat.
2. Add one roast half. Brown on all sides for about 5 minutes. Remove and repeat with remaining beef half.
3. Meanwhile, in a bowl, whisk the coconut milk with peanut butter, curry paste, honey, beef stock, soy sauce, and ginger root.
4. Put all the beef halves into the Instant Pot, then add red pepper and pour the coconut milk mixture over the beef.
5. Lock the lid. Select the Manual setting and set the cooking time for 35 minutes at High Pressure.
6. When timer beeps, quick release the pressure. Carefully open the lid.
7. Add the sugar snap peas and set the cooking time for 5 minutes at High Pressure.
8. When timer beeps, naturally release the pressure for 10 minutes, then release any remaining pressure. Unlock the lid.
9. Remove beef from the pot. Skim fat from cooking juices. Shred beef with forks. Stir in cilantro and serve.

## Beef Empanadas

**Prep time: 20 minutes | Cook time: 20 minutes | Serves 4**

2 tablespoons olive oil, divided
¼ pound (113 g) ground beef
1 garlic clove, minced
½ white onion, chopped
6 green olives, pitted and chopped
¼ teaspoon cumin
powder
¼ teaspoon paprika
¼ teaspoon cinnamon powder
2 small tomatoes, chopped
1 cup water
8 square wonton wrappers
1 egg, beaten

1. Select the Sauté mode of the Instant Pot and heat 1 tablespoon of olive oil.
2. Add and sauté the ground beef, garlic, and onion for 5 minutes or until fragrant and the beef is no longer pink.
3. Stir in olives, cumin, paprika, and cinnamon, and cook for 3 minutes.
4. Add the tomatoes and water, and cook for 1 minute.
5. Seal the lid, then select the Manual mode and set the time for 8 minutes on High Pressure.
6. When timer beeps, allow a natural release for 10 minutes, then release any remaining pressure. Carefully open the lid.
7. Spoon the beef mixture onto a plate and let cool for a few minutes. Lay the wonton wrappers on a flat surface.
8. Place 2 tablespoons of the beef mixture in the middle of each wrapper. Brush the edges of the wrapper with egg and fold in half to form a triangle. Pinch the edges together to seal.
9. Heat the remaining oil in the Instant Pot and fry the empanadas for a minute each. Work in batches to avoid overcrowding.
10. Remove to paper towels to soak up excess fat before serving.

## Beery Back Ribs

**Prep time: 20 minutes | Cook time: 50 minutes | Serves 2 to 4**

| | |
|---|---|
| ½ pound (227 g) back ribs | 1-inch piece fresh ginger, minced |
| 4 ounces (113 g) beers | 2 tablespoons tamari |
| ½ cup BBQ sauce | 1 tablespoon agave nectar |
| ½ red chili, sliced | Sea salt and ground black pepper, to taste |
| ½ onion, chopped | |
| 1 garlic clove, minced | 1 teaspoon toasted sesame seeds |

1. Place the back ribs, beers, BBQ sauce, red chili, onion, garlic, and ginger in the Instant Pot.
2. Secure the lid. Choose the Manual mode and set the cooking time for 40 minutes at High pressure.
3. Once cooking is complete, perform a natural pressure release for 10 minutes, then release any remaining pressure. Carefully open the lid.
4. Add the tamari sauce, agave, salt and pepper and place the beef ribs under the broiler.
5. Broil ribs for 10 minutes or until well browned. Serve with sesame seeds.

## Beef and Lush Vegetable Pot

**Prep time: 15 minutes | Cook time: 21 minutes | Serves 4**

| | |
|---|---|
| 2 tablespoons olive oil | 1 garlic clove, minced |
| 1 pound (454 g) ground beef | 1 tablespoon Worcestershire Sauce |
| ¾ cup chopped baby Bella mushrooms | 2 tablespoons tomato paste |
| 1 carrot, peeled and chopped | 1 teaspoon cinnamon powder |
| 1 small onion, finely chopped | 2 cups beef stock |
| 1 celery stick, chopped | 2 sweet potatoes, chopped |

1. Set the Instant Pot to the Sauté mode, then heat the olive oil.
2. Brown the beef in the pot for 5 minutes. Mix in mushrooms, carrot, onion, celery, and garlic. Sauté for 5 minutes or until softened.
3. Mix in Worcestershire sauce, tomato paste, and cinnamon. Cook for 1 minute.
4. Pour in the beef stock and add the potatoes. Seal the lid, then select the Manual mode and set the cooking time for 10 minutes.
5. Once cooking is complete, allow a natural release for 5 minutes, then release any remaining pressure and unlock the lid.
6. Serve warm.

## Apricot Preserved Flank Steak

**Prep time: 10 minutes | Cook time: 45 minutes | Serves 4**

| | |
|---|---|
| ¼ cup apricot preserves | pepper |
| ⅛ cup apple cider vinegar | ¼ teaspoon ground black pepper |
| ¼ cup ketchup | 1 (2-pound / 907-g) flank steak |
| ⅛ cup honey | 2 tablespoons avocado oil, divided |
| ¼ cup soy sauce | 1 large sweet onion, peeled and sliced |
| 1 teaspoon ground mustard | |
| ⅛ teaspoon cayenne | 1½ cups beef broth |

1. In a small bowl, combine the preserves, vinegar, ketchup, honey, soy sauce, mustard, cayenne pepper, and pepper. Spread half of the mixture on all sides of the flank steak on a clean work surface. Set the remaining mixture aside.
2. Press the Sauté button on Instant Pot. Heat 1 tablespoon of avocado oil. Add and sear the meat on each side for about 5 minutes. Remove the meat and set aside.
3. Add remaining 1 tablespoon of avocado oil and onions. Sauté for 3 to 5 minutes or until translucent.
4. Pour in the beef broth. Set meat on the onions. Pour the remaining preserve mixture over. Lock the lid.
5. Press the Meat / Stew button and set the cooking time for 35 minutes at High Pressure.
6. When timer beeps, let pressure release naturally for 15 minutes, then release any remaining pressure. Unlock the lid.
7. Transfer the meat to a serving platter. Thinly slice and serve immediately.

## Classic Sloppy Joes

**Prep time: 10 minutes | Cook time: 19 minutes | Serves 4**

1 pound (454 g) ground beef, divided
½ cup chopped onion
½ cup chopped green bell pepper
¼ cup water
2 teaspoons Worcestershire sauce
1 garlic clove, minced
1 tablespoon Dijon mustard
¾ cup ketchup
2 teaspoons brown sugar
¼ teaspoon sea salt
½ teaspoon hot sauce
4 soft hamburger buns

1. Select the Sauté mode of the Instant Pot. Put about ½ cup of the ground beef in the pot and cook for about 4 minutes or until browned.
2. Stir in the onion, bell pepper, and water. Add the remaining beef and cook for about 3 minutes or until well browned.
3. Mix in the Worcestershire sauce, garlic, mustard, ketchup, brown sugar, and salt.
4. Lock the lid. Select the Manual mode. Set the time for 12 minutes at High Pressure.
5. When timer beeps, quick release the pressure, then unlock the lid.
6. Stir in the hot sauce. Select the Sauté mode and simmer until lightly thickened. Spoon the meat and sauce into the buns. Serve immediately.

## Beef and Bacon Fig Chutney

**Prep time: 20 minutes | Cook time: 35 minutes | Serves 4**

3 bacon slices, chopped
1 teaspoon olive oil
4 pounds (1.8 kg) beef short ribs
Salt and black pepper, to taste
1 pound (454 g) cherry tomatoes, halved
1 medium white onion, chopped
3 garlic cloves, minced
1 cup Marsala wine
¼ cup fig preserves
2 cups beef broth
3 tablespoons thyme leaves

1. Set the Instant Pot to Sauté mode and brown the bacon for 5 minutes until crispy. Place the bacon on a paper towel-lined plate and set aside.
2. Heat the olive oil, then season beef ribs with salt, and pepper. Sear the beef in the pot for 5 minutes on both sides or until brown. Transfer the beef next to bacon.
3. Add the cherry tomatoes, onion, and garlic to Instant Pot, then sauté for 5 minutes or until soft.
4. Stir in Marsala wine, fig preserves, beef broth, and thyme. Return beef and bacon to the pot.
5. Seal the lid, then select the Manual mode and set the time for 20 minutes at High Pressure.
6. Once cooking is complete, allow a natural release for 10 minutes, then release any remaining pressure. Unlock the lid.
7. Serve immediately.

## New York Strip with Heavy Cream

**Prep time: 15 minutes | Cook time: 30 minutes | Serves 4**

1 tablespoon sesame oil
1 pound (454 g) New York strip, sliced into thin strips
½ leek, sliced
1 carrot, sliced
$1/_3$ cup dry red wine
½ tablespoon tamari
½ cup cream of mushroom soup
1 clove garlic, sliced
Kosher salt and ground black pepper, to taste
¼ cup heavy cream

1. Press the Sauté button of the Instant Pot. Heat the sesame oil until sizzling.
2. Add and brown the beef strips in batches for 4 minutes. Stir in the remaining ingredients, except for the heavy cream.
3. Secure the lid. Choose the Manual mode and set the cooking time for 20 minutes at High pressure.
4. Once cooking is complete, use a quick pressure release. Carefully open the lid.
5. Transfer the beef on a serving plate. Mash the vegetables in the pot with a potato masher.
6. Press the Sauté button. Bring to a boil, then Stir in the heavy cream.
7. Spoon the mixture over the New York strip and serve immediately.

## Beef Meatballs with Roasted Tomatoes

**Prep time: 15 minutes | Cook time: 16 minutes | Serves 4**

2 tablespoons avocado oil
1 pound (454 g) ground beef
½ teaspoon dried basil
½ teaspoon crushed red pepper
½ teaspoon ground

cayenne pepper
½ teaspoon kosher salt
½ teaspoon freshly ground black pepper
2 (14-ounce / 397-g) cans fire roasted tomatoes

1. Set the Instant Pot to Sauté mode and heat the avocado oil.
2. In a large bowl, mix the remaining ingredients, except for the tomatoes. Form the mixture into 1½-inch meatballs and place them into the Instant Pot. Spread the tomatoes evenly over the meatballs.
3. Close the lid. Select the Manual mode, set the cooking time for 16 minutes on High Pressure.
4. When timer beeps, perform a natural pressure release for 5 minutes, then release any remaining pressure.
5. Open the lid and serve.

## Beef Lasagna

**Prep time: 20 minutes | Cook time: 20 minutes | Serves 4**

1 cup water
1 pound (454 g) ground beef
1 cup spinach, chopped
1 (14-ounce / 397-g) can fire roasted tomatoes
1 egg
¼ (4-ounce / 113-g) small onion, sliced
¾ cup Mozzarella cheese, shredded
½ cup Parmesan

cheese, grated
1½ cups whole milk ricotta cheese
2 tablespoons coconut oil
½ teaspoon garlic
½ teaspoon dried basil
½ teaspoon fennel seeds
½ teaspoon dried parsley
½ teaspoon dried oregano

1. Pour the water into the Instant Pot, then insert the trivet.

2. In a large bowl, combine the remaining ingredients in the pot. Transfer the mixture into a baking pan.
3. Place the pan onto the trivet, and cover with aluminum foil.
4. Close the lid, then select the Manual mode. Set the cooking time for 20 minutes on High Pressure.
5. When timer beeps, naturally release the pressure for about 10 minutes, then release any remaining pressure. Carefully open the lid.
6. Let cool and serve.

## Beef and Yogurt Pitas

**Prep time: 15 minutes | Cook time: 28 minutes | Serves 4**

1 tablespoon olive oil
1 pound (454 g) beef stew meat, cut into strips
Salt and black pepper, to taste
1 small white onion, chopped
3 garlic cloves, minced
2 teaspoons hot sauce

1 cup beef broth
1 cucumber, deseeded and chopped
1 medium tomato, chopped
4 whole pita bread, warmed
1 cup Greek yogurt
1 teaspoon chopped dill

1. Set the Instant Pot to Sauté mode, then heat the olive oil until shimmering.
2. Season the beef with salt, pepper, and brown the beef in the pot for 5 minutes. Remove the beef from the pot and set aside.
3. Add the onion and garlic to oil and sauté for 3 minutes or until softened,. Return the beef to the pot, stir in hot sauce and beef broth.
4. Seal the lid, then select the Manual mode and set the time for 20 minutes at High Pressure.
5. Once cooking is complete, allow a natural release for 5 minutes, then release any remaining pressure. Unlock the lid.
6. Transfer the beef into a bowl. Mix in the cucumber, tomatoes, and spoon the beef mixture into pita bread.
7. In a medium bowl, mix yogurt and dill. Top beef with yogurt mixture and serve immediately.

## Beef and Broccoli

**Prep time: 15 minutes | Cook time: 25 minutes | Serves 4**

½ cup grass-fed bone broth
1 pound (454 g) chuck steak, sliced
1 jalapeño pepper, sliced
1 green onion, chopped
½ teaspoon ginger, grated
½ teaspoon garlic
2 tablespoons coconut oil
½ teaspoon crushed red pepper
½ teaspoon kosher salt
½ teaspoon freshly ground black pepper
½ teaspoon dried parsley
1 cup broccoli, chopped
1 teaspoon sesame seeds

1. Pour the bone broth into the Instant Pot, then add the steak, jalapeño, green onion, ginger, garlic, coconut oil, red pepper, salt, black pepper, and parsley.
2. Close the lid and select the Manual mode. Set the cooking time for 20 minutes on High Pressure.
3. When timer beeps, let the pressure naturally release for about 10 minutes, then release any remaining pressure. Carefully open the lid.
4. Transfer the steak mixture on a plate. Add the broccoli and set to the Sauté mode. Cook for 5 minutes or until tender. Remove the broccoli from the pot.
5. Top the beef with the sesame seeds, serve with the broccoli.

## Beef and Spinach Tagliatelle

**Prep time: 15 minutes | Cook time: 18 minutes | Serves 4**

1 tablespoon olive oil
1 pound (454 g) ground beef
1 cup sliced cremini mushrooms
1 small yellow onion, chopped
2 garlic cloves, minced
8 ounces (227 g) tagliatelle
2 (26-ounce / 737-g) jars tomato pasta sauce
1 tablespoon Italian seasoning
1 teaspoon dried basil
6 cups water
Salt and black pepper, to taste
1 cup baby spinach

1. Set the Instant Pot to Sauté mode, heat the olive oil and brown the beef for 5 minutes.
2. Add the mushrooms, onion, garlic, and sauté for 3 minutes or until soft.
3. Stir in tagliatelle, tomato sauce, Italian seasoning, basil, water, salt, and pepper.
4. Seal the lid, then select the Manual mode and set the time for 5 minutes at High Pressure.
5. Once cooking is complete, do a quick release, then unlock the lid.
6. Select the Sauté mode and add the spinach. Cook for 5 minutes or until wilted. Serve warm.

## Beef Rice Noodles

**Prep time: 15 minutes | Cook time: 16 minutes | Serves 4**

6 cups boiled water
8 ounces (227 g) rice noodles
1 tablespoon sesame oil
1 pound (454 g) ground beef
2 cups sliced shitake mushrooms
½ cup julienned carrots
1 yellow onion, sliced
1 cup shredded green cabbage
¼ cup sliced scallions, for garnish
Sesame seeds, for garnish

**Sauce:**
¼ cup tamarind sauce
1 tablespoon hoisin sauce
1 teaspoon grated ginger
1 teaspoon maple syrup

1. In a medium bowl, whisk together the ingredients for the sauce. Set aside.
2. Pour boiling water into a bowl and add rice noodles. Cover the bowl and allow the noodles to soften for 5 minutes. Drain and set aside.
3. Set the Instant Pot to Sauté mode and heat the sesame oil.
4. Cook the beef in the pot for 5 minutes or until browned.
5. Stir in the mushrooms, carrots, onion, and cabbage. Cook for 5 minutes or until softened.
6. Add the noodles. Top with the sauce and mix well. Cook for 1 more minute. Garnish with scallions and sesame seeds and serve immediately.

## Cheesy and Creamy Delmonico Steak

**Prep time: 10 minutes | Cook time: 20 minutes | Serves 4**

1 tablespoon butter
1 pound (454 g) Delmonico steak, cubed
½ cup double cream
½ cup beef broth
1 clove garlic, minced
¼ cup sour cream
1 teaspoon cayenne pepper
Sea salt and ground black pepper, to taste
¼ cup gorgonzola cheese, shredded

1. Press the Sauté button of the Instant Pot. Melt the butter and brown the beef cubes in batches for about 4 minutes per batch.
2. Add the double cream, broth, garlic, and sour cream to the Instant Pot, then season with cayenne pepper, salt, and black pepper.
3. Secure the lid. Choose the Manual mode and set the cooking time for 10 minutes at High pressure.
4. Once cooking is complete, use a quick pressure release. Carefully open the lid.
5. Top with gorgonzola cheese and serve.

## Ground Beef and Mushroom Stroganoff

**Prep time: 25 minutes | Cook time: 20 minutes | Serves 8**

2 pounds (907 g) ground beef, divided
1½ teaspoons salt, divided
1 teaspoon ground black pepper, divided
½ pound (227 g) sliced fresh mushrooms
1 tablespoon butter
2 medium onions, chopped
2 garlic cloves, minced
1 (10½-ounce / 298-g) can condensed beef consomme, undiluted
⅓ cup all-purpose flour
2 tablespoons tomato paste
1½ cups sour cream
Hot cooked noodles, for serving

1. Select the Sauté setting of the Instant Pot. Add half of ground beef, salt and pepper. Sauté for 8 minutes or until no longer pink. Remove the beef. Repeat with remaining ground beef, salt and pepper.
2. Add mushrooms, butter, and onions to Instant Pot. Sauté for 6 minutes or until mushrooms are tender. Add garlic and sauté for 1 minute more until fragrant. Return the beef to the pot.
3. Lock the lid. Select the Manual setting and set the cooking time for 5 minutes at High Pressure.
4. When timer beeps, quick release pressure. Carefully open the lid. Select the Sauté setting.
5. In a small bowl, whisk together consomme, flour and tomato paste. Pour over the beef and stir to combine.
6. Sauté for 3 more minutes or until thickened. Stir in sour cream; cook for a minute more until heated through. Serve with noodles.

## Indian Spicy Beef with Basmati

**Prep time: 15 minutes | Cook time: 15 minutes | Serves 4**

1 tablespoon olive oil
1 pound (454 g) beef stew meat, cubed
Salt and black pepper, to taste
½ teaspoon garam masala powder
½ teaspoon grated ginger
2 white onions, sliced
2 garlic cloves, minced
1 tablespoon cilantro
leaves
½ teaspoon red chili powder
1 teaspoon cumin powder
¼ teaspoon turmeric powder
1 cup basmati rice
1 cup grated carrots
2 cups beef broth
¼ cup cashew nuts
¼ cup coconut yogurt, for serving

1. Set the Instant Pot to Sauté mode, then heat the olive oil.
2. Season the beef with salt and pepper, and brown both sides for 5 minutes. Transfer to a plate and set aside.
3. Add and sauté the garam masala, ginger, onions, garlic, cilantro, red chili, cumin, turmeric, salt, and pepper for 2 minutes.
4. Stir in beef, rice, carrots, and broth. Seal the lid, select the Manual mode, and set the time to 6 minutes on High Pressure.
5. When cooking is complete, do a natural pressure release for 5 minutes, then release any remaining pressure. Unlock the lid.
6. Fluff the rice and stir in cashews. Serve with coconut yogurt.

## Citrus Beef Carnitas

**Prep time: 15 minutes | Cook time: 25 minutes | Serves 8**

2½ pounds (1.1 kg) bone-in country ribs
Salt, to taste
¼ cup orange juice
1½ cups beef stock
1 onion, cut into wedges
2 garlic cloves, smashed and peeled
1 teaspoon chili powder
1 cup shredded Jack cheese

1. Season the ribs with salt on a clean work surface.
2. In the Instant Pot, combine the orange juice and stock. Fold in the onion and garlic. Put the ribs in the pot. Sprinkle with chili powder.
3. Seal the lid, select the Manual mode and set the cooking time for 25 minutes at High Pressure.
4. Once cooking is complete, do a natural pressure release for 10 minutes, then release any remaining pressure. Carefully open the lid. Transfer beef to a plate to cool.
5. Remove and discard the bones. Shred the ribs with two forks. Top the beef with the sauce remains in the pot. Sprinkled with cheese and serve.

## Beef Roast with Cauliflower

**Prep time: 10 minutes | Cook time: 15 minutes | Serves 2**

2 teaspoons sesame oil
12 ounces (340 g) sliced beef roast
Freshly ground black pepper, to taste
½ small onion, chopped
3 garlic cloves, minced
½ cup beef stock
¼ cup soy sauce
2 tablespoons brown sugar
Pinch red pepper flakes
1 tablespoon cornstarch
8 ounces (227 g) fresh cauliflower, cut into florets

1. Set the Instant Pot pot on Sauté mode. Add the sesame oil, beef, and black pepper. Sear for 2 minutes on all sides. Transfer the beef to a plate and set aside.
2. Add the onion and garlic to the pot and sauté for 2 minutes or until softened.
3. Stir in the stock, soy sauce, brown sugar, and red pepper flakes. Stir until the sugar is dissolved, then return the beef to the pot.
4. Secure the lid and set to the Manual mode. Set the cooking time for 10 minutes on High Pressure.
5. When timer beeps, quick release the pressure and open the lid. Set to the Sauté mode.
6. Transfer 2 tablespoons of liquid from the pot to a small bowl. Whisk it with the cornstarch, then add back to the pot along with the cauliflower.
7. Cover the lid and let simmer for 3 to 4 minutes, or until the sauce is thickened and the cauliflower is softened.
8. Serve the beef and cauliflower.

## Ribeye Steak with Cauliflower Rice

**Prep time: 15 minutes | Cook time: 20 minutes | Serves 4**

1 cup water
1 ribeye steak
½ teaspoon dried parsley
½ teaspoon ground cumin
½ teaspoon ground turmeric
½ teaspoon paprika
½ teaspoon freshly ground black pepper
½ teaspoon kosher salt
1 head cauliflower, riced
2 tablespoons butter, softened

1. Pour the water into the Instant Pot, then insert a trivet.
2. In a small bowl, mix the parsley, cumin, turmeric, paprika, black pepper, and salt. Coat the steak evenly with the mixture.
3. Place the steak into a greased baking pan. Arrange the cauliflower rice beside the steak.
4. Place the pan onto the trivet, and cover with aluminum foil. Close the lid, then select the Manual mode. Set the cooking time for 20 minutes on High Pressure.
5. When timer beeps, naturally release the pressure for about 10 minutes, then release any remaining pressure. Carefully open the lid.
6. Remove the pan. Add the butter to the steak. Serve immediately.

## Greek Beef and Spinach Ravioli

**Prep time: 15 minutes | Cook time: 20 minutes | Serves 4**

1 cup cheese ravioli
3 cups water
Salt, to taste
1 tablespoon olive oil
1 pound (454 g) ground beef
1 cup canned diced tomatoes
1 tablespoon dried mixed herbs
3 cups chicken broth
1 cup baby spinach
¼ cup Kalamata olives, sliced
¼ cup crumbled feta cheese

1. Put ravioli, water, and salt in Instant Pot. Seal the lid, select the Manual mode and set the time for 3 minutes at High Pressure.
2. Once cooking is complete, do a quick pressure release. Carefully open the lid. Drain the ravioli through a colander and set aside.
3. Set the pot to Sauté mode, then heat the olive oil. Add and brown the beef for 5 minutes.
4. Mix in the tomatoes, mixed herbs, and chicken broth. Seal the lid, select the Manual mode and set cooking time for 10 minutes on High Pressure.
5. When timer beeps, do a quick pressure release. Carefully open the lid.
6. Set the pot to Sauté mode, then mix in ravioli, spinach, olives and cook for 2 minutes or until spinach wilts. Stir in the feta cheese and serve.

## Beef with Red and Green Cabbage

**Prep time: 20 minutes | Cook time: 22 minutes | Serves 4**

1 tablespoon olive oil
1 pound (454 g) ground beef
1 tablespoon grated ginger
3 garlic cloves, minced
Salt and black pepper, to taste
1 medium red cabbage, shredded
1 medium green cabbage, shredded
1 red bell pepper,
chopped
1 cup water
2 tablespoons tamarind sauce
½ tablespoon honey
1 tablespoon hot sauce
1 tablespoon sesame oil
2 tablespoons walnuts
1 teaspoon toasted sesame seeds

1. Set the Instant Pot to Sauté mode and heat the olive oil.
2. Add the beef, then season with ginger, garlic, salt, black pepper. Cook for 5 minutes.
3. Add the red and green cabbage, bell pepper, and sauté for 5 minutes.
4. Pour in the water and seal the lid. Select the Manual mode and set the time to 10 minutes on High Pressure.
5. When timer beeps, allow a natural release for 10 minutes, then release any remaining pressure. Unlock the lid.
6. Meanwhile, in a bowl, combine the tamarind sauce, honey, hot sauce, and sesame oil. Stir in the pot, add walnuts, and cook for 1 to 2 minutes on Sauté mode.
7. Dish out and garnish with sesame seeds. Serve warm.

## Mexican Beef Shred

**Prep time: 20 minutes | Cook time: 30 minutes | Serves 4**

1 pound (454 g) tender chuck roast, cut into half
3 tablespoons chipotle sauce
1 (8-ounce / 227-g) can tomato sauce
1 cup beef broth
½ cup chopped cilantro
1 lime, zested and
juiced
2 teaspoons cumin powder
1 teaspoon cayenne pepper
Salt and ground black pepper, to taste
½ teaspoon garlic powder
1 tablespoon olive oil

1. In the Instant Pot, add the beef, chipotle sauce, tomato sauce, beef broth, cilantro, lime zest, lime juice, cumin powder, cayenne pepper, salt, pepper, and garlic powder.
2. Seal the lid, then select the Manual mode and set the cooking time for 30 minutes at High Pressure.
3. Once cooking is complete, allow a natural pressure release for 10 minutes, then release any remaining pressure.
4. Unlock the lid and using two forks to shred the beef into strands. Stir in the olive oil. Serve warm.

## Easy Japanese Beef Shanks

**Prep time: 15 minutes | Cook time: 30 minutes | Serves 4**

1 pound (454 g) beef shank
½ teaspoon Five-spice powder
1 teaspoon instant dashi granules
½ teaspoon garlic, minced
1 tablespoon tamari or soy sauce
¼ cup rice wine
1 clove star anise
½ dried red chili, sliced
1 tablespoon sesame oil
¾ cup water

1. Combine all ingredients to the Instant Pot.
2. Secure the lid. Choose the Manual mode and set the cooking time for 30 minutes at High pressure.
3. Once cooking is complete, use a natural pressure release for 10 minutes, then release any remaining pressure. Carefully open the lid.
4. Slice the beef shank and serve hot.

## Beef Tips with Portobello Mushrooms

**Prep time: 20 minutes | Cook time: 16 minutes | Serves 4**

2 teaspoons olive oil
1 beef top sirloin steak (1-pound / 454-g), cubed
½ teaspoon salt
¼ teaspoon ground black pepper
$1/3$ cup dry red wine
½ pound (227 g) sliced baby portobello mushrooms
1 small onion, halved and sliced
2 cups beef broth
1 tablespoon Worcestershire sauce
3 to 4 tablespoons cornstarch
¼ cup cold water

1. Select the Sauté setting of the Instant Pot. Add the olive oil.
2. Sprinkle the beef with salt and pepper. Brown meat in batches in the pot for 10 minutes. Flip constantly. Transfer meat to a bowl.
3. Add the wine to the pot. Return beef to the pot and add mushrooms, onion, broth, and Worcestershire sauce.
4. Lock the lid. Select the Manual setting and set the cooking time for 15 minutes at High Pressure.

5. When timer beeps, quick release the pressure. Carefully open the lid.
6. Select the Sauté setting and bring to a boil.
7. Meanwhile, in a small bowl, mix cornstarch and water until smooth.
8. Gradually stir the cornstarch into beef mixture. Sauté for 1 more minute or until sauce is thickened. Serve immediately.

## Steak and Bell Pepper Fajitas

**Prep time: 15 minutes | Cook time: 45 minutes | Serves 6**

1 (2-pound / 907-g) skirt steak
1 medium red bell pepper, deseeded and diced
**Sauce:**
1 tablespoon fish sauce
¼ cup soy sauce
1 teaspoon ground cumin
2 tablespoons tomato
1 medium green bell pepper, deseeded and diced
1 small onion, diced
1 cup beef broth
paste
1 teaspoon chili powder
½ teaspoon sea salt
⅛ cup avocado oil

1. In a small bowl, combine the ingredients for the sauce. Spread ¾ of the sauce on all sides of the beef on a clean work surface. Reserve the remaining sauce.
2. Press the Sauté button on Instant Pot. Add skirt steak and sear on each side for about 5 minutes. Remove the meat and set aside.
3. Add the bell peppers and onion with reserved sauce. Sauté for 3 to 5 minutes or until the onions are translucent.
4. Pour in the beef broth. Set the beef over the onion and peppers. Lock the lid.
5. Press the Meat / Stew button and set the cooking time for 35 minutes at High Pressure.
6. When timer beeps, let the pressure release naturally for 15 minutes, then release any remaining pressure. Unlock the lid.
7. Using a slotted spoon, remove the meat and vegetables to a serving platter. Thinly slice the skirt steak and serve.

## Simple Herbed Beef Chuck Roast

**Prep time: 15 minutes | Cook time: 1 hour | Serves 8**

| | |
|---|---|
| 2 tablespoons coconut oil | ½ teaspoon chili powder |
| 3 pounds (1.4 kg) beef chuck roast | ½ teaspoon fresh paprika |
| 1 cup water | 1 cup butter |
| ½ teaspoon dried parsley | ½ teaspoon kosher salt |
| ½ teaspoon dried basil | ½ teaspoon freshly ground black pepper |

1. Set the Instant Pot to Sauté mode and melt the coconut oil.
2. Add and sear the roast for 4 minutes or until browned on both sides. Flip the roast halfway through, then remove from the pot.
3. Pour the water into the Instant Pot, then add the parsley, basil, chili powder, paprika, butter, salt, and black pepper. Return the beef to the pot.
4. Close the lid. Select the Manual mode, set the cooking time for 55 minutes on High Pressure.
5. When timer beeps, naturally release the pressure for about 10 minutes, then release any remaining pressure. Open the lid.
6. Serve immediately.

## Sumptuous Beef and Tomato Biryani

**Prep time: 10 minutes | Cook time: 25 minutes | Serves 6**

| | |
|---|---|
| 1 tablespoon ghee | cloves |
| 1 small onion, sliced | ½ teaspoon ground cumin |
| 1 pound (454 g) top round, cut into strips | ½ teaspoon ground coriander |
| 1 (28-ounce / 794-g) can whole stewed tomatoes, with juice | ½ teaspoon ground cinnamon |
| 1 cup plain Greek yogurt | ½ teaspoon ground cardamom |
| 1 tablespoon minced fresh ginger root | 1 teaspoon salt |
| 2 cloves garlic, minced | ½ teaspoon ground black pepper |
| ½ teaspoon ground | 2 cups cooked basmati rice |

1. Press the Sauté button on Instant Pot. Melt the ghee.
2. Add the onion and sauté for 3 to 5 minutes or until translucent.
3. Add the remaining ingredients, except for the rice, to the Instant Pot. Lock the lid.
4. Press the Manual button and set the cooking time for 10 minutes at High Pressure.
5. When timer beeps, quick release the pressure, then unlock the lid.
6. Press the Sauté button and simmer for about 10 minutes or until most of the liquid has evaporated. Serve over cooked basmati rice.

## Philly Steak Sub

**Prep time: 20 minutes | Cook time: 13 minutes | Serves 4**

| | |
|---|---|
| 1½ pounds (680 g) flat iron steak | 1-inch-wide strips |
| 1 tablespoon olive oil | 2 tablespoons soy sauce |
| 4 teaspoons garlic seasoning | 4 crusty sub sandwich rolls, split lengthwise |
| 1 cup beef broth | |
| 1 large red bell pepper, cut into | 4 slices provolone cheese |

1. Select the Sauté mode. Brush the steak with the olive oil and rub with garlic seasoning.
2. Add the steaks in batches to the pot and cook for 8 minutes until well browned. Flip the steaks halfway through.
3. Transfer the steaks to a cutting board and slice into ¼- to ½-inch-thick slices. Return the meat to the pot. Add the broth, bell peppers, and soy sauce.
4. Lock the lid, select the Manual function, and set the cooking time for 5 minutes on High Pressure.
5. When timer beeps, let the pressure release naturally for 10 minutes, then release any remaining pressure. Carefully open the lid.
6. Remove the beef and vegetables from the pot. Mound the beef and peppers on the rolls. Top with slices of cheese and serve.

## Tequila Short Ribs

**Prep time: 3 hours 25 minutes | Cook time: 35 minutes | Serves 4**

1 pound (454 g) chuck short ribs
1 shot tequila
½ tablespoon stone ground mustard
½ tablespoon Sriracha sauce
½ cup apple cider
1 tablespoon tomato paste
1 tablespoon honey
½ teaspoon

marjoram
½ teaspoon garlic powder
½ teaspoon shallot powder
½ teaspoon paprika
Kosher salt and cracked black pepper, to taste
¾ cup beef bone broth

1. Place all ingredients, except for the beef broth, in a large bowl. Cover with a foil and let it marinate for 3 hours in the refrigerator.
2. Pour the beef along with the marinade in the Instant Pot. Pour in the beef bone broth.
3. Secure the lid. Choose the Meat / Stew mode and set the cooking time for 35 minutes at High pressure.
4. Once cooking is complete, do a natural pressure release for 15 minutes, then release any remaining pressure. Carefully open the lid.
5. Serve immediately.

## Hot Sirloin with Snap Peas

**Prep time: 15 minutes | Cook time: 8 minutes | Serves 4**

½ teaspoon hot sauce
1 teaspoon balsamic vinegar
1 cup chicken stock
¼ cup soy sauce
2 tablespoons sesame oil, divided
2 tablespoons maple syrup

½ cup plus 2 teaspoons cornstarch, divided
1 pound (454 g) beef sirloin, sliced
2 cups snap peas
3 garlic cloves, minced
3 scallions, sliced

1. In a bowl, combine the hot sauce, vinegar, stock, soy sauce, 1 tablespoon of sesame oil, maple syrup, and 2 tablespoons of cornstarch. Set aside.
2. Pour the remaining cornstarch on a plate. Season beef with salt, and pepper; toss lightly in cornstarch.
3. Set the Instant Pot to Sauté mode, heat the remaining sesame oil and fry the beef in batches for 5 minutes or until browned and crispy. Remove the beef from the pot and set aside.
4. Wipe the Instant Pot clean and pour in hot sauce mixture. Return meat to the pot, then add snow peas and garlic.
5. Seal the lid, select the Manual mode and set the time for 3 minutes on High Pressure.
6. When cooking is complete, perform natural pressure release for 10 minutes, then release the remaining pressure. Unlock the lid.
7. Dish out and garnish with scallions.

## Saucy Italian Beef Chuck

**Prep time: 10 minutes | Cook time: 19 minutes | Serves 6**

1 tablespoon olive oil
1 pound (454 g) 95% lean ground chuck
1 medium yellow onion, chopped
3 tablespoons tomato paste
3 medium garlic cloves, chopped

2 teaspoons Italian seasoning
1 (28-ounce / 794-g) can tomatoes, chopped, with juice
½ cup beef broth
Salt and freshly ground black pepper, to taste

1. Put the olive oil in the pot, select the Sauté mode.
2. Add the ground beef and onion and sauté for 8 minutes or until the beef is browned.
3. Push the meat and onion mixture to one side of the pot. Add the tomato paste, garlic, and Italian seasoning to the other side of the pot and sauté for 1 minute or until fragrant.
4. Add the tomatoes and the broth to the pot. Lock on the lid, select the Manual function, and set the cooking time for 10 minutes on High Pressure.
5. When the cooking time is up, quick release the pressure. Season with salt and pepper and serve.

## Winter Beef Roast Pot

**Prep time: 15 minutes | Cook time: 40 minutes | Serves 6**

2 tablespoons olive oil
1 (3-pound / 1.4-kg) chuck roast
½ cup dry red wine
1 (1-pound / 454-g) butternut squash, chopped
2 carrots, chopped
¾ cup pearl onions
1 teaspoon dried oregano leaves
1 bay leaf
1½ cups beef broth
Salt and black pepper, to taste
1 small red onion, quartered

1. Select the Sauté mode of the Instant Pot and heat the olive oil.
2. Season the beef with salt and sear in the pot for 3 minutes per side or until well browned.
3. Mix in the wine. Bring to a boil and cook for 2 more minutes or until the wine has reduced by half.
4. Mix in the butternut squash, carrots, pearl onions, oregano, bay leaf, broth, black pepper, and red onion. Stir to combine and add the beef.
5. Seal the lid, then select the Manual mode and set the time for 35 minutes on High Pressure.
6. Once cooking is complete, do a quick pressure release. Carefully open the lid.
7. Remove the beef and slice. Spoon over the sauce and vegetables to serve.

## Saucy Short Ribs

**Prep time: 20 minutes | Cook time: 40 minutes | Serves 4**

2 tablespoons olive oil
1½ pounds (680 g) large beef short ribs
Salt and ground black pepper, to taste
3 garlic cloves, minced
1 medium onion,
finely chopped
½ cup apple cider vinegar
1 tablespoon honey
1 cup beef broth
2 tablespoons tomato paste
1 tablespoon cornstarch

1. Select the Sauté mode of the Instant Pot, then heat the olive oil.
2. Season ribs with salt and pepper, and fry in the pot for 8 minutes or until browned. Remove from the pot and set aside.

3. Sauté the garlic, onion, and cook for 4 minutes until fragrant.
4. Stir in apple cider vinegar, honey, broth, tomato paste. Bring to a simmer.
5. Add ribs. Seal the lid, then select the Manual mode and set the time for 25 minutes at High Pressure.
6. Once cooking is complete, allow a natural pressure release for 10 minutes, then release any remaining pressure. Unlock the lid.
7. Transfer the ribs to serving plates. Stir cornstarch into the sauce in the pot and stir for 1 minute or until thickened, on Sauté mode.
8. Spoon sauce over ribs and serve.

## Mongolian Arrowroot Glazed Beef

**Prep time: 15 minutes | Cook time: 20 minutes | Serves 4**

1 tablespoon sesame oil
1 (2-pound / 907-g) skirt steak, sliced into thin strips
½ cup pure maple syrup
¼ cup soy sauce
4 cloves garlic,
minced
1-inch knob fresh ginger root, peeled and grated
½ cup plus 2 tablespoons water, divided
2 tablespoons arrowroot powder

1. Press the Sauté button on the Instant Pot. Heat the sesame oil.
2. Add and sear the steak strips for 3 minutes on all sides.
3. In a medium bowl, whisk together maple syrup, soy sauce, garlic, ginger, and ½ cup water. Pour the mixture over beef. Lock the lid.
4. Press the Manual button and set the cooking time for 10 minutes at High Pressure.
5. When timer beeps, quick release the pressure, then unlock the lid.
6. Meanwhile, in a small dish, whisk together the arrowroot and 2 tablespoons water until smooth and chunky.
7. Stir the arrowroot into the beef mixture. Press the Sauté button and simmer for 5 minutes or until the sauce thickens.
8. Ladle the beef and sauce on plates and serve.

## Korean Flavor Beef Ribs

**Prep time: 10 minutes | Cook time: 15 minutes | Serves 6**

| | |
|---|---|
| 3 pounds (1.4 kg) beef short ribs | sliced |
| 1 cup beef broth | 1 tablespoon toasted sesame seeds |
| 2 green onions, | |

**Sauce:**

| | |
|---|---|
| ½ teaspoon gochujang | ginger |
| ½ cup rice wine | ½ cup pure maple syrup |
| ½ cup soy sauce | 1 teaspoon white pepper |
| ½ teaspoon garlic powder | 1 tablespoon sesame oil |
| ½ teaspoon ground | |

1. In a large bowl, combine the ingredients for the sauce. Dunk the rib in the bowl and press to coat well. Cover the bowl in plastic and refrigerate for at least an hour.
2. Add the beef broth to the Instant Pot. Insert a trivet. Arrange the ribs standing upright over the trivet. Lock the lid.
3. Press the Manual button and set the cooking time for 25 minutes at High Pressure.
4. When timer beeps, let pressure release naturally for 10 minutes, then release any remaining pressure. Unlock the lid.
5. Transfer ribs to a serving platter and garnish with green onions and sesame seeds. Serve immediately.

## Steak, Pepper, and Lettuce Salad

**Prep time: 20 minutes | Cook time: 25 minutes | Serves 4**

| | |
|---|---|
| ¾ pound (340 g) steak | vinegar |
| ¼ cup red wine | 1 sweet pepper, cut into strips |
| ½ teaspoon red pepper flakes | ½ red onion, sliced |
| Sea salt and ground black pepper, to taste | 1 butterhead lettuce, separate into leaves |
| ¾ cup water | ¼ cup feta cheese, crumbled |
| 2 tablespoons olive oil | ¼ cup black olives, pitted and sliced |
| 1 tablespoon wine | |

1. Add the steak, red wine, red pepper, salt, black pepper, and water to the Instant Pot.
2. Secure the lid. Choose the Manual mode and set the cooking time for 25 minutes at High pressure.
3. Once cooking is complete, perform a natural pressure release for 10 minutes. Carefully open the lid.
4. Thinly slice the steak and transfer to a salad bowl. Toss with the olive oil and vinegar.
5. Add the peppers, red onion, and lettuce, then toss to combine well. Top with cheese and olives and serve.

## Herbed Beef Ribs with Leek

**Prep time: 40 minutes | Cook time: 1 hour 40 minutes | Serves 4**

| | |
|---|---|
| 1 pound (454 g) beef short ribs, bone-in | 1 clove garlic, sliced |
| ½ medium leek, sliced | 1 sprig thyme |
| | 1 sprig rosemary |
| ½ teaspoon celery seeds | 1 tablespoon olive oil |
| 1 teaspoon onion soup mix | Sea salt and ground black pepper, to taste |
| | 1 cup water |

1. Place all ingredients in the Instant Pot.
2. Secure the lid. Choose the Manual mode and set the cooking time for 90 minutes at High pressure.
3. Once cooking is complete, do a natural pressure release for 30 minutes, then release any remaining pressure. Carefully open the lid.
4. Transfer the short ribs in the broiler and broil for 10 minutes or until crispy.
5. Transfer the ribs to a platter and serve.

## Lemongrass Beef and Rice Pot

**Prep time: 45 minutes | Cook time: 15 minutes | Serves 4**

1 pound (454 g) beef stew meat, cut into cubes
2 tablespoons olive oil
1 green bell pepper, chopped
1 red bell pepper, chopped
1 lemongrass stalk, sliced
1 onion, chopped
2 garlic cloves, minced
1 cup jasmine rice
2 cups chicken broth
2 tablespoons chopped parsley, for garnish

**Marinade:**

1 tablespoon rice wine
½ teaspoon Five-spice
½ teaspoon miso paste
1 teaspoon garlic purée
1 teaspoon chili powder
1 teaspoon cumin
powder
1 tablespoon soy sauce
1 teaspoon plus ½ tablespoon ginger paste, divided
½ teaspoon sesame oil
Salt and black pepper, to taste

1. In a bowl, add beef and top with the ingredients for the marinade. Mix and wrap the bowl in plastic. Marinate in the refrigerate for 30 minutes.
2. Set the Instant Pot to Sauté mode, then heat the olive oil.
3. Drain beef from marinade and brown in the pot for 5 minutes. Flip frequently.
4. Stir in bell peppers, lemongrass, onion, and garlic. Sauté for 3 minutes.
5. Stir in rice, cook for 1 minute. Pour in the broth. Seal the lid, select the Manual mode and set the time for 5 minutes on High Pressure.
6. When timer beeps, perform a quick pressure release. Carefully open the lid.
7. Dish out and garnish with parsley. Serve warm.

## Beef Steaks with Mushrooms

**Prep time: 15 minutes | Cook time: 25 minutes | Serves 2**

2 beef steaks, boneless
Salt and black pepper, to taste
2 tablespoons olive oil
4 ounces (113 g) mushrooms, sliced
½ onion, chopped
1 garlic clove, minced
1 cup vegetable soup
1½ tablespoons cornstarch
1 tablespoon half-and-half

1. Rub the beef steaks with salt and pepper on a clean work surface.
2. Set the Instant Pot to Sauté mode and warm the olive oil until shimmering.
3. Sear the beef for 2 minutes per side until browned. Transfer to a plate.
4. Add the mushrooms and sauté for 5 minutes or until soft. Add the onion and garlic and sauté for 2 minutes until fragrant.
5. Return the steaks to the pot and pour in the soup. Seal the lid, select the Manual mode, and set the time to 15 minutes on High Pressure.
6. When cooking is complete, do a quick pressure release and unlock the lid and transfer the chops to a plate. Press the Sauté button.
7. In a bowl, combine the cornstarch and half-and-half and mix well. Pour the mixture into the pot and cook until the sauce is thickened. Serve warm.

# Chapter 11 Lamb

## Braised Lamb Ragout

**Prep time: 10 minutes | Cook time: 1 hour 8 minutes | Serves 4 to 6**

1½ pounds (680 g) lamb, bone-in
1 teaspoon vegetable oil
4 tomatoes, chopped
2 carrots, sliced
½ pound (227 g) mushrooms, sliced
1 small yellow onion, chopped
6 cloves garlic,

minced
2 tablespoons tomato paste
1 teaspoon dried oregano
Water, as needed
Salt and ground black pepper, to taste
Handful chopped parsley

1. Press the Sauté button on the Instant Pot and heat the olive oil. Add the lamb and sear for 4 minutes per side, or until browned.
2. Stir in the tomatoes, carrots, mushrooms, onion, garlic, tomato paste, oregano and water. Season with salt and pepper.
3. Set the lid in place. Select the Manual mode and set the cooking time for 60 minutes on High Pressure. Once cooking is complete, perform a quick pressure release. Carefully open the lid.
4. Transfer the lamb to a plate. Discard the bones and shred the meat. Return the shredded lamb to the pot, add the parsley and stir.
5. Serve warm.

## Milky Lamb with Potatoes

**Prep time: 10 minutes | Cook time: 1 hour | Serves 4**

2 pounds (907 g) boneless lamb shoulder, cubed
1 pound (454 g) potatoes, cubed
3 carrots, cubed
5 garlic cloves

2 rosemary sprigs
4 cups milk
2 cups water
1 tablespoon Vegeta seasoning
Salt and black pepper, to taste

1. Add all the ingredients to the Instant Pot and stir to combine.
2. Lock the lid. Select the Manual mode and set the cooking time for 60 minutes on High Pressure. Once cooking is complete, use a natural pressure release for 10 minutes, then release any remaining pressure.
3. Carefully open the lid. Remove and discard the rosemary springs. Divide the dish among four serving bowls and serve warm.

## Indian Lamb Curry

**Prep time: 15 minutes | Cook time: 1 hour 3 minutes | Serves 4**

2 tablespoons olive oil
1 pound (454 g) lamb meat, cubed
2 tomatoes, chopped
1 onion, chopped
1-inch piece ginger, grated
2 garlic cloves, minced
½ tablespoon ground cumin
½ tablespoon chili

flakes
½ tablespoon ground turmeric
½ teaspoon garam masala
1 cup chicken stock
½ cup coconut milk
¼ cup rice, rinsed
1 tablespoon fish sauce
¼ cup chopped cilantro

1. Set the Instant Pot on the Sauté mode. Heat the olive oil and sear the lamb shoulder on both sides for 8 minutes, or until browned. Transfer the lamb to a plate and set aside.
2. Add the tomatoes, onion, ginger and garlic to the pot and sauté for 5 minutes. Stir in the cumin, chili flakes, turmeric and garam masala. Cook for 10 minutes, or until they form a paste. Whisk in the chicken stock, coconut milk, rice and fish sauce. Return the lamb back to the pot.
3. Lock the lid. Select Meat/Stew mode and set the cooking time for 35 minutes on High Pressure. Once cooking is complete, do a natural pressure release for 10 minutes, then release any remaining pressure. Open the lid and select the Sauté mode. Cook the curry for 5 minutes, or until thickened.
4. Top with the chopped cilantro and serve warm in bowls.

## Garlicky Lamb Leg

**Prep time: 35 minutes | Cook time: 50 minutes | Serves 6**

2 pounds (907 g) lamb leg
6 garlic cloves, minced
1 teaspoon sea salt
1½ teaspoons black pepper

2½ tablespoons olive oil
1½ small onions
1½ cups bone broth
¾ cup orange juice
6 sprigs thyme

1. In a bowl, whisk together the garlic, salt and pepper. Add the lamb leg to the bowl and marinate for 30 minutes.
2. Press the Sauté button on the Instant Pot and heat the olive oil. Add the onions and sauté for 4 minutes. Transfer the onions to a separate bowl.
3. Add the marinated lamb to the pot and sear for 3 minutes on each side, or lightly browned. Whisk in the cooked onions, broth, orange juice and thyme.
4. Close and secure the lid. Set the Instant Pot to the Meat/Stew mode and set the cooking time for 40 minutes on High Pressure. When the timer beeps, use a natural pressure release for 10 minutes, then release any remaining pressure. Carefully open the lid.
5. Divide the dish among 6 serving bowls and serve hot.

## Lamb Curry with Tomatoes

**Prep time: 15 minutes | Cook time: 59 minutes | Serves 4**

¼ cup olive oil, divided
2 pounds (907 g) lamb shoulder, cubed
4 green onions, sliced
2 tomatoes, peeled and chopped
2 tablespoons garlic paste
1 tablespoon ginger paste
1½ cups vegetable stock
2 teaspoons ground

coriander
2 teaspoons allspice
1 teaspoon ground cumin
½ teaspoon ground red chili pepper
½ teaspoon curry powder
1 large carrot, sliced
1 potato, cubed
2 bay leaves
Salt, to taste
2 tablespoons mint leaves, chopped

1. Press the Sauté button on the Instant Pot and heat 2 tablespoons of the olive oil. Add the green onions and sauté for 3 minutes, or until softened, stirring constantly. Transfer the green onions to a blender. Mix in the tomatoes, garlic paste and ginger paste. Blend until smooth.
2. Heat the remaining 2 tablespoons of the olive oil in the pot and add the lamb to the pot. Cook for 6 minutes. Stir in the vegetable stock, coriander, allspice, cumin, red chili pepper, curry powder, carrot, potato, bay leaves and salt.
3. Lock the lid. Select the Manual function and set the cooking time for 50 minutes on High Pressure. When the timer beeps, use a natural pressure release for 10 minutes, then release any remaining pressure. Open the lid. Discard the bay leaves.
4. Top with the mint leaves and serve immediately.

## Spicy Lamb Shoulder

**Prep time: 10 minutes | Cook time: 50 minutes | Serves 4**

2 pounds (907 g) lamb shoulder
1 cup chopped fresh thyme
¼ cup rice wine
¼ cup chicken stock
1 tablespoon turmeric

1 tablespoon ground black pepper
1 teaspoon oregano
1 teaspoon paprika
1 teaspoon sugar
1 tablespoon olive oil
½ cup water
4 tablespoons butter

1. In a large bowl, whisk together the thyme, rice wine, chicken stock, turmeric, black pepper, oregano, paprika and sugar. Rub all sides of the lamb shoulder with the spice mix.
2. Press the Sauté button on the Instant Pot and heat the oil. Add the lamb to the pot and sear for 5 minutes on both sides, or until browned. Add the remaining spice mixture, water and butter to the pot. Stir until the butter is melted.
3. Lock the lid. Select the Manual mode and set the cooking time for 45 minutes on High Pressure. Once cooking is complete, do a natural pressure release for 10 minutes, then release any remaining pressure. Carefully open the lid.
4. Serve hot.

## Lamb with Peppers and Tomatoes

**Prep time: 10 minutes | Cook time: 30 minutes | Serves 10**

2 tablespoons olive oil
2 pounds (907 g) boneless lamb, trimmed
Salt and black pepper, to taste
4 cups chopped tomatoes
3 cups sugar-free tomato sauce
2 cups water
2 teaspoons crushed

dried rosemary
6 garlic cloves, minced
2 large yellow bell peppers, deseeded and sliced
2 large red bell peppers, deseeded and sliced
2 large green bell peppers, deseeded and sliced

1. Press the Sauté button on the Instant Pot and heat the olive oil. Add the lamb meat to the pot and season with salt and pepper. Cook for 5 minutes. Transfer the lamb meat to a plate.
2. Stir together all the remaining ingredients in the pot and add the lamb meat.
3. Lock the lid. Select the Manual function and set the cooking time for 25 minutes at High Pressure.
4. Once cooking is complete, use a quick pressure release. Open the lid. Serve hot.

## Lamb Tagine with Carrots

**Prep time: 15 minutes | Cook time: 32 to 34 minutes | Serves 4**

2 tablespoons ghee
1½ pounds (680 g) lamb stew meat, cubed
4 large carrots, peeled and chopped
1 large red onion, chopped
6 cloves garlic, minced
2 teaspoons coriander powder
2 teaspoons ginger powder
2 teaspoons cumin powder
½ teaspoon turmeric

¼ teaspoon clove powder
¼ teaspoon cinnamon powder
¼ teaspoon red chili flakes
2 bay leaves
1 lemon, zested and juiced
Salt and black pepper, to taste
2 cups vegetable stock
2 cups green olives, pitted
3 tablespoons chopped parsley

1. Select the Sauté setting. Melt the ghee and add the lamb to the pot. Cook for 6 to 7 minutes, or until the lamb is lightly browned. Stir in the carrots, onion and garlic and cook for 5 minutes, or until the vegetables are tender.
2. Add the coriander, ginger, cumin, turmeric, clove, cinnamon, red chili flakes, bay leaves, lemon zest, lemon juice, salt and pepper to the pot. Cook for 1 to 2 minutes, or until fragrant. Pour the vegetable stock into the pot.
3. Lock the lid. Select Manual mode and set the cooking time for 20 minutes on High Pressure. Once cooking is complete, use a natural pressure release for 10 minutes, then release any remaining pressure. Open the lid. Discard the bay leaves and stir in the green olives and parsley.
4. Divide the dish among 4 serving bowls and serve warm.

## Black Bean Minced Lamb

**Prep time: 10 minutes | Cook time: 25 minutes | Serves 4 to 6**

1 pound (454 g) ground lamb
2 tablespoons vegetable oil
½ cup chopped onion
½ teaspoon salt
2 cans drained black beans
1 can undrained diced tomatoes
1 can chopped and

undrained green chillies
1½ cups chicken broth
1½ tablespoons tomato paste
1½ tablespoons chili powder
2 teaspoons cumin
½ teaspoon cayenne

1. Set the Instant Pot to the Sauté mode and heat the oil. Add the lamb, onion and salt to the pot and sauté for 5 minutes, stirring constantly. Add the remaining ingredients to the pot and stir well.
2. Select the Manual setting and set the cooking time for 20 minutes on High Pressure. Once the timer goes off, use a natural pressure release for 10 minutes, then release any remaining pressure. Carefully open the lid.
3. Serve immediately.

## Greek Lamb Loaf

**Prep time: 5 minutes | Cook time: 15 minutes | Serves 2**

| | |
|---|---|
| 1 pound (454 g) ground lamb meat | marjoram |
| 4 garlic cloves | 1 teaspoon rosemary |
| ½ small onion, chopped | ¾ teaspoon salt |
| | ¼ teaspoon black pepper |
| 1 teaspoon ground | ¾ cup water |

1. In a blender, combine the lamb meat, garlic, onions, marjoram, rosemary, salt and pepper. Pulse until well mixed. Shape the lamb mixture into a compact loaf and cover tightly with aluminium foil. Use a fork to make some holes.
2. Pour the water into the Instant Pot and put a trivet in the pot. Place the lamb loaf on the trivet and lock the lid.
3. Select the Manual mode and set the cooking time for 15 minutes on High Pressure. When the timer goes off, use a quick pressure release.
4. Carefully open the lid. Serve warm.

## Slow Cooked Lamb Shanks

**Prep time: 10 minutes | Cook time: 55 minutes | Serves 4**

| | |
|---|---|
| 2 tablespoons olive oil | 1 cup chicken broth |
| 2 pounds (907 g) lamb shanks | ¾ cup red wine |
| | 2 cups crushed tomatoes |
| Salt and black pepper, to taste | 1 teaspoon dried oregano |
| 6 garlic cloves, minced | ¼ cup chopped parsley, for garnish |

1. Press the Sauté button on the Instant Pot. Heat the olive oil and add the lamb to the pot. Season with salt and pepper. Sear the lamb on both sides for 6 minutes, or until browned. Transfer the lamb to a plate and set aside.
2. Add the garlic to the pot and sauté for 30 seconds, or until fragrant. Stir in the chicken broth and red wine and cook for 2 minutes, stirring constantly. Add the tomatoes and oregano. Stir and cook for 2 minutes. Return the lamb to the pot and baste with the chicken broth mixture.

3. Lock the lid. Select the Manual setting and set the cooking time for 45 minutes on High Pressure.
4. When the timer beeps, do a natural pressure release for 15 minutes, then release any remaining pressure. Open the lid. Top with the chopped parsley and adjust the taste with salt and pepper.
5. Divide among 4 plates and serve warm.

## Sauce Glazed Lamb Chops

**Prep time: 10 minutes | Cook time: 29 minutes | Serves 2**

| | |
|---|---|
| 1½ tablespoons butter | free tomatoes |
| | ½ cup bone broth |
| 1 pound (454 g) lamb loin chops | ¾ teaspoon crushed dried rosemary |
| ½ small onion, sliced | Salt and black pepper, to taste |
| 1 garlic clove, crushed | 1 tablespoon arrowroot starch |
| 1 cup carrots, peeled and sliced | ½ tablespoon cold water |
| ¾ cup diced sugar- | |

1. Select the Sauté mode and heat the butter in the Instant Pot. Add the lamb chops to the pot and cook for 3 minutes on each side, or until lightly browned. Transfer the lamb chops to plates.
2. Add the onion and garlic to the pot and cook for 3 minutes. Stir in the carrots, tomatoes, bone broth, rosemary, salt and pepper.
3. Lock the lid. Select the Manual mode and set the cooking time for 15 minutes at High Pressure. When the timer goes off, do a quick pressure release. Carefully open the lid.
4. In a small bowl, whisk together the arrowroot starch and water. Pour the slurry in the pot. Select the Sauté mode and cook for 5 minutes.
5. Spread the sauce over the cooked chops and serve hot.

## Lamb Curry with Zucchini

**Prep time: 40 minutes | Cook time: 25 minutes | Serves 3**

| | |
|---|---|
| 1 pound (454 g) cubed lamb stew meat | pepper |
| | 1 tablespoon olive oil |
| 2 garlic cloves, minced | 1½ medium carrots, sliced |
| ½ cup coconut milk | ½ medium onion, diced |
| 1 tablespoon grated fresh ginger | ¾ cup diced tomatoes |
| ½ teaspoon lime juice | ½ teaspoon turmeric powder |
| ¼ teaspoon salt | ½ medium zucchini, diced |
| ¼ teaspoon black | |

1. In a bowl, stir together the garlic, coconut milk, ginger, lime juice, salt and pepper. Add the lamb to the bowl and marinate for 30 minutes.
2. Combine the remaining ingredients, except for the zucchini, in the Instant Pot. Add the meat and the marinade to the pot.
3. Set the lid in place. Select the Manual mode and set the cooking time for 20 minutes on High Pressure. Once the timer goes off, use a natural pressure release for 15 minutes, then release any remaining pressure.
4. Open the lid. Add the zucchini to the pot. Select the Sauté mode and cook for 5 minutes.
5. Serve hot.

## Spicy Lamb with Anchovies

**Prep time: 10 minutes | Cook time: 1 hour 5 minutes | Serves 4**

| | |
|---|---|
| 2 tablespoons olive oil | purée |
| | 3 green chilies, minced |
| 2 pounds (907 g) boneless lamb shoulder, cut into 4 pieces | 1 sprig rosemary |
| | 1 teaspoon dried oregano |
| 2 cups chicken stock | Salt, to taste |
| 6 tinned anchovies, chopped | 2 tablespoons chopped parsley |
| 1 teaspoon garlic | |

1. Press the Sauté button on the Instant Pot. Heat the olive oil and sear the lamb shoulder on both sides for 5 minutes, or until browned. Transfer the lamb to a plate and set aside.
2. Pour the chicken stock into the Instant Pot and add the anchovies and garlic. Return the lamb to the pot and sprinkle the green chilies, rosemary, oregano and salt on top.
3. Set the lid in place, select the Manual mode and set the cooking time for 60 minutes on High Pressure.
4. When the timer goes off, use a natural pressure release for 15 minutes, then release any remaining pressure.
5. Open the lid, shred the lamb with two forks and top with the chopped parsley. Serve warm.

## Sumptuous Lamb Casserole

**Prep time: 15 minutes | Cook time: 41 minutes | Serves 2 to 4**

| | |
|---|---|
| 1 pound (454 g) lamb stew meat, cubed | 2 tablespoons red wine |
| | 2 tablespoons ketchup |
| 1 tablespoon olive oil | 1 teaspoon ground cumin |
| 3 cloves garlic, minced | |
| 2 tomatoes, chopped | 1 teaspoon sweet paprika |
| 2 carrots, chopped | |
| 1 onion, chopped | ¼ teaspoon dried rosemary |
| 1 pound (454 g) baby potatoes | ¼ teaspoon dried oregano |
| 1 celery stalk, chopped | Salt and ground |
| 2 cups chicken stock | black pepper, to taste |

1. Press the Sauté button on the Instant Pot and heat the oil. Add the lamb to the pot and sear for 5 minutes, or until lightly browned. Add the garlic and sauté for 1 minute. Add all the remaining ingredients to the pot.
2. Set the lid in place. Select the Manual mode and set the cooking time for 35 minutes on High Pressure. Once cooking is complete, perform a natural pressure release for 10 minutes, then release any remaining pressure. Carefully open the lid.
3. Serve hot.

## Spicy Minced Lamb Meat

**Prep time: 10 minutes | Cook time: 20 minutes | Serves 2**

| | |
|---|---|
| ½ pound (227 g) ground lamb meat | ½ teaspoon salt |
| ½ cup onion, chopped | ¼ teaspoon ground coriander |
| ½ tablespoon minced ginger | ¼ teaspoon cayenne pepper |
| ½ tablespoon garlic | ¼ teaspoon cumin |
| | ¼ teaspoon turmeric |

1. Press the Sauté button on the Instant Pot. Add the onion, ginger and garlic to the pot and sauté for 5 minutes. Add the remaining ingredients to the pot and lock the lid.
2. Select the Manual mode and set the cooking time for 15 minutes on High Pressure. Once the timer goes off, perform a natural pressure release for 15 minutes.
3. Open the lid and serve immediately.

## Lamb Chops in Picante Sauce

**Prep time: 5 minutes | Cook time: 40 minutes | Serves 6**

| | |
|---|---|
| 6 lamb chops, bone-in | 1¼ cups Picante sauce |
| 3 tablespoons all-purpose flour | 3 tablespoons brown sugar |
| 1¼ apples, peeled and sliced | 3 tablespoons olive oil |

1. In a bowl, place the flour and dip the lamb chops in it to coat well.
2. In another bowl, combine the apples, Picante sauce and brown sugar until well mixed.
3. Press the Sauté button on the Instant Pot and heat the olive oil. Add the coated chops to the pot and sear for 5 minutes, or until lightly browned.
4. Lock the lid. Select the Meat/Stew mode and set the cooking time for 35 minutes on High Pressure.
5. When the timer beeps, use a natural pressure release for 10 minutes, then release any remaining pressure.
6. Open the lid and serve warm.

## Instant Pot Lamb Meatballs

**Prep time: 10 minutes | Cook time: 38 minutes | Serves 3**

| | |
|---|---|
| ¾ pound (340 g) ground lamb meat | peeled |
| 1 teaspoon adobo seasoning | ½ small yellow onion, chopped roughly |
| ½ tablespoon olive oil | ½ cup sugar-free tomato sauce |
| 2 small tomatoes, chopped roughly | ¼ teaspoon crushed red pepper flakes, |
| 5 mini bell peppers, deseeded and halved | Salt and freshly ground black pepper, to taste |
| 2 garlic cloves, | |

1. Mix the lamb meat and adobo seasoning in a bowl until well combined. Shape the meat mixture into small meatballs.
2. Set the Instant Pot on the Sauté mode and heat the olive oil. Add the meatballs to the pot and cook for 3 minutes, or until golden brown. Transfer the meatballs to bowls.
3. Stir together all the remaining ingredients in the pot. Lock the lid. Select the Meat/Stew mode and set the cooking time for 35 minutes on High Pressure. When the timer beeps, use a natural pressure release for 10 minutes, then release any remaining pressure.
4. Carefully open the lid. Transfer the vegetable mixture to a blender and pulse until smooth. Spread the vegetable paste over the meatballs and serve hot.

## Traditional Lamb Rogan Josh

**Prep time: 15 minutes | Cook time: 35 to 37 minutes | Serves 4**

2 tablespoons ghee
1 large onion, chopped
2 pounds (907 g) boneless lamb shoulder, cubed
4 teaspoons chili powder
3 teaspoons coriander powder
2 teaspoons minced ginger
1 teaspoon garam masala
1 teaspoon turmeric
½ teaspoon cinnamon powder
½ teaspoon cardamom powder
¼ teaspoon ground cloves
¼ teaspoon cumin powder
10 garlic cloves, minced
1 bay leaf
Salt and black pepper, to taste
1 (15-ounce / 425-g) can tomato sauce
8 tablespoons plain yogurt
1 cup water
3 tablespoons chopped cilantro

1. Select the Sauté mode. Melt the ghee and add the onion and lamb to the pot. Cook for 6 to 7 minutes, or until the lamb is lightly browned.
2. Add the chili powder, coriander, ginger, garam masala, turmeric, cinnamon, cardamom, cloves, cumin, garlic, bay leaf, salt and pepper to the pot. Cook for 3 minutes, or until fragrant.
3. Stir in the tomato sauce and cook for 2 to 3 minutes. Add the yogurt, 1 tablespoon at a time, stirring to combine. Pour the water in the pot.
4. Lock the lid. Select Manual mode and set the cooking time for 20 minutes on High Pressure.
5. When the timer goes off, do a natural pressure release for 10 minutes, then release any remaining pressure. Open the lid and select the Sauté mode. Cook for another 4 minutes to boil off some liquid until the consistency is stew-like.
6. Divide the dish among 4 bowls. Top with the chopped cilantro and serve warm.

## Lamb Biryani with Raisins

**Prep time: 45 minutes | Cook time: 16 to 17 minutes | Serves 4**

1 pound (454 g) lamb leg steak, cut into cubes
1 large brown onion, thinly sliced
1 green bell pepper, sliced
Juice of ½ lime
½ cup Greek yogurt
4 tablespoons ghee, divided
1 tablespoon garlic paste
1 tablespoon grated ginger
3 teaspoons garam masala
1 teaspoon paprika
¼ teaspoon cayenne pepper
½ teaspoon cardamom powder
½ teaspoon turmeric
Salt, to taste
2 cups warm water
1 cup basmati rice, rinsed
½ cup chopped cilantro
½ teaspoon saffron, soaked in 3 tablespoons of hot water
2 tablespoons red raisins

1. In a bowl, stir together the lamb, brown onion and bell pepper.
2. In another bowl, whisk together the lime juice, yogurt, 2 tablespoons of the ghee, garlic, ginger, garam masala, paprika, cayenne pepper, cardamom, turmeric and salt.
3. Spread the mixture over the meat and vegetables. Stir and cover in plastic. Let marinate in the refrigerator for 30 minutes.
4. Remove the meat from the refrigerator and drain the marinade.
5. Press the Sauté button on the Instant Pot and melt the remaining 2 tablespoons of the ghee. Add the lamb and sear for 6 to 7 minutes, or lightly browned. Add the warm water, basmati rice, cilantro and saffron liquid to the pot. Do not stir.
6. Close and secure the lid. Select the Manual mode and set the cooking time for 10 minutes on High Pressure. When the timer goes off, use a natural pressure release for 10 minutes, then release any remaining pressure.
7. Carefully open the lid and stir in raisins. Serve immediately.

# Chapter 12 Vegetarian and Vegan

## Brussels Sprouts with Peanuts

**Prep time: 10 minutes | Cook time: 8 minutes | Serves 4**

3 tablespoons sesame oil
1½ pounds (680 g) Brussels sprouts, halved

2 tablespoons fish sauce
1 cup chicken stock
½ cup chopped roasted peanuts

1. Set the Instant Pot to Sauté and heat the sesame oil until shimmering.
2. Add and fry Brussels sprouts for 5 minutes or until golden. Mix in the fish sauce and chicken stock.
3. Seal the lid. Select the Manual mode and set the time for 3 minutes.
4. Once cooking is complete, do a quick pressure release, then unlock the lid.
5. Mix in the peanuts. Serve immediately.

## Bok Choy with Rice Wine Vinegar

**Prep time: 5 minutes | Cook time: 6 minutes | Serves 4**

1 teaspoon sesame oil
1 clove garlic, pressed
1 pound (454 g) Bok choy

½ cup water
1 tablespoon rice wine vinegar
2 tablespoons soy sauce

1. Press the Sauté button and heat the sesame oil in the Instant Pot.
2. Add the garlic and sauté for 1 minute or until fragrant. Add the Bok choy and pour in the water.
3. Secure the lid. Choose the Manual mode and set the cooking time for 5 minutes at High pressure.
4. Meanwhile, in a small bowl, whisk the rice vinegar and soy sauce.
5. Once cooking is complete, do a quick pressure release. Carefully open the lid.
6. Drizzle the sauce over the Bok choy and serve immediately.

## Broccoli, Spinach, and Avocado Mash

**Prep time: 15 minutes | Cook time: 3 minutes | Serves 4**

1 medium broccoli, cut into florets
2 cups spinach
1 cup vegetable broth
2 avocados, halved, pitted, and peeled
2 tablespoons chopped parsley

2 tablespoons butter
Salt and black pepper, to taste
3 tablespoons Greek yogurt
2 tablespoons toasted pine nuts, for topping

1. Add the broccoli, spinach, and broth to the Instant Pot. Stir to mix well.
2. Seal the lid. Select the Manual mode and set the cooking time for 3 minutes on High Pressure.
3. Once cooking is complete, do a quick pressure release. Carefully open the lid. Stir in the avocado, parsley, butter, salt, pepper, and Greek yogurt.
4. Pour the mixture in a food processor and pulse until smooth. Spoon into serving bowls and top with pine nuts. Serve immediately.

## Cauliflower and Celeriac Mix

**Prep time: 10 minutes | Cook time: 2 minutes | Serves 4**

1 cup water
1 head cauliflower, cut into florets
1 carrot, sliced

½ cup celeriac, sliced
2 tablespoons butter
Salt and black pepper, to taste

1. Pour the water into the Instant Pot and fit in a steamer basket. Place the cauliflower, carrots, and celeriac in the basket.
2. Seal the lid. Select the Steam mode, then set the cooking time for 2 minutes at High Pressure.
3. Once cooking time is complete, perform a quick pressure release. Unlock the lid and transfer the veggies to a bowl.
4. Stir in the butter and sprinkle with salt and pepper before serving.

## Hearty Vegetable Burgers

**Prep time: 20 minutes | Cook time: 55 minutes | Serves 2**

2 tablespoons olive oil, divided
½ medium red bell pepper, deseeded and chopped
½ medium yellow onion, chopped
½ medium zucchini, chopped
½ cup chopped yellow squash
4 cloves garlic, minced

1 cup dried black beans
8 cups water
1 teaspoon salt
½ cup panko bread crumbs
½ jalapeño, deseeded and minced
Pinch freshly ground black pepper
2 burger buns

1. Press the Sauté button on the Instant Pot and heat 1 tablespoon of olive oil until shimmering.
2. Add the bell pepper and onion and sauté for 3 minutes or until the onion is translucent.
3. Add the zucchini, squash, and garlic and sauté for 3 minutes. Transfer the vegetables in the pot to a small bowl and set aside.
4. Add the beans, water, and salt to the pot. Lock the lid. Press the Bean button and set the cooking time for 30 minutes at High Pressure.
5. When the timer beeps, let pressure release naturally for 10 minutes. Release any remaining pressure, then unlock lid.
6. Press the Sauté button on the pot and simmer bean mixture for 10 minutes to thicken.
7. Transfer the mixture to a large bowl and mash with forks. When cool enough to handle, quickly mix in the vegetable mixture, panko, jalapeño, and pepper and blend thoroughly.
8. Form the mixture into 2 patties. Cook in a skillet over remaining 1 tablespoon of olive oil for 2 to 3 minutes on each side until browned.
9. Remove from heat and assemble each patty with a bun. Serve warm.

## Cheesy Asparagus

**Prep time: 10 minutes | Cook time: 8 minutes | Serves 4**

1 cup water
1 pound (454 g) asparagus, chopped
2 garlic cloves, minced
2 tablespoons butter, softened

Salt and black pepper, to taste
1 tablespoon olive oil
½ lemon, juiced
2 tablespoons grated Parmesan cheese

1. In the Instant pot, pour the water and fit in a trivet. Cut out a foil sheet, place the asparagus on top with garlic and butter. Season with salt and black pepper. Wrap the foil and place on the trivet.
2. Seal the lid. Select the Manual mode and set to 8 minutes on High Pressure.
3. Once cooking is complete, do a quick pressure release. Carefully open the lid.
4. Remove the foil, then transfer the asparagus onto a platter. Drizzle with lemon juice, and top with Parmesan cheese to serve.

## Easy Green Beans with Toasted Peanuts

**Prep time: 10 minutes | Cook time: 1 minutes | Serves 4**

1 cup water
1 pound (454 g) green beans, trimmed
1 lemon, juiced
2 tablespoons olive

oil
Salt and black pepper, to taste
2 tablespoons toasted peanuts

1. Pour the water in the Instant Pot, then fit in a steamer basket and arrange the green beans on top.
2. Seal the lid. Select the Manual mode and set the time for 1 minute on High Pressure.
3. Once cooking is complete, do a quick pressure release. Unlock the lid.
4. Transfer the green beans onto a plate and mix in lemon juice, olive oil, salt, pepper, and toasted peanuts. Serve immediately.

## Mexican Bell Peppers with Tomato Sauce

**Prep time: 10 minutes | Cook time: 5 minutes | Serves 4**

4 large mixed bell peppers, sliced into strips
1 (15-ounce / 425-g) can tomato sauce
½ teaspoon Mexican seasoning
2 large white onions, sliced
2 teaspoons chili powder
½ teaspoon garlic powder
Salt and black pepper, to taste
1 cup water

1. Combine all the ingredients in the Instant Pot. Stir to mix well.
2. Seal the lid. Select the Manual mode and set the time for 5 minutes at High Pressure.
3. Once cooking is complete, do a quick pressure release, then unlock the lid.
4. Serve warm.

## Gold Potato and Boiled Egg Salad

**Prep time: 20 minutes | Cook time: 12 minutes | Serves 4**

1 cup water
1 pound (454 g) small Yukon Gold potatoes
2 boiled eggs, peeled and chopped
1 celery rib, diced
¼ cup pickle relish
½ yellow onion, sliced
1 garlic clove,
minced
$1/3$ cup mayonnaise
½ teaspoon fresh rosemary, chopped
½ tablespoon yellow mustard
$1/3$ teaspoon cayenne pepper
Sea salt and ground black pepper, to taste

1. Pour the water in the Instant Pot and fit in a steamer basket. Place the potatoes in the steamer basket.
2. Secure the lid. Choose the Manual mode and set the cooking time for 12 minutes at High pressure.
3. Once cooking is complete, do a quick pressure release. Carefully remove the lid. Allow to cool for a few minutes until cool enough to handle.
4. Peel and slice the potatoes, then place them in a large bowl and toss with the remaining ingredients. Stir to combine.
5. Serve immediately.

## Sweet Potato Casserole with Marshmallows

**Prep time: 20 minutes | Cook time: 25 minutes | Serves 4**

3 medium-sized sweet potatoes, peeled and cut into 1-inch pieces
1½ cup water, divided
½ cup milk
1 egg, whisked
3 tablespoons butter, softened
½ teaspoon vanilla paste
¼ cup granulated sugar
Topping:
½ cup mini marshmallows
¼ cup chopped pecans
¼ cup all-purpose flour
¼ teaspoon cinnamon
⅛ teaspoon salt
$1/3$ cup brown sugar
2 tablespoons butter, at room temperature

1. Add the sweet potatoes and ½ cup of water to the Instant Pot.
2. Secure the lid. Choose the Manual mode and set the cooking time for 8 minutes at High pressure.
3. Once cooking is complete, perform a quick pressure release. Carefully open the lid.
4. Drain the potatoes and transfer them to a mixing bowl. Add the milk, egg, butter, vanilla, and granulated sugar to the bowl. Pour them in a food processor.
5. Pulse to mash the potatoes. Scrape the mashed potatoes into a lightly greased baking pan.
6. Mix the ingredients for the topping in a small bowl. Top the baking pan with the topping mixture.
7. Pour 1 cup of water in the Instant Pot, then fit in a trivet. Lower the baking dish into the trivet.
8. Secure the lid. Choose the Manual mode and set the cooking time for 15 minutes at High pressure.
9. Once cooking is complete, perform a quick pressure release. Carefully open the lid. Serve immediately.

## Italian Potato and Carrot Medley

**Prep time: 15 minutes | Cook time: 11 minutes | Serves 4**

2 tablespoons olive oil
1 cup potatoes, peeled and chopped
3 carrots, peeled and chopped
3 garlic cloves, minced
1 cup vegetable broth
1 teaspoon Italian seasoning
Salt and black pepper, to taste
1 tablespoon chopped parsley
1 tablespoon chopped oregano

1. Set the Instant Pot to the Sauté mode. Heat the olive oil until shimmering.
2. Add and sauté the potatoes and carrots for 5 minutes or until tender.
3. Add the garlic and cook for a minute or until fragrant. Pour in the vegetable broth, season with Italian seasoning, salt, and black pepper.
4. Seal the lid. Select the Manual mode and set the time for 5 minutes at High Pressure.
5. Once cooking is complete, do a quick pressure release, then unlock the lid.
6. Spoon the potatoes and carrots into a serving bowl and mix in the parsley and oregano. Serve warm.

## Cheesy Broccoli Stuffed Potatoes

**Prep time: 10 minutes | Cook time: 20 minutes | Serves 4**

1 cup water
1 head broccoli, cut into florets
4 small russet potatoes
¾ cup half-and-half
1 tablespoon butter
2 cups Gruyere cheese, grated
1 teaspoon cornstarch
¼ cup chopped fresh chives

1. Pour the water in the Instant Pot and fit in a steamer basket.
2. Add the broccoli. Seal the lid. Select the Manual mode and set the cooking time for 1 minute at High Pressure.
3. Once cooking is complete, do a quick pressure release, then unlock the lid and transfer the broccoli to a bowl.
4. In the steamer basket, place the potatoes. Seal the lid again. Select the Manual mode and set the cooking time for 15 minutes on High Pressure.
5. Once cooking is complete, do a quick pressure release. Unlock the lid and let the potatoes cool.
6. Take out the steamer basket and discard the water. Press the Sauté button and warm half-and-half and butter until the butter melts.
7. In a bowl, mix the cheese with cornstarch and pour the mixture into the pot. Stir until the cheese melts. Transfer the mixture in a large bowl.
8. Toss the broccoli with the mixture to combine well. Cut a slit into each potato and stuff with the broccoli mixture. Scatter with chives to serve.

## Cheesy Cabbage and Pepper Bake

**Prep time: 15 minutes | Cook time: 25 minutes | Serves 2**

1 tablespoon olive oil, divided
½ pound (227 g) green cabbage, shredded
1 garlic clove, sliced
1 onion, thinly sliced
1 Serrano pepper, chopped
1 sweet pepper, thinly sliced
Sea salt and ground black pepper, to taste
1 teaspoon paprika
1 cup cream of mushroom soup
4 ounces (113 g) Colby cheese, shredded
1 cup water

1. Grease a baking dish with ½ tablespoon of olive oil. Add the cabbage, garlic, onion, and peppers. Stir to combine.
2. Drizzle with remaining oil and season with salt, black pepper, and paprika. Pour in the mushroom soup. Top with the shredded cheese and cover with aluminum foil.
3. Pour the water in the Instant Pot and fit in a trivet. Lower the dish onto the trivet.
4. Secure the lid. Choose the Manual mode and set the cooking time for 25 minutes at High pressure.
5. Once cooking is complete, perform a quick pressure release. Carefully open the lid. Serve warm.

## Cherry and Pecan Stuffed Pumpkin

**Prep time: 20 minutes | Cook time: 20 minutes | Serves 4**

1 (2-pound / 907-g) pumpkin, halved lengthwise, stems trimmed
2 tablespoons olive oil
1 cup water
½ cup dried cherries
1 teaspoon dried parsley
5 toasted bread slices, cubed
1 teaspoon onion powder
1½ cups vegetable broth
Salt and black pepper, to taste
½ cup chopped pecans, for topping

1. Brush the pumpkin with olive oil. Pour the water in the Instant Pot and fit in a trivet. Place the pumpkin, skin-side down, on the trivet.
2. Seal the lid. Select the Manual mode and set the cooking time for 15 minutes at High Pressure.
3. Once cooking is complete, do a quick pressure release. Carefully open the lid.
4. Remove the pumpkin and water. Press the Sauté button, add the remaining ingredients. Stir for 5 minutes or until the liquid is reduced by half.
5. Divide the mixture between pumpkin halves and top with pecans.

## Butternut Squash and Mushrooms

**Prep time: 10 minutes | Cook time: 40 minutes | Serves 4**

1 tablespoon olive oil
2 cups butternut squash, peeled and diced
1 red bell pepper, diced
½ cup onion, chopped
3 garlic cloves, minced
8 ounces (227 g) white mushrooms, sliced
1½ cups Arborio rice
3½ cup vegetable soup
¼ teaspoon oregano
2 teaspoons ground coriander
1 teaspoon salt
1 teaspoon black pepper
½ cup dry white wine
1½ tablespoons nutritional yeast

1. Put the oil to the Instant Pot and select the Sauté function.
2. Add the butternut squash, bell pepper, onion, and garlic to the oil and sauté for 5 minutes.
3. Stir in the mushrooms, rice, soup, oregano, coriander, salt, pepper, and wine.
4. Secure the lid and select the Bean / Chili function and set the cooking time for 30 minutes at High Pressure.
5. When the timer beeps, do a natural pressure release for 10 minutes, then release any remaining pressure. Open the lid.
6. Mix in the nutritional yeast, then cook for another 5 minutes on Sauté setting. Serve warm.

## Beet Thoran Keralite Sadhya

**Prep time: 10 minutes | Cook time: 20 minutes | Serves 4**

1 cup water
½ pound (227 g) small beets
2 tablespoons olive oil
½ chili pepper, chopped
1 garlic clove, minced
½ cup shallots, chopped
5 curry leaves
$1/3$ teaspoon turmeric powder
Sea salt and ground black pepper, to taste

1. Pour the water in the Instant Pot and fit in a steamer basket. Place the beets in the steamer basket.
2. Secure the lid. Choose the Steam mode and set the cooking time for 15 minutes at High pressure.
3. Once cooking is complete, perform a quick pressure release. Carefully open the lid. Allow the beets to cool for a few minutes.
4. Once the beets are cool enough to touch, transfer them to a cutting board, then peel and chop them into small pieces.
5. Press the Sauté button and heat the olive oil until shimmering.
6. Add and sauté the chili pepper, garlic, shallots, and curry leaves for about 4 minutes or until softened.
7. Sprinkle with the turmeric, salt, and black pepper. Fold in the cooked beets. Serve warm.

## Beet and Walnut Burgers

**Prep time: 10 minutes | Cook time: 45 minutes | Serves 4**

5 medium beets, quartered
1½ cups water
1½ cups chopped walnuts
4 teaspoons cornstarch, combined with ¼ cup warm water
½ cup chopped yellow onions
⅛ cup all-purpose flour
1 cup shredded Cheddar cheese
2 tablespoons soy sauce
2 tablespoons olive oil
Salt and ground black pepper, to taste
4 burger buns

1. Add the beets and water to the Instant Pot. Lock the lid, then press the Manual button, and set the timer to 15 minutes at High Pressure.
2. When the timer beeps, let pressure release naturally for 5 minutes, then release any remaining pressure. Unlock lid.
3. Drain the beets and add to a large bowl. Add the remaining ingredients, except for the buns, and mash the mixture with a potato masher. Form the beet mixture into 4 patties.
4. Preheat the oven to 350ºF (180ºC). Spray a baking pan with cooking spray.
5. Place the patties on the prepared baking pan and bake for 25 to 30 minutes.
6. Allow the patties to cool, then assemble the patties with buns and serve.

## Instant Pot Spanish Pisto

**Prep time: 15 minutes | Cook time: 15 minutes | Serves 2 to 4**

1 tablespoon olive oil
½ onion, diced
2 cloves garlic, sliced
¼ cup Spanish wine
1 pound (454 g) zucchini, cut into 1-inch cubes
½ (14-ounce / 397-g) can tomatoes with
juice
1 Guajillo chili pepper, minced
1 cup cream of mushrooms soup
1 bell pepper, diced
Sea salt and ground black pepper, to taste

1. Press the Sauté button and heat the olive oil in the Instant Pot.

2. Add and sauté the onion for 3 minutes or until translucent.
3. Add the garlic and sauté for a minute or until fragrant. Add the wine to deglaze the pan. Stir in the remaining ingredients.
4. Secure the lid. Choose the Manual mode and set the cooking time for 10 minutes at High pressure.
5. Once cooking is complete, perform a quick pressure release. Carefully open the lid. Serve immediately.

## Golden Cauliflower Tots

**Prep time: 30 minutes | Cook time: 10 minutes | Serves 4**

1 cup water
1 large cauliflower
1 egg, beaten
1 cup almond meal
1 cup grated Parmesan cheese
1 cup grated Gruyere
cheese
2 garlic cloves, minced
Salt, to taste
3 tablespoons olive oil

1. Pour the water in the Instant Pot, then fit in a trivet and place the cauliflower on top.
2. Seal the lid. Select the Manual mode and set the time for 3 minutes at High Pressure.
3. Once cooking is complete, do a quick pressure release. Carefully open the lid.
4. Transfer the cauliflower to a food processor and pulse to rice the cauliflower.
5. Pour the cauliflower rice into a bowl. Mix in the egg, almond meal, cheeses, garlic, and salt.
6. Make the tots: Form the mixture into 2-inch oblong balls. Place on a baking sheet and chill in the refrigerator for 20 minutes.
7. Set the Instant Pot on Sauté mode. Heat the olive oil until shimmering.
8. Remove tots from refrigerator and fry in the oil for 6 minutes on all sides until golden brown. Flip the tots in the oil during the frying. Work in batches to avoid overcrowding.
9. Place the tots on a paper towel-lined plate to pat dry and serve.

## Maple Cinnamon Acorn Squash Slices

**Prep time: 10 minutes | Cook time: 2 minutes | Serves 4**

1 cup water
1 acorn squash, cut into 1-inch slices
1 teaspoon cinnamon
powder
2 tablespoons maple syrup

1. Pour the water in the Instant Pot, then fit in a steamer basket. Add the acorn squash in the basket.
2. Seal the lid. Select the Manual mode and set the time for 2 minutes at high Pressure.
3. Once cooking is complete, do a quick pressure release, then unlock the lid; set aside.
4. Combine cinnamon powder and maple syrup in a deep plate and coat each squash slice in the mixture. Serve immediately.

## Cauliflower and Olive Salad

**Prep time: 10 minutes | Cook time: 2 minutes | Serves 4**

1 cup water
½ pound (227 g) cauliflower, cut into florets
1 bell pepper, thinly sliced
½ red onion, thinly sliced
¼ cup fresh flat-leaf parsley, coarsely chopped
¼ cup green olives, pitted and coarsely chopped
2 ounces (57 g) Mozzarella cheese, crumbled
Dressing:
1 teaspoon hot mustard
2 tablespoons fresh lime juice
3 tablespoons extra-virgin olive oil
Sea salt and ground black pepper, to taste

1. Pour the water in the Instant Pot and fit in a steamer basket. Place the cauliflower in the steamer basket.
2. Secure the lid. Choose the Steam mode and set the cooking time for 2 minutes at High pressure.
3. Once cooking is complete, perform a quick pressure release. Carefully open the lid.

4. Toss the cooked cauliflower with pepper, onion, parsley, and olives in a large bowl.
5. In a small bowl, combine the ingredients for the dressing.
6. Dress the salad and serve garnished with the crumbled Mozzarella cheese.

## Potatoes with Raisin Ketchup

**Prep time: 20 minutes | Cook time: 20 minutes | Serves 4**

1 pound (454 g) potatoes, peeled and chopped
1½ pounds (680 g) tomatoes, quartered
¼ cup raisins
1 onion, cut into wedges
6 tablespoons apple cider vinegar
1 tablespoon honey
¼ teaspoon celery seeds
¼ teaspoon
cinnamon powder
½ teaspoon Dijon mustard
¼ teaspoon clove powder
¼ teaspoon garlic powder
1 cup chicken broth
1 tablespoon paprika
Salt, to taste
1 tablespoon cornstarch, mixed with 1 tablespoon water

1. In the Instant Pot, cover the potatoes with salted water: Seal the lid. Select the Manual mode and set the cooking time for 10 minutes on High Pressure.
2. Once cooking is complete, do a quick pressure release. Carefully open the lid and drain potatoes; set aside.
3. Add the remaining ingredients, except for the cornstarch, to the Instant Pot. Stir to combine well.
4. Seal the lid. Select the Manual mode and set the cooking time for 5 minutes on High Pressure.
5. Once cooking is complete, perform a quick pressure release. Carefully open the lid.
6. Using an immersion blender to purée the mixture in the Instant Pot. Then select the Sauté mode. Mix in the cornstarch and cook for 5 minutes or until thickened.
7. Allow to cool for a few minutes and serve with potatoes.

## Easy Khoreshe Karafs

**Prep time: 20 minutes | Cook time: 11 minutes | Serves 2**

| | |
|---|---|
| 1 tablespoon unsalted butter | chopped |
| ½ onion, chopped | 1 tablespoon fresh mint, finely chopped |
| 1 garlic clove, minced | ½ teaspoon mustard seeds |
| ½ pound (227 g) celery stalks, diced | 2 cups vegetable broth |
| 1 Persian lime, prick a few holes | ½ teaspoon cayenne pepper |
| 1 tablespoon fresh cilantro, roughly | Sea salt and ground black pepper, to taste |

1. Press the Sauté button of the Instant Pot. Add and melt the butter.
2. Add and sauté the onions and garlic for about 3 minutes or until tender and fragrant.
3. Stir in the remaining ingredients, except for the basmati rice.
4. Secure the lid. Choose the Manual mode and set the cooking time for 18 minutes at High pressure.
5. Once cooking is complete, use a natural pressure release for 15 minutes, then release any remaining pressure. Carefully open the lid.
6. Serve hot.

## Mushroom and Swiss Cheese Tarts

**Prep time: 20 minutes | Cook time: 27 minutes | Serves 4**

| | |
|---|---|
| 5 ounces (142 g) oyster mushrooms, sliced | pepper, to taste |
| | ¼ cup dry white wine |
| 1 small white onion, sliced | 1 sheet puff pastry |
| | 1 cup shredded Swiss cheese, divided |
| 2 tablespoons melted butter, divided | 1 cup water |
| Salt and black | 1 tablespoon sliced green onions |

1. Set the Instant Pot to the Sauté mode, then add the mushrooms, onion, and 1 tablespoon of butter. Sauté for 5 minutes or until tender.
2. Season with salt and pepper, pour in white wine and cook for 2 minutes or until evaporated. Set aside.
3. Unwrap the puff pastry and cut into 4 squares. Pierce the dough with a fork and brush both sides with the remaining butter.
4. Scatter half of the Swiss cheese evenly over the puff pastry squares. Spread the mushroom mixture over the pastry squares and top with the remaining cheese. Place in a baking pan.
5. Pour the water in the pot, then arrange a trivet in the pot. Lay the pan on the trivet.
6. Seal the lid. Select the Manual mode and set the time for 20 minutes on High Pressure.
7. Once cooking is complete, do a natural release for 10 minutes, then release any remaining pressure. Carefully open the lid.
8. Transfer the tart to a plate. Garnish with the green onions and serve.

## Broccoli, Raisin, and Seed Salad

**Prep time: 10 minutes | Cook time: 1 minutes | Serves 2 to 4**

| | |
|---|---|
| 1 cup water | toasted |
| ½ pound (227 g) broccoli, cut into florets | 2 tablespoons sunflower seeds, to toasted |
| 2 tablespoons raisins | 1 tablespoon balsamic vinegar |
| 2 scallion stalks, chopped | ⅓ cup mayonnaise |
| Sea salt and ground black pepper, to taste | 1 tablespoon fresh lemon juice |
| 2 tablespoons sesame seeds, | ⅓ cup sour cream |

1. Pour the water in the Instant Pot and fit in a steamer basket. Place the broccoli in the steamer basket.
2. Secure the lid. Choose the Manual mode and set the cooking time for 1 minute at High pressure.
3. Once cooking is complete, perform a quick pressure release. Carefully open the lid. Allow to cool for a few minutes.
4. Transfer the broccoli florets to a serving bowl. Toss in the raisins, scallions, salt, black pepper, and seeds.
5. Stir in the balsamic vinegar, mayo, lemon juice, and sour cream. Serve immediately.

## Honey Carrot Salad with Dijon Mustard

**Prep time: 10 minutes | Cook time: 3 minutes | Serves 2 to 4**

1 cup water
1 pound (454 g) carrots, sliced to 2-inch chunks
1 scallion, finely sliced
½ tablespoon Dijon mustard
½ tablespoon lime
juice
1 teaspoon honey
¼ teaspoon red pepper flakes
½ teaspoon Himalayan salt
¼ teaspoon ground white pepper
1 tablespoon olive oil

1. Pour the water in the Instant Pot and fit in a steamer basket. Place the carrots in the steamer basket.
2. Secure the lid. Choose the Steam mode and set the cooking time for 3 minutes at High pressure.
3. Once cooking is complete, perform a quick pressure release. Carefully open the lid.
4. Toss the carrots with the remaining ingredients in a serving bowl and serve chilled.

## Pumpkin Oatmeal

**Prep time: 20 minutes | Cook time: 4 minutes | Serves 4**

¾ cup steel-cut oats
1 tablespoon pumpkin pie spice
½ cup pumpkin purée
2 tablespoons honey
1 teaspoon vanilla
essence
1 teaspoon ground cinnamon
Pinch grated nutmeg
1½ cups water
Salt, to taste

1. Add all ingredients to the Instant Pot. Stir to mix well.
2. Secure the lid. Choose the Manual mode and set the cooking time for 4 minutes at High pressure.
3. Once cooking is complete, use a natural pressure release for 15 minutes, then release any remaining pressure. Carefully open the lid.
4. Ladle the oatmeal into serving bowls and serve immediately.

## Lemony Artichoke

**Prep time: 5 minutes | Cook time: 10 minutes | Serves 4**

½ tablespoon peppercorns
2 cups water
4 artichokes, trimmed
2 lemons, one juiced and one sliced
1½ garlic cloves, minced
½ tablespoon olive oil
Salt and ground black pepper, to taste

1. Put the peppercorns and water into the Instant Pot. Place the steamer trivet inside. Arrange the artichokes over the trivet.
2. Secure the lid and select the Manual function and set the cooking time for 5 minutes on Low Pressure.
3. When the timer beeps, do a natural pressure release for 5 minutes, then release any remaining pressure and open the lid.
4. Strain the artichokes and return them back to the pot.
5. Add the remaining ingredients into the Instant Pot, and then sauté for 5 minutes on the Sauté mode.
6. Serve hot.

## Steamed Lemony Cabbage

**Prep time: 10 minutes | Cook time: 2 minutes | Serves 2 to 4**

1 cup water
1 large cabbage, cut into wedges
Juice of 1 lemon
2 tablespoons melted
butter
Salt and black pepper, to taste
¼ teaspoon red chili flakes

1. Pour the water in the Instant Pot, then fit in a trivet. Place the cabbage in the trivet.
2. Seal the lid. Select the Manual mode and set the time for 2 minutes at High Pressure.
3. Once cooking is complete, do a quick pressure release, then unlock the lid. Transfer the cabbage on a plate.
4. In a bowl, whisk together the lemon juice, butter, salt, pepper, and chili flakes.
5. Drizzle the mixture all over the cabbage and serve.

## Mediterranean Herbed Cabbage

**Prep time: 10 minutes | Cook time: 6 minutes | Serves 4**

1 (1-pound / 454-g) head cabbage, cut into wedges
1 bell pepper, chopped
1 carrot, chopped
1 bay leaf
1 sprig thyme
1 sprig rosemary
1 cup roasted vegetable broth
½ teaspoon cayenne pepper
2 tablespoons olive oil
Sea salt and ground black pepper, to taste

1. Add all ingredients to the Instant Pot. Stir to combine.
2. Secure the lid. Choose the Manual mode and set the cooking time for 6 minutes at High pressure.
3. Once cooking is complete, perform a quick pressure release. Carefully open the lid. Discard the bay leaf, thyme, and rosemary.
4. Divide them into bowls and serve warm.

## Ritzy Vegetable Mix

**Prep time: 10 minutes | Cook time: 5 minutes | Serves 4**

1 tablespoon butter, at room temperature
1 clove garlic, minced
½ pound (227 g) broccoli, cut into florets
2 medium waxy potatoes, peeled and
cubed
2 cups acorn squash
1 parsnip, cut into 1-inch pieces
1 carrot, cut into 1-inch pieces
1 cup roasted vegetable broth

1. Press the Sauté button of the Instant Pot and melt the butter.
2. Add and sauté the garlic for 1 minute or until fragrant. Stir in the remaining ingredients.
3. Secure the lid. Choose the Manual mode and set the cooking time for 4 minutes at High pressure.
4. Once cooking is complete, perform a quick pressure release. Carefully open the lid.
5. Serve warm.

## Winter Vegetables Salad

**Prep time: 10 minutes | Cook time: 8 minutes | Serves 4**

1 cup water
1 cup Brussels sprouts, trimmed and halved lengthwise
1 head cauliflower, cut into bite-size pieces
1 sweet potato, cubed
Dressing:
1½ teaspoons yellow miso paste
Juice of ½ lemon
1 tablespoon olive oil
Salt and black pepper, to taste
2 tablespoons peanut oil

1. Pour the water in the Instant Pot, fit in a steamer basket. Place the Brussels sprouts, cauliflower, and sweet potato into the basket.
2. Seal the lid. Select the Manual mode and set the time for 8 minutes at High Pressure.
3. Once cooking is complete, do a quick pressure release. Carefully open the lid.
4. In a bowl, whisk the miso paste, lemon juice, olive oil, salt, black pepper, and peanut oil to make the dressing.
5. Toss the cooked vegetables in the dressing to serve.

## Simple Molasses Glazed Carrots

**Prep time: 5 minutes | Cook time: 5 minutes | Serves 4**

1 cup water
1 pound (454 g) baby carrots
2 tablespoons butter
1 tablespoon molasses
¼ teaspoon kosher salt
⅛ teaspoon white pepper
1/3 teaspoon cayenne pepper

1. Pour the water in the Instant Pot and fit in a steamer basket. Place the carrots in the steamer basket.
2. Secure the lid. Choose the Steam mode and set the cooking time for 3 minutes at High pressure.
3. Once cooking is complete, perform a quick pressure release. Carefully open the lid.
4. Discard the water and press the Sauté button. Add the butter to melt.
5. Stir in the cooked carrots, molasses, salt, white pepper, and cayenne pepper.
6. Sauté for about 2 minutes or until the carrots are well glazed and tender. Serve warm.

## Squash and Carrot Curry with Tofu

**Prep time: 10 minutes | Cook time: 12 minutes | Serves 4**

1 tablespoon canola oil
1 large onion, sliced
4 cubes (about 2⅝ ounces / 74 g in total) mild Japanese curry sauce mix
1½ cups water
1 pound (454 g) winter squash, peeled and cut into 1-inch chunks
2 large carrots, peeled and cut into 1-inch-thick slices
1 pound (454 g) extra-firm tofu, cut into 1-inch cubes

1. Select the Sauté mode of the Instant Pot. Heat the canola oil until shimmering.
2. Add the onions and sauté for 4 minutes or until translucent.
3. Add the curry mix and water in the pot. Break up the curry cubes with a wooden spoon.
4. Add the squash and carrots and stir to combine. Arrange the tofu cubes on top.
5. Lock the lid. Select the Manual function, and set the cooking time for 8 minutes on High Pressure.
6. When the cooking time is up, quick release the pressure. Carefully open the lid. Stir gently to combine the tofu and other ingredients. Serve immediately.

## Mushroom and Swiss Chard Risotto

**Prep time: 15 minutes | Cook time: 20 minutes | Serves 4**

3 tablespoons olive oil
½ cup mushrooms, sliced
1 small bunch Swiss chard, chopped
1 cup short-grain rice
½ cup white wine
2 cups vegetable soup
Salt, to taste
½ cup caramelized onions
½ cup grated Pecorino Romano cheese

1. Set the Instant Pot to Sauté mode. Heat the olive oil until shimmering.
2. Add and sauté the mushrooms for 5 minutes or until soft. Add and sauté Swiss chard for 2 minutes or until wilted. Transfer the mushrooms and chard in a bowl and set aside.

3. Add the rice to the pot and cook for about 1 minute. Add the white wine and cook for 2 to 3 minutes, stir constantly until the wine has evaporated. Add the vegetable soup and salt; stir to combine.
4. Seal the lid. Select the Manual mode and set the time for 8 minutes at High Pressure.
5. Once cooking is complete, perform a quick pressure release and unlock the lid.
6. Add the mushroom, Swiss chard, and onions and cook for 1 minute on Sauté mode.
7. Mix the cheese into the rice until melted. Serve immediately.

## Okra Bhindi Masala

**Prep time: 10 minutes | Cook time: 8 minutes | Serves 2 to 4**

1 tablespoon coconut oil, at room temperature
½ yellow onion, sliced
1 teaspoon ginger garlic paste
½ pound (227 g) okra, cut into small pieces
½ cup tomato purée
1/3 teaspoon cumin
seeds
1/3 teaspoon ground turmeric
½ teaspoon Gram masala
½ teaspoon mango powder
½ teaspoon Sriracha sauce
Himalayan salt, to taste

1. Press the Sauté button and heat the coconut oil until shimmering.
2. Add and sauté the onion for 3 minutes or until translucent.
3. Stir in the ginger-garlic paste and cook for 1 minute. Stir the remaining ingredients into the pot.
4. Secure the lid. Choose the Manual mode and set the cooking time for 4 minutes at High pressure.
5. Once cooking is complete, perform a quick pressure release. Carefully open the lid.
6. Serve warm.

## Rutabaga, Apple, and Cabbage Salad

**Prep time: 10 minutes | Cook time: 6 minutes | Serves 4**

1 cup water
½ pound (227 g) rutabaga, peeled and cut into ¼-inch chunks
1 apple, cored and

diced
$1/_3$ pound (136 g) cabbage, shredded
4 tablespoons almonds, slivered

**Dressing:**

1 teaspoon Dijon mustard
1 tablespoon fresh lemon juice

½ tablespoon agave syrup
3 tablespoons olive oil

1. Pour the water in the Instant Pot and fit in a steamer basket. Place the rutabaga in the steamer basket.
2. Secure the lid. Choose the Manual mode and set the cooking time for 6 minutes at High pressure.
3. Once cooking is complete, perform a quick pressure release. Carefully open the lid.
4. Toss the rutabaga chunks with the apple, cabbage, and almonds in a large bowl.
5. In a small bowl, combine the ingredients for the dressing.
6. Dress the salad and serve chilled.

## Ritzy Eggplant with Tomato Chickpeas

**Prep time: 45 minutes | Cook time: 10 minutes | Serves 4**

1 pound (454 g) eggplant, cut into cubes
1 tablespoon sea salt
1 tablespoon olive oil
1 red onion, chopped
2 bell peppers, deseeded and diced
1 garlic clove, sliced
6 ounces (170 g) chickpeas, boiled and

rinsed
4 vine-ripened tomatoes, puréed
$1/_3$ teaspoon ground turmeric
1 teaspoon basil
½ teaspoon oregano
½ teaspoon paprika
¼ teaspoon sea salt
¼ teaspoon ground black pepper

1. Toss the eggplant with the sea salt in a colander. Let sit for 30 minutes, then squeeze out the excess liquid.

2. Press the Sauté button and heat the olive oil in the Instant Pot.
3. Add and sauté the onion for 3 minutes or until translucent.
4. Add the eggplant, bell peppers and garlic and sauté for an additional 1 minute or until fragrant.
5. Add the remaining ingredients to the Instant Pot. Stir to combine well.
6. Secure the lid. Choose the Manual mode and set the cooking time for 3 minutes at High pressure.
7. Once cooking is complete, perform a quick pressure release. Carefully open the lid. Ladle them into bowls and serve immediately.

## Simple Broccoli with Mushroom

**Prep time: 10 minutes | Cook time: 8 minutes | Serves 4**

1 cup water
1 large head broccoli, cut into bite-size pieces
2 tablespoons olive oil
1 cup chopped

mushrooms
2 teaspoons hot sauce
Salt and black pepper, to taste
2 tablespoons chopped almonds

1. Pour the water in the Instant Pot, then fit in a steamer basket, and put in broccoli.
2. Seal the lid. Select the Manual mode and set the cooking time for 2 minutes at High Pressure.
3. Once cooking is complete, do a quick pressure release, then unlock the lid. Transfer the broccoli to a bowl. Set aside.
4. Wipe clean the Instant Pot and set to the Sauté mode. Heat the olive oil until shimmering.
5. Add and sauté the mushrooms for 5 minutes or until softened.
6. Add broccoli, hot sauce, salt, and pepper. Sauté until well coated in hot sauce. Stir in almonds. Serve immediately.

## Sumptuous Broccoli and Zucchini Tarts

**Prep time: 15 minutes | Cook time: 10 minutes | Serves 4**

1 cup water
2 cups broccoli florets
3 large zucchinis, grated
5 eggs, beaten
1 onion, diced
6 large carrots, grated
½ cup all-purpose
flour
½ cup panko bread crumbs
½ teaspoon baking powder
Salt and black pepper, to taste
½ cup grated Cheddar cheese

1. Pour the water in the Instant Pot. Place a trivet in the pot. Grease a springform pan with cooking spray and set aside.
2. In a bowl, mix the broccoli, zucchini, eggs, onion, carrots, flour, panko bread crumbs, baking powder, salt, pepper, and Cheddar cheese. Pour the mixture into the pan, cover with aluminum foil, and place on the trivet.
3. Seal the lid. Select the Manual mode and set the time for 10 minutes on High Pressure.
4. Once cooking is complete, do a quick pressure release. Carefully open the lid and remove the pan. Let cool to firm up.
5. Release the pan, then slice the tart and serve.

## Sumptuous Ratatouille with Pinot Noir

**Prep time: 45 minutes | Cook time: 6 minutes | Serves 4**

½ pound (227 g) eggplant, sliced
1 teaspoon sea salt
½ pound (227 g) zucchini, sliced
½ pound (227 g) tomatoes, puréed
2 tablespoons Pinot Noir
2 sweet peppers, deseeded and sliced
1 onion, sliced
½ teaspoon basil
$1/_3$ teaspoon oregano
½ teaspoon rosemary
2 cloves garlic, minced
½ cup vegetable broth
2 tablespoons extra-virgin olive oil
Sea salt and ground cayenne pepper, to taste

1. Toss the eggplant with salt in a colander. Let sit for 30 minutes, then squeeze out the excess liquid.
2. Transfer the eggplant to the Instant Pot. Add the remaining ingredients.
3. Secure the lid. Choose the Manual mode and set the cooking time for 6 minutes at High pressure.
4. Once cooking is complete, perform a quick pressure release. Carefully open the lid.
5. Serve warm.

## Sweet Potato and Kale Curry

**Prep time: 15 minutes | Cook time: 15 minutes | Serves 4**

½ tablespoon grapeseed oil
½ onion, chopped
2 medium sweet potatoes, diced
1 tablespoon tomato paste
½ cup vegetable broth
1 teaspoon ginger-garlic paste
1 teaspoon ground cumin
½ teaspoon ground
turmeric
½ tablespoon ground coriander
Sea salt and freshly ground black pepper, to taste
½ cup tomatoes juice
1 cinnamon stick
2 cups kale, torn into pieces
½ cup coconut milk
1 tablespoon fresh cilantro, chopped

1. Press the Sauté button of the Instant Pot and heat the grapeseed oil until shimmering.
2. Add and sauté the onion for 3 minutes or until tender.
3. Stir in the sweet potatoes, tomato paste, vegetable broth, ginger-garlic paste, cinnamon stick, spices, and tomato juice.
4. Secure the lid. Choose the Manual mode and set the cooking time for 6 minutes at High pressure.
5. Once cooking is complete, perform a quick pressure release. Carefully open the lid.
6. Add the kale and coconut milk. Press the Sauté button and let it simmer for 5 to 6 minutes or until heated.
7. Discard the cinnamon stick. Ladle into bowls and serve garnished with fresh cilantro.

## Scrambled Eggs with Broccoli and Pepper

**Prep time: 10 minutes | Cook time: 7 minutes | Serves 2**

2 teaspoons olive oil
½ cup chopped broccoli
1 orange bell pepper, diced
1 garlic clove, minced
4 large eggs
3 tablespoons milk
¼ cup crumbled goat cheese
½ teaspoon dried oregano
Salt and black pepper, to taste

1. Set the Instant Pot to the Sauté mode. Heat the olive oil until shimmering.
2. Add and sauté the broccoli and bell pepper for 4 minutes or until softened.
3. Add the garlic and cook for 1 more minute until fragrant. Beat the eggs with milk and pour the mixture over the vegetables.
4. Scrambling the eggs with a spatula for 2 minutes until set. Mix in the goat cheese, oregano, salt, and pepper until well combined.
5. Transfer the scrambled eggs with vegetables to plates and serve warm.

## Vegetable Salad with Tahini Sauce

**Prep time: 15 minutes | Cook time: 4 minutes | Serves 4**

½ pound (227 g) cauliflower, cut into florets
2 medium potatoes, diced
2 carrots, sliced
¼ teaspoon sea salt
1 tablespoon olive oil
½ cup vegetable broth

**Tahini Sauce:**
¼ cup tahini
1 tablespoon fresh parsley, chopped
1 tablespoon fresh lime juice
1 clove garlic, minced
2 tablespoons olive oil
¼ cup water

1. Combine the vegetables, salt, olive oil, and vegetable broth in the Instant Pot.
2. Secure the lid. Choose the Manual mode and set the cooking time for 4 minutes at High pressure.
3. Meanwhile, mix the ingredients for the tahini sauce in a small bowl.

4. Once cooking is complete, perform a quick pressure release. Carefully open the lid.
5. Serve the warm vegetables with the tahini sauce on the side.

## Tortellini Alfredo with Peas

**Prep time: 5 minutes | Cook time: 12 minutes | Serves 4**

1 pound (454 g) dried cheese tortellini
3 cups vegetable broth
2 medium garlic cloves, chopped
2 teaspoons olive oil
Salt and freshly ground black pepper,
to taste
1½ cups heavy cream
¾ cup peas
2 teaspoons lemon zest
½ cup grated Parmesan cheese

1. Combine the tortellini, broth, garlic, olive oil, salt, and pepper in the Instant Pot. Stir to mix well.
2. Lock the lid. Select the Manual function, and set the cooking time for 10 minutes on High Pressure.
3. When the cooking time is up, release the pressure naturally for 10 minutes and then release the remaining pressure. Carefully open the lid.
4. Add the cream, peas, and lemon zest. Select the Sauté mode. Sauté for 2 minutes or until the sauce thickens. Mix in the cheese. Serve immediately.

## Sumptuous Cioppino

**Prep time: 15 minutes | Cook time: 23 minutes | Serves 8**

2 tablespoons unsalted butter
1 medium red bell pepper, deseeded and diced
1 medium yellow onion, peeled and diced
2 stalks celery, chopped
3 cloves garlic, minced
1 teaspoon dried oregano
½ teaspoon Italian seasoning
½ teaspoon salt
½ teaspoon black pepper
2 tablespoons tomato paste
1 cup white wine

1 (15-ounce / 425-g) can crushed tomatoes
4 cups seafood stock
1 bay leaf
1 pound (454 g) fresh mussels, scrubbed clean and beards removed
1 pound (454 g) fresh clams, scrubbed clean
½ pound (227 g) large shrimp, peeled and deveined
½ pound (227 g) fresh scallops
½ pound (227 g) calamari rings
1 tablespoon lemon juice

1. Press the Sauté button on the Instant Pot and melt the butter. Add the bell pepper, onion and celery to the pot and sauté for 8 minutes, or until tender. Add the garlic, oregano, Italian seasoning, salt and black pepper to the pot and cook for 30 seconds.
2. Add the tomato paste and cook for 1 minute. Pour in the white wine and scrape the bottom of the pot well. Stir in the tomatoes, seafood stock and bay leaf.
3. Set the lid in place. Select the Manual mode and set the cooking time for 5 minutes on High Pressure. When the timer goes off, perform a quick pressure release. Carefully open the lid.
4. Stir in the remaining ingredients, except for the lemon juice. Select the Sauté mode and allow the soup to simmer for 10 minutes, or until the seafood is cooked through. Remove and discard the bay leaf and stir in the lemon juice. Serve hot.

## Vegetable and Lamb Stew

**Prep time: 25 minutes | Cook time: 33 minutes | Serves 6**

2 pounds (907 g) boneless lean lamb shoulder, cut into cubes
¼ teaspoon salt
¼ teaspoon ground black pepper
2 tablespoons olive oil
1 large onion, peeled and chopped
1 clove garlic, minced
¼ cup dry white wine
4 cups chicken stock

1 bay leaf
1 teaspoon dried thyme
2 pounds (907 g) small red potatoes, scrubbed and quartered
16 ounces (454 g) sliced button mushrooms
8 ounces (227 g) baby-cut carrots
8 ounces (227 g) frozen peas, thawed

1. In a bowl, season the lamb shoulder with salt and pepper. Cover in plastic and set in a refrigerator for 15 minutes.
2. Press the Sauté button on the Instant Pot and heat the oil. Arrange half the lamb in an even layer in the pot, making sure there is space between pieces to prevent steam from forming. Sear the lamb for 3 minutes on each side, or until lightly browned. Transfer the lamb to a plate. Repeat with the remaining lamb.
3. Add the onion and garlic to the pot and cook for 1 minute. Pour in the wine and scrape any bits from bottom of the pot. Stir in the lamb along with the remaining ingredients, except for the peas.
4. Lock the lid, select the Manual mode and set the cooking time for 20 minutes at High Pressure. When the timer goes off, do a natural pressure release for 20 minutes, then release any remaining pressure. Open the lid.
5. Remove and discard the bay leaf. Whisk in the peas and let it sit in the residual heat for 10 minutes. Serve warm.

## Chuck Roast with Onions

**Prep time: 20 minutes | Cook time: 1 hour 2 minutes | Serves 6**

2½ pounds (1.1 kg) boneless chuck roast, cut into pieces
1 teaspoon salt
1 teaspoon ground black pepper
1 tablespoon olive oil
2 medium yellow onions, peeled and chopped
2 medium red bell peppers, deseeded and chopped
6 cloves garlic, peeled and minced
2 teaspoons ground cumin
2 teaspoons dried oregano
2 teaspoons smoked paprika
½ teaspoon cayenne pepper
½ cup white wine
1 (14.5-ounce / 411-g) can diced tomatoes
1 bay leaf
½ cup halved Spanish olives
2 teaspoons distilled white vinegar

1. Season the chuck roast with the salt and pepper on all sides. Set aside.
2. Press the Sauté button on the Instant Pot and heat the oil. Add half the seasoned meat to the pot and sear for 7 minutes on both sides, or until well browned. Transfer the browned meat to a platter and set aside. Repeat with the remaining meat.
3. Add the onions and bell peppers to the pot and sauté for 5 minutes, or until just softened. Add the garlic, cumin, oregano, paprika and cayenne pepper to the pot and sauté for 1 minute, or until fragrant.
4. Pour in the white wine and cook for 2 minutes, or until the liquid is reduced by half. Return the browned meat back to the pot along with the tomatoes and bay leaf.
5. Close and secure the lid. Select the Manual setting and set the cooking time for 40 minutes at High Pressure. Once the timer goes off, use a quick pressure release. Carefully open the lid.
6. Remove and discard the bay leaf. Stir in the olives and vinegar. Serve hot.

## Beef and Vegetable Stew

**Prep time: 15 minutes | Cook time: 46 minutes | Serves 6**

2 tablespoons olive oil
2 pounds (907 g) beef stew cubes
1 medium sweet onion, peeled and diced
4 cloves garlic, peeled and minced
3 cups beef broth
½ cup dry red wine
1 (14.5-ounce / 411-g) can crushed tomatoes, undrained
2 medium carrots, peeled and diced
2 medium Russet potatoes, scrubbed and small-diced
1 stalk celery, chopped
2 tablespoons chopped fresh rosemary
1 teaspoon salt
½ teaspoon ground black pepper
2 tablespoons gluten-free all-purpose flour
4 tablespoons water
¼ cup chopped fresh Italian flat-leaf parsley

1. Press the Sauté button on the Instant Pot and heat the oil. Add the beef and onion to the pot and sauté for 5 minutes, or until the beef is seared and the onion is translucent. Add the garlic and sauté for 1 minute.
2. Pour in the beef broth and wine and deglaze the pot by scraping up any bits from the sides and bottom of the pot.
3. Stir in the tomatoes with juice, carrots, potatoes, celery, rosemary, salt and pepper.
4. Set the lid in place. Select the Meat/ Stew setting and set the cooking time for 35 minutes on High Pressure. When the timer goes off, perform a natural pressure release for 10 minutes, then release any remaining pressure. Open the lid.
5. Create a slurry by whisking together the flour and water in a small bowl. Add the slurry to the pot. Select the Sauté mode and let simmer for 5 minutes, stirring constantly.
6. Ladle the stew into 6 bowls and serve topped with the parsley.

## Bean and Carrot Chili

**Prep time: 10 minutes | Cook time: 41 minutes | Serves 4**

1 tablespoon olive oil
1 small red onion, peeled and diced
1 medium green bell pepper, deseeded and diced
1 large carrot, peeled and diced
4 cloves garlic, peeled and minced
1 small jalapeño, deseeded and diced
1 (28-ounce / 794-g) can diced tomatoes, undrained
1 (15-ounce / 425-g)
can cannellini beans, drained and rinsed
1 (15-ounce / 425-g) can kidney beans, drained and rinsed
1 (15-ounce / 425-g) can black beans, drained and rinsed
2 tablespoons chili powder
1 teaspoon ground cumin
1 teaspoon salt
¼ cup vegetable broth

1. Press the Sauté button on the Instant Pot and heat the oil. Add the onion, bell pepper and carrot to the pot and sauté for 5 minutes, or until the onion is translucent. Add the garlic and sauté for 1 minute.
2. Stir in the remaining ingredients.
3. Set the lid in place. Select the Meat/ Stew setting and set the cooking time for 35 minutes on High Pressure. When the timer goes off, perform a natural pressure release for 15 minutes, then release any remaining pressure. Open the lid.
4. Ladle the chili into 4 bowls and serve warm.

## Beef and Pork Chili

**Prep time: 10 minutes | Cook time: 40 minutes | Serves 4**

1 tablespoon olive oil
½ pound (227 g) ground beef
½ pound (227 g) ground pork
1 medium onion, peeled and diced
1 (28-ounce / 794-g) can puréed tomatoes, undrained
1 large carrot, peeled and diced
1 small green bell pepper, deseeded and diced
1 small jalapeño, deseeded and diced
3 cloves garlic, minced
2 tablespoons chili powder
1 teaspoon sea salt
2 teaspoons ground black pepper

1. Press the Sauté button on the Instant Pot and heat the olive oil. Add the ground beef, ground pork and onion to the pot and sauté for 5 minutes, or until the pork is no longer pink.
2. Stir in the remaining ingredients.
3. Close and secure the lid. Select the Meat/Stew setting and set the cooking time for 35 minutes on High Pressure. Once cooking is complete, use a natural pressure release for 15 minutes, then release any remaining pressure. Open the lid.
4. Serve warm.

## Beef Chili with Pinto Beans

**Prep time: 20 minutes | Cook time: 40 minutes | Serves 8**

1 pound (454 g) 80% lean ground beef
1 medium onion, peeled and chopped
2 cloves garlic, peeled and minced
¼ cup chili powder
2 tablespoons brown sugar
1 teaspoon ground cumin
½ teaspoon ground coriander
½ teaspoon salt
½ teaspoon ground black pepper
1 (14.5-ounce / 411-g) can diced tomatoes
2 cups dried pinto beans, soaked overnight in water and drained
2 cups beef broth
1 tablespoon lime juice

1. Press the Sauté button on the Instant Pot and brown the beef for 10 minutes, or until no pink remains. Add the onion, garlic, chili powder, brown sugar, cumin, coriander, salt and pepper to the pot and sauté for 10 minutes, or until the onion is just softened.
2. Stir in the tomatoes, soaked beans and beef broth.
3. Lock the lid. Select the Manual mode and set the cooking time for 20 minutes on High Pressure. When the timer goes off, do a natural pressure release for 20 minutes, then release any remaining pressure. Carefully open the lid.
4. Add the lime juice and stir well. Serve hot.

## Chickpea and Lamb Soup

**Prep time: 10 minutes | Cook time: 13 minutes | Serves 4**

1 tablespoon olive oil
1 pound (454 g) ground lamb
1 medium red onion, peeled and diced
1 medium carrot, peeled and shredded
3 cloves garlic, peeled and minced
1 (15-ounce / 425-g) can diced tomatoes, undrained
1 (15.5-ounce / 439-g) can chickpeas, rinsed and drained
4 cups chicken broth
½ teaspoon ground ginger
½ teaspoon turmeric
½ teaspoon salt
¼ teaspoon ground cinnamon
½ cup chopped fresh cilantro
4 tablespoons plain full-fat Greek yogurt

1. Set the Instant Pot to the Sauté mode and heat the olive oil. Add the lamb and onion to the pot and sauté for 5 minutes, or until the lamb is lightly browned. Add the carrot and garlic to the pot and sauté for 1 minute.
2. Stir in the remaining ingredients, except for the cilantro and Greek yogurt.
3. Set the lid in place. Select the Manual mode and set the cooking time for 7 minutes on High Pressure. When the timer goes off, perform a quick pressure release. Carefully open the lid.
4. Ladle the soup into 4 bowls and garnish with the cilantro and yogurt. Serve warm.

## Black Bean and Quinoa Chili

**Prep time: 10 minutes | Cook time: 16 minutes | Serves 6**

1 tablespoon vegetable oil
1 medium onion, peeled and chopped
1 medium red bell pepper, deseeded and chopped
2 cloves garlic, peeled and minced
3 tablespoons chili powder
1 teaspoon ground
cumin
½ teaspoon salt
½ teaspoon ground black pepper
2 cups vegetable broth
1 cup water
¾ cup quinoa
2 (15-ounce / 425-g) cans black beans, drained and rinsed

1. Press the Sauté button on the Instant Pot and heat the oil. Add the onion and bell pepper to the pot and sauté for 5 minutes, or until tender. Add the garlic, chili powder, cumin, salt and black pepper to the pot and sauté for 1 minute, or until fragrant.
2. Stir in the remaining ingredients.
3. Lock the lid. Select the Manual mode and set the cooking time for 10 minutes on High Pressure. When the timer goes off, do a quick pressure release. Carefully open the lid.
4. Serve hot.

## Beef and Mushroom Chili

**Prep time: 15 minutes | Cook time: 40 minutes | Serves 6**

1 tablespoon olive oil
1 pound (454 g) beef stew cubes
1 medium onion, peeled and diced
4 cloves garlic, minced
½ cup beef broth
1 (16-ounce / 454-g) can chili beans, undrained
1 (14.5-ounce / 411-g) can diced tomatoes, undrained
2 cups sliced mushrooms
2 tablespoons tomato paste
2 tablespoons chili powder
1 tablespoon Italian seasoning
1 teaspoon red pepper flakes
1 teaspoon sea salt
½ teaspoon ground black pepper

1. Press the Sauté button on the Instant Pot and heat the oil. Add the beef stew cubes and onion to the pot and sauté for 3 minutes, or until the beef is lightly browned and the onion is translucent. Add the garlic to the pot and sauté for 2 minutes.
2. Pour in the beef broth and deglaze by scraping any of the bits from the bottom and sides of the pot. Stir in the remaining ingredients.
3. Set the lid in place. Select the Meat/Stew setting and set the cooking time for 35 minutes on High Pressure. Once cooking is complete, do a natural pressure release for 15 minutes, then release any remaining pressure. Open the lid.
4. Ladle the chili into individual bowls and serve warm.

## Ham Hock and Bean Soup

**Prep time: 5 minutes | Cook time: 45 minutes | Serves 4**

1 ham hock
½ pound (227 g) dried great northern beans, rinsed
1 (8-ounce / 227-g) can tomato sauce
1 large carrot, peeled and diced
1 small yellow onion, peeled and diced
4 cloves garlic, peeled and minced
2 stalks celery, chopped
1 bay leaf
4 cups chicken broth
4 tablespoons fresh thyme leaves
½ teaspoon salt

1. Add all the ingredients to the Instant Pot and stir to combine.
2. Set the lid in place. Select the Manual mode and set the cooking time for 45 minutes at High Pressure. Once the timer goes off, use a natural pressure release for 10 minutes, then release any remaining pressure. Carefully open the lid.
3. Remove and discard the bay leaf. Use two forks to shred the meat off the ham bone. Discard the bone.
4. Divide the soup among 4 bowls and serve warm.

## Creamy Crab Soup

**Prep time: 10 minutes | Cook time: 21 minutes | Serves 4**

4 tablespoons unsalted butter
2 large carrots, peeled and diced
1 cup chopped leeks
2 stalks celery, chopped
4 cloves garlic, peeled and minced
2 teaspoons Italian seasoning
1 teaspoon salt
5 cups vegetable broth
1 pound (454 g) lump crabmeat, divided
2 tablespoons cooking sherry
¼ cup heavy cream
2 tablespoons fresh thyme leaves

1. Press the Sauté button on the Instant Pot and melt the butter. Add the carrots, leeks and celery to the pot and sauté for 5 minutes, or until the leeks are translucent. Add the garlic and sauté for 1 minute.
2. Stir in the Italian seasoning, salt, vegetable broth and ½ pound (227 g) of the crabmeat.
3. Lock the lid, select the Manual mode and set the cooking time for 15 minutes on High Pressure. Once cooking is complete, use a natural pressure release for 10 minutes, then release any remaining pressure. Carefully open the lid.
4. Use an immersion blender to blend the soup in the pot until smooth. Stir in the remaining ½ pound (227 g) of the crabmeat, sherry and heavy cream.
5. Ladle soup into four bowls and serve garnished with the thyme

## Carrot and Cabbage Beef Stew

**Prep time: 10 minutes | Cook time: 19 minutes | Serves 4 to 6**

3 tablespoons extra-virgin olive oil
2 large carrots, peeled and sliced into ¼-inch disks and then quartered
1 large Spanish onion, diced
2 pounds (907 g) ground beef
3 cloves garlic, minced
1 (46-ounce / 1.3-kg) can tomato juice
2 cups vegetable broth
Juice of 2 lemons
1 head cabbage, cored and roughly chopped
½ cup jasmine rice
¼ cup dark brown sugar
1 tablespoon Worcestershire sauce
2 teaspoons seasoned salt
1 teaspoon black pepper
3 bay leaves

1. Set the Instant Pot to the Sauté mode and heat the oil for 3 minutes. Add the carrots and onion to the pot and sauté for 3 minutes, or until just tender. Add the ground beef and garlic to the pot and sauté for 3 minutes, or until the beef is lightly browned. Stir in the remaining ingredients.
2. Lock the lid. Select the Manual mode and set the cooking time for 10 minutes on High Pressure. When the timer goes off, perform a quick pressure release. Carefully open the lid.
3. Let rest for 5 minutes to thicken and cool before serving.

## Cheesy Veggie Orzo Soup

**Prep time: 15 minutes | Cook time: 10 minutes | Serves 4**

1 medium potato, peeled and small-diced
1 medium zucchini, diced
1 small carrot, peeled and diced
1 small yellow onion, peeled and diced
2 stalks celery, diced
1 (15-ounce / 425-g) can diced tomatoes, undrained
2 cloves garlic, peeled and minced
½ cup gluten-free orzo
5 cups vegetable broth
2 teaspoons dried oregano leaves
2 teaspoons dried thyme leaves
1 teaspoon salt
1 teaspoon ground black pepper
3 cups fresh baby spinach
4 tablespoons grated Parmesan cheese

1. Add all the ingredients, except for the spinach and Parmesan cheese, to the Instant Pot.
2. Lock the lid. Select the Manual setting and set the cooking time for 10 minutes at High Pressure. Once the timer goes off, use a quick pressure release. Carefully open the lid.
3. Stir in the spinach until wilted.
4. Ladle the soup into four bowls and garnish with the Parmesan cheese. Serve warm.

## Potato Bisque with Bacon

**Prep time: 10 minutes | Cook time: 20 minutes | Serves 4**

2 tablespoons unsalted butter
1 slice bacon, diced
3 leeks, trimmed, rinsed and diced
6 cups diced Yukon Gold potatoes
4 cups chicken broth
2 teaspoons dried thyme leaves
1 teaspoon sriracha
½ teaspoon sea salt
¼ cup whole milk

1. Set the Instant Pot on the Sauté mode and melt the butter. Add the bacon and leeks to the pot and sauté for 5 minutes, or until the fat is rendered and leeks become tender.
2. Stir in the remaining ingredients, except for the milk.

3. Lock the lid. Select the Manual mode and set the cooking time for 15 minutes at High Pressure. When the timer goes off, use a natural pressure release for 5 minutes, then release any remaining pressure. Carefully open the lid.
4. Pour the milk into the pot. Use an immersion blender to blend the soup in the pot until it achieves the desired consistency.
5. Ladle the bisque into 4 bowls and serve warm.

## Chicken Soup with Egg Noodles

**Prep time: 15 minutes | Cook time: 24 minutes | Serves 8**

1 (3½-pound / 1.5-kg) chicken, cut into pieces
4 cups low-sodium chicken broth
3 stalks celery, chopped
2 medium carrots, peeled and chopped
1 medium yellow onion, peeled and chopped
1 clove garlic, and smashed
1 bay leaf
1 teaspoon poultry seasoning
½ teaspoon dried thyme
1 teaspoon salt
¼ teaspoon ground black pepper
4 ounces (113 g) dried egg noodles

1. Add all the ingredients, except for the egg noodles, to the Instant Pot and stir to combine.
2. Set the lid in place. Select the Soup mode and set the cooking time for 20 minutes at High Pressure. Once cooking is complete, use a natural pressure release for 20 to 25 minutes, then release any remaining pressure. Carefully open the lid.
3. Remove and discard the bay leaf. Transfer the chicken to a clean work surface. Shred chicken and discard the skin and bones. Return the shredded chicken to the pot and stir to combine. Stir in the noodles.
4. Lock the lid. Select the Manual mode and set the cooking time for 4 minutes at High Pressure. Once cooking is complete, use a quick pressure release. Carefully open the lid.
5. Serve hot.

## Fish Stew with Carrot

**Prep time: 10 minutes | Cook time: 14 minutes | Serves 4**

1 tablespoon olive oil
1 large carrot, peeled and diced
1 stalk celery, diced
1 small yellow onion, peeled and diced
4 cloves garlic, peeled and minced
2 cups baby red potatoes, scrubbed and small-diced
1 (28-ounce / 794-g) can diced tomatoes, undrained
1 pound (454 g) skinless cod, cut into cubes
1 (8-ounce / 227-g) bottle clam juice
2 cups water
1 tablespoon Italian seasoning
1 teaspoon salt
1 bay leaf

1. Press the Sauté button on the Instant Pot and heat the oil. Add the carrot, celery and onion to the pot and sauté for 5 minutes, or until the onion is translucent. Add the garlic and sauté for 1 minute. Stir in the remaining ingredients.
2. Set the lid in place. Select the Manual setting and set the cooking time for 8 minutes on High Pressure. Once cooking is complete, perform a natural pressure release for 10 minutes, then release any remaining pressure. Open the lid.
3. Ladle the stew into 4 bowls and serve warm.

## Venison Chili with Kidney Beans

**Prep time: 20 minutes | Cook time: 50 minutes | Serves 8**

2 pounds (907 g) ground venison
1 medium yellow onion, peeled and chopped
1 medium poblano pepper, deseeded and chopped
2 cloves garlic, peeled and minced
1 (28-ounce / 794-g) can diced tomatoes
¼ cup chili powder
1 teaspoon ground cumin
1 teaspoon smoked paprika
½ teaspoon dried oregano
½ teaspoon salt
½ teaspoon ground black pepper
4 cups beef broth
1 cup dried kidney beans, soaked overnight in water and drained
1 teaspoon Worcestershire sauce

1. Press the Sauté button on the Instant Pot. Add the venison to the pot and sear for 10 minutes, or until browned.
2. Add the onion, poblano pepper, garlic, tomatoes, chili powder, cumin, paprika, oregano, salt and black pepper to the pot and cook for 10 minutes, or until the onion is just softened. Stir in the remaining ingredients.
3. Set the lid in place. Select the Bean/Chili setting and set the cooking time for 30 minutes at High Pressure. Once the timer goes off, do a quick pressure release. Carefully open the lid.
4. Serve hot.

## Coconut Red Bean Soup

**Prep time: 10 minutes | Cook time: 50 minutes | Serves 4**

2 teaspoons olive oil
3 slices bacon, diced
2 large carrots, peeled and diced
5 green onions, sliced
1 stalk celery, chopped
1 Scotch bonnet, deseeded, veins removed and minced
1 (15-ounce / 425-g) can diced tomatoes, undrained
½ pound (227 g) dried small red beans
1 (13.5-ounce / 383-g) can coconut milk
2 cups chicken broth
1 tablespoon Jamaican jerk seasoning
1 teaspoon salt
4 cups cooked basmati rice
1 cup chopped fresh parsley
1 lime, quartered

1. Press the Sauté button on the Instant Pot and heat the oil. Add the bacon, carrots, onions, celery and Scotch bonnet to the pot and sauté for 5 minutes, or until the onions are translucent.
2. Stir in the tomatoes with juice, red beans, coconut milk, chicken broth, Jamaican jerk seasoning and salt.
3. Lock the lid. Select the Manual mode and set the cooking time for 45 minutes on High Pressure. When the timer goes off, do a natural pressure release for 10 minutes, then release any remaining pressure. Carefully open the lid.
4. Ladle the soup into four bowls over cooked rice and garnish with parsley. Squeeze a quarter of lime over each bowl. Serve warm.

## Beer Chipotle Chili

**Prep time: 15 minutes | Cook time: 55 minutes | Serves 8**

2 pounds (907 g) chili meat, made from chuck roast
1 medium onion, peeled and chopped
3 cloves garlic, peeled and minced
3 tablespoons minced chipotle in adobo
2 tablespoons chili powder
2 tablespoons light brown sugar
1 teaspoon ground cumin
½ teaspoon ground coriander
½ teaspoon salt
½ teaspoon ground black pepper
2 cups beef broth
1 (12-ounce / 340-g) bottle lager-style beer
½ cup water
¼ cup corn masa
1 tablespoon lime juice

1. Press the Sauté button on the Instant Pot and brown the chili meat for 10 minutes. Add the onion, garlic, chipotle, chili powder, brown sugar, cumin, coriander, salt and pepper to the pot and cook for 10 minutes, or until the onion is just softened.
2. Pour in the beef broth and beer and stir well.
3. Lock the lid. Select the Bean/Chili mode and set the cooking time for 30 minutes on High Pressure. When the timer goes off, perform a quick pressure release. Carefully open the lid.
4. Select the Sauté mode. Whisk in the water and masa and cook for 5 minutes, stirring constantly, or until it starts to thicken.
5. Stir in the lime juice. Serve hot.

## Beef Chili with Onions

**Prep time: 20 minutes | Cook time: 19 minutes | Serves 8**

2 pounds (907 g) 90% lean ground beef
3 large yellow onions, peeled and diced, divided
3 cloves garlic, peeled and minced
2 (16-ounce / 454-g) cans kidney beans, rinsed and drained
1 (15-ounce / 425-g) can tomato sauce
1 cup beef broth
2 tablespoons semisweet chocolate chips
2 tablespoons honey
2 tablespoons red wine vinegar
2 tablespoons chili powder
1 tablespoon pumpkin pie spice
1 teaspoon ground cumin
½ teaspoon ground cardamom
½ teaspoon salt
½ teaspoon freshly cracked black pepper
¼ teaspoon ground cloves
1 pound (454 g) cooked spaghetti
4 cups shredded Cheddar cheese

1. Press the Sauté button on the Instant Pot. Add the ground beef and ¾ of the diced onions to the pot and sauté for 8 minutes, or until the beef is browned and the onions are transparent. Drain the beef mixture and discard any excess fat. Add the garlic to the pot and sauté for 30 seconds.
2. Stir in the remaining ingredients, except for the reserved onions, spaghetti and cheese. Cook for 1 minute, or until fragrant.
3. Set the lid in place. Select the Manual mode and set the cooking time for 10 minutes on High Pressure. When the timer goes off, perform a quick pressure release. Carefully open the lid.
4. Serve over the cooked spaghetti and top with the reserved onions and cheese.

## Creamy Broccoli Soup with Bacon

**Prep time: 15 minutes | Cook time: 30 minutes | Serves 4**

2 teaspoons unsalted butter
6 slices bacon, diced
1 large carrot, peeled and diced
1 medium sweet onion, peeled and diced
1 small Russet potato, scrubbed and diced
1 pound (454 g) fresh broccoli, chopped
¼ cup grated Cheddar cheese
1 tablespoon Dijon mustard
1 teaspoon salt
1 teaspoon ground black pepper
4 cups chicken broth
¼ cup whole milk
4 tablespoons sour cream

1. Set the Instant Pot to the Sauté mode and melt the butter. Add the bacon to the pot and sear for 5 minutes, or until crispy. Transfer the bacon to a plate lined with paper towels and let rest for 5 minutes. Crumble the bacon when cooled.
2. Add the carrot, onion and potato to the pot. Sauté for 5 minutes, or until the onion is translucent. Stir in the remaining ingredients, except for the milk and sour cream.
3. Set the lid in place. Select the Soup mode and set the cooking time for 20 minutes at High Pressure. Once cooking is complete, use a quick pressure release. Carefully open the lid.
4. Pour the milk into the pot. Use an immersion blender to blend the soup in the pot until it achieves the desired smoothness.
5. Ladle the soup into 4 bowls and garnish with the crumbled bacon and sour cream. Serve warm.

## Cheesy Beef Soup

**Prep time: 10 minutes | Cook time: 16 minutes | Serves 4**

1 tablespoon olive oil
1 pound (454 g) ground beef
1 medium yellow onion, peeled and diced
1 small green bell pepper, deseeded and diced
1 medium carrot peeled and shredded
1 (15-ounce / 425-g) can diced tomatoes, undrained
2 teaspoons yellow mustard
1 teaspoon garlic powder
1 teaspoon smoked paprika
½ teaspoon salt
4 cups beef broth
2 cups shredded iceberg lettuce
1 cup shredded Cheddar cheese, divided
½ cup diced dill pickles

1. Set the Instant Pot to the Sauté mode and heat the olive oil for 30 seconds. Add the beef, onion and green bell pepper to the pot and sauté for 5 minutes, or until the beef is lightly browned. Add the carrot and sauté for 1 minute.
2. Stir in the tomatoes with juice, mustard, garlic powder, paprika, salt and beef broth.
3. Close and secure the lid. Select the Manual mode and set the cooking time for 7 minutes on High Pressure. When the timer goes off, use a quick pressure release. Carefully open the lid.
4. Whisk in the lettuce and ½ cup of the cheese. Select the Sauté mode and cook for 3 minutes.
5. Divide the soup among 4 bowls and serve topped with the remaining ½ cup of the cheese and dill pickles.

## Chinese Pork Belly Stew

**Prep time: 10 minutes | Cook time: 42 minutes | Serves 8**

½ cup plus 2 tablespoons soy sauce, divided
¼ cup Chinese cooking wine
½ cup packed light brown sugar
2 pounds (907 g) pork belly, skinned and cubed
12 scallions, cut into

pieces
3 cloves garlic, minced
3 tablespoons vegetable oil
1 teaspoon Chinese five-spice powder
2 cups vegetable broth
4 cups cooked white rice

1. In a large bowl, whisk together ½ cup of the soy sauce, wine and brown sugar. Place the pork into the bowl and turn to coat evenly. Cover in plastic and refrigerate for at least 4 hours. Drain the pork and pat dry. Reserve the marinade.
2. Press the Sauté button on the Instant Pot and heat the oil. Add half the pork to the pot in an even layer, making sure there is space between pork cubes to prevent steam from forming. Sear the pork for 3 minutes on each side, or until lightly browned. Transfer the browned pork to a plate. Repeat with the remaining pork.
3. Stir in the remaining ingredients, except for the rice. Return the browned pork to the pot with the reserved marinade.
4. Lock the lid. Select the Manual mode and set the cooking time for 30 minutes on High Pressure. When the timer beeps, perform a natural pressure release for 20 minutes, then release any remaining pressure. Carefully open the lid.
5. Serve hot over cooked rice.

## Guinness Beef Stew

**Prep time: 15 minutes | Cook time: 52 minutes | Serves 8**

2 pounds (907 g) boneless beef chuck steak, cubed
2 tablespoons all-purpose flour
½ teaspoon salt
¼ teaspoon black pepper
2 tablespoons vegetable oil
1 medium onion, peeled and chopped
1 clove garlic,

chopped
½ teaspoon dried thyme
1 cup Guinness stout
1 cup beef broth
2 large carrots, peeled and chopped
2 medium Russet potatoes, chopped
1 bay leaf
¼ cup chopped fresh flat-leaf parsley

1. In a medium bowl, whisk together the flour, salt and pepper. Add the beef to the bowl and toss until well coated. Set aside.
2. Press the Sauté button on the Instant Pot and heat the oil. Arrange half the beef in the pot in an even layer, making sure there is space between beef cubes to prevent steam from forming. Sear the beef for 6 minutes on both sides, or until lightly browned. Transfer the beef to a plate. Repeat with the remaining beef.
3. Add the onion, garlic and thyme to the pot and cook for 5 minutes, or until the onion is tender. Pour in half the Guinness and scrape off all the browned bits from the bottom of the pot. Stir in the remaining half of the Guinness, beef broth, carrots, potatoes, bay leaf and the cooked beef.
4. Lock the lid. Select the Manual mode and set the cooking time for 35 minutes at High Pressure. When the timer goes off, use a natural pressure release for 20 minutes, then release any remaining pressure. Carefully open the lid.
5. Remove and discard the bay leaf and serve hot with the fresh parsley on top.

## Green Lentil Chicken Sausage Stew

**Prep time: 10 minutes | Cook time: 36 minutes | Serves 6**

2 tablespoons vegetable oil
1 pound (454 g) chicken sausage, sliced
3 stalks celery, cut into pieces
2 medium carrots, peeled and cut into pieces
1 medium yellow onion, peeled and roughly chopped
2 cloves garlic, peeled and minced
½ teaspoon salt
1 large Russet potato, peeled and cut into pieces
4 cups chicken stock
2 cups green lentils
¼ cup chopped fresh flat-leaf parsley

1. Press the Sauté button on the Instant Pot and heat the oil. Add the sausage and cook for 8 minutes, or until the edges are browned. Transfer the sausage to a plate and set aside.
2. Add the celery, carrots and onion to the pot and sauté for 3 minutes, or until just softened. Add the garlic and salt to the pot and cook for 30 seconds, or until fragrant.
3. Place the sausage back to the pot along with the remaining ingredients.
4. Lock the lid, select the Manual mode and set the cooking time for 25 minute on High Pressure. When the timer goes off, do a natural pressure release for 15 minutes, then release any remaining pressure. Open the lid.
5. Serve warm.

## Lamb Stew with Apricots

**Prep time: 15 minutes | Cook time: 39 to 41 minutes | Serves 6**

2 tablespoons olive oil
2 pounds (907 g) cubed boneless lamb
1 medium onion, peeled and diced
4 garlic cloves, minced
2 cups beef broth
¼ cup freshly squeezed orange juice
1 cup crushed tomatoes
¼ cup diced dried apricots
¼ cup diced pitted dates
2 teaspoons ground cumin
2 teaspoons minced fresh ginger
¼ teaspoon cayenne pepper
¼ teaspoon ground cinnamon
1 teaspoon sea salt
½ teaspoon ground black pepper
½ cup chopped fresh cilantro

1. Press the Sauté button on the Instant Pot and heat the olive oil. Add the lamb cubes and onion to the pot and sauté for 3 to 5 minutes, or until the onion is translucent. Add the garlic and sauté for 1 minute.
2. Pour in the beef broth and orange juice and deglaze by scraping any of the bits from the side of the pot. Stir in the remaining ingredients, except for the cilantro.
3. Lock the lid, select the Meat/Stew mode and set the cooking time for 35 minutes on High Pressure. When the timer goes off, do a natural pressure release for 10 minutes, then release any remaining pressure. Open the lid.
4. Ladle into individual bowls and serve garnished with the cilantro.

## Pork Meatball Soup

**Prep time: 15 minutes | Cook time: 19 minutes | Serves 4**

**Meatballs:**

½ pound (227 g) ground pork
2 tablespoons gluten-free bread crumbs
2 tablespoons grated Parmesan cheese
1 tablespoon Italian seasoning

½ teaspoon cayenne pepper
½ teaspoon salt
1 large egg, whisked
2 cloves garlic, peeled and minced
2 tablespoons olive oil, divided

**Soup:**

1 tablespoon olive oil
1 medium carrot, peeled and shredded
1 Russet potato, scrubbed and small-diced
1 small red onion, peeled and diced
1 (15-ounce / 425-g) can diced fire-

roasted tomatoes, undrained
4 cups beef broth
½ teaspoon salt
½ teaspoon ground black pepper
½ teaspoon red pepper flakes
½ cup chopped fresh basil leaves

1. In a medium bowl, stir together all the ingredients for the meatballs, except for the olive oil. Shape the mixture into 24 meatballs.
2. Set the Instant Pot to the Sauté mode and heat 1 tablespoon of the olive oil for 30 seconds. Add half the meatballs to the pot and sear for 3 minutes, turning them to brown all sides. Remove the first batch and set aside. Add the remaining 1 tablespoon of the olive oil to the pot and repeat with the remaining meatballs. Remove the meatballs from the pot.
3. Select the Sauté mode and heat the olive oil for 30 seconds. Add the carrot, potato and onion to the pot and sauté for 5 minutes, or until the onion becomes translucent.
4. Add the meatballs to the pot along with the remaining ingredients for the soup.
5. Close and secure the lid. Select the Manual mode and set the cooking time for 7 minutes at High Pressure. Once cooking is complete, use a quick pressure release. Carefully open the lid.
6. Serve warm.

## Potato and Fish Stew

**Prep time: 15 minutes | Cook time: 28 minutes | Serves 8**

2 tablespoons unsalted butter
2 stalks celery, chopped
1 medium carrot, peeled and diced
1 medium yellow onion, peeled and diced
2 cloves garlic, peeled and minced
1 teaspoon Italian seasoning
¼ teaspoon dried thyme
¼ teaspoon salt

¼ teaspoon ground black pepper
1 cup lager-style beer
1 (28-ounce / 794-g) can diced tomatoes
2 large Russet potatoes, peeled and diced
3 cups seafood stock
1 bay leaf
2 pounds (907 g) cod, cut into pieces
2 tablespoons lemon juice

1. Set the Instant Pot to the Sauté mode and melt the butter. Add the celery, carrot and onion to the pot and sauté for 8 minutes, or until softened. Add the garlic, Italian seasoning, thyme, salt and pepper to the pot and cook for 30 seconds.
2. Pour in the beer and scrape the bottom of the pot well. Stir in the tomatoes, potatoes, seafood stock and bay leaf.
3. Set the lid in place. Select the Manual mode and set the cooking time for 10 minutes on High Pressure. When the timer goes off, perform a quick pressure release. Carefully open the lid.
4. Stir in the fish. Select the Sauté mode and allow the soup to simmer for 10 minutes, or until the fish is cooked through. Remove and discard the bay leaf and stir in lemon juice. Serve hot.

## Peppery Chicken Chili

**Prep time: 15 minutes | Cook time: 36 minutes | Serves 8**

2 tablespoons unsalted butter
1 medium yellow onion, peeled and chopped
½ pound (227 g) Anaheim peppers, deseeded and roughly chopped
½ pound (227 g) poblano peppers, deseeded and roughly chopped
½ pound (227 g) tomatillos, husked and quartered
2 small jalapeño peppers, deseeded and roughly chopped
2 cloves garlic, peeled and minced
1 teaspoon ground cumin
6 bone-in, skin-on chicken thighs (2½ pounds / 1.1 kg total)
2 cups chicken stock
2 cups water
⅓ cup roughly chopped fresh cilantro
3 (15-ounce / 425-g) cans Great Northern beans, drained and rinsed

1. Press the Sauté button on the Instant Pot and melt the butter. Add the onion and sauté for 3 minutes, or until tender. Add Anaheim peppers, poblano peppers, tomatillos and jalapeño peppers to the pot and sauté for 3 minutes.
2. Add the garlic and cumin to the pot and sauté for 30 seconds, or until fragrant. Stir in the chicken thighs, stock and water.
3. Lock the lid. Select the Bean/Chili mode and set the cooking time for 30 minutes on High Pressure. When the timer goes off, perform a quick pressure release. Carefully open the lid.
4. Transfer the chicken thighs to a clean work surface. Use two forks to remove the skin off the chicken and shred the meat.
5. Use an immersion blender to purée the mixture in the pot until smooth. Stir in the shredded chicken, cilantro and beans. Serve warm.

## Pork Chili with Black-Eyed Peas

**Prep time: 15 minutes | Cook time: 49 minutes | Serves 6**

2 tablespoons vegetable oil
2 pounds (907 g) boneless pork shoulder, cut into pieces
1 medium onion, peeled and finely chopped
3 cloves garlic, peeled and minced
1 (14.5-ounce / 411-g) can diced tomatoes, drained
3 tablespoons chili powder
1 teaspoon ground cumin
½ teaspoon ground coriander
½ teaspoon salt
½ teaspoon ground black pepper
4 cups chicken broth
2 cups dried black-eyed peas, soaked overnight in water and drained
1 tablespoon lime juice

1. Set the Instant Pot to the Sauté mode and heat the oil. Add half the pork to the pot in an even layer, working in batches to prevent meat from steaming. Sear the pork for 3 minutes on each side, or until lightly browned. Transfer the browned pork to a plate. Repeat with the remaining pork.
2. Add the onion to the pot and sauté for 5 minutes, or until softened. Add the garlic, tomatoes, chili powder, cumin, coriander, salt and pepper to the pot and cook for 2 minutes, or until fragrant.
3. Stir in the browned pork, chicken broth and black-eyed peas.
4. Lock the lid. Select the Manual mode and set the cooking time for 30 minutes on High Pressure. Once the timer goes off, perform a natural pressure release for 20 minutes, then release any remaining pressure. Carefully open the lid.
5. Stir in the lime juice. Serve hot.

## Peppery Red Kidney Bean Chili

**Prep time: 20 minutes | Cook time: 14 minutes | Serves 4 to 6**

3 tablespoons salted butter
1 medium yellow onion, finely diced
1 Scotch bonnet pepper, deseeded and sliced in half
1 jalapeño pepper, deseeded and diced
1 poblano pepper, deseeded and diced
3 cloves garlic, minced
1½ pounds (680 g) ground beef
½ cup beer
1 (14.5-ounce / 411-g) can diced tomatoes
1 (10-ounce / 284-g) can Rotel tomatoes
1 (8-ounce / 227-g) can tomato sauce
¼ cup taco sauce
1 tablespoon hoisin sauce
1 teaspoon Worcestershire sauce
2 tablespoons cumin
1½ teaspoons seasoned salt
1 teaspoon dried cilantro
1 teaspoon Italian seasoning
1 teaspoon celery salt
½ teaspoon chili powder
1 teaspoon Tony Chachere's Creole Seasoning
2 (15.5-ounce / 439-g) cans red kidney beans, drained and rinsed

1. Press the Sauté button on the Instant Pot and melt the butter. Add the onion, Scotch bonnet pepper, jalapeño pepper and poblano pepper to the pot and sauté for 5 minutes, or until tender. Add the garlic and sauté for 1 minute.
2. Add the ground beef to the pot and sauté for 3 minutes, crumbling and breaking the pieces up with a wooden spoon, or until slightly browned.
3. Stir in the beer, diced tomatoes, Rotel tomatoes, tomato sauce, taco sauce, hoisin sauce and Worcestershire sauce. Scrape up any browned bits from the bottom of the pot.
4. Stir in the cumin, seasoned salt, dried cilantro, Italian seasoning, celery salt, chili powder and Creole seasoning. Gently fold in the kidney beans.
5. Set the lid in place. Select the Manual mode and set the cooking time for 5 minutes on High Pressure. When the timer goes off, do a quick pressure release. Carefully open the lid.
6. Serve warm.

## Spicy Ground Chicken Chili

**Prep time: 15 minutes | Cook time: 40 minutes | Serves 8**

1 tablespoon olive oil
1 pound (454 g) ground chicken
1 medium yellow onion, peeled and diced
3 cloves garlic, minced
1 (30-ounce / 850-g) can diced tomatoes, undrained
1 (4-ounce / 113-g) can diced green chilies, undrained
1 (15-ounce / 425-g) can dark red kidney beans, drained and rinsed
1 (15-ounce / 425-g) can black beans, drained and rinsed
3 canned chipotle chilies in adobo sauce
2 teaspoons hot sauce
1 teaspoon smoked paprika
1 teaspoon chili powder
1 teaspoon Worcestershire sauce
1 teaspoon sea salt

1. Press the Sauté button on the Instant Pot and heat the oil. Add the ground chicken and onion to the pot and sauté for 5 minutes, or until the chicken is no longer pink.
2. Stir in the remaining ingredients.
3. Set the lid in place. Select the Meat/Stew setting and set the cooking time for 35 minutes on High Pressure. When the timer goes off, perform a natural pressure release for 15 minutes, then release any remaining pressure. Open the lid.
4. Ladle the chili into individual bowls and serve warm.

## Spicy Turkey Chili

**Prep time: 15 minutes | Cook time: 43 minutes | Serves 8**

2 pounds (907 g) ground turkey
1 medium carrot, peeled and finely chopped
1 medium onion, peeled and chopped
3 cloves garlic, peeled and minced
1 small jalapeño pepper, deseeded and minced
¼ cup chili powder
1 teaspoon ground cumin
½ teaspoon smoked paprika
1 tablespoon light brown sugar
½ teaspoon salt
½ teaspoon ground black pepper
2 cups chicken broth
1 cup water
1 (15-ounce / 425-g) can kidney beans, drained and rinsed
1 tablespoon lime juice

1. Set the Instant Pot to the Sauté mode. Add the turkey to the pot and sear for 10 minutes, or until browned. Add the carrot, onion, garlic, jalapeño pepper, chili powder, cumin and paprika to the pot and sauté for 3 minutes, or until fragrant. Season with the brown sugar, salt and pepper and cook for 30 seconds.
2. Pour in the chicken broth and water and stir well.
3. Close and secure the lid. Select the Bean/Chili mode and set the cooking time for 30 minutes at High Pressure. When the timer goes off, use a quick pressure release. Carefully open the lid.
4. Stir in the kidney beans and lime juice and let sit in the residual heat for 10 minutes until the beans are heat through.
5. Serve warm.

## Spicy Corn and Bean Chili

**Prep time: 15 minutes | Cook time: 44 minutes | Serves 4**

1 tablespoon olive oil
1 medium red bell pepper, deseeded and diced
2 stalks celery, chopped
1 small yellow onion, peeled and diced
½ pound (227 g) ground pork
4 cloves garlic, peeled and minced
1 cup sliced white mushrooms
1 (28-ounce / 794-g) can diced tomatoes, undrained
1 (15.5-ounce / 439-g) can corn, drained
1 (15-ounce / 425-g) can black beans, drained and rinsed
2 tablespoons chili powder
1 teaspoon smoked paprika
1 teaspoon adobo sauce
1 teaspoon salt
¼ cup beef broth
2 chipotles in adobo sauce, finely diced
1 cup shredded Cheddar cheese

1. Set the Instant Pot to the Sauté mode and heat the oil. Add the bell pepper, celery and onion to the pot and sauté for 3 minutes, or until the onion is tender. Add the pork to the pot and sauté for 5 minutes, or until the pork is no longer pink. Add the garlic and sauté for 1 minute.
2. Stir in the remaining ingredients, except for the cheese.
3. Set the lid in place. Select the Meat/Stew setting and set the cooking time for 35 minutes on High Pressure. Once cooking is complete, do a natural pressure release for 15 minutes, then release any remaining pressure. Open the lid.
4. Ladle the chili into 4 bowls and serve warm garnished with the cheese.

## Tomato and Red Pepper Bisque

**Prep time: 10 minutes | Cook time: 15 minutes | Serves 4**

1 tablespoon olive oil
2 teaspoons balsamic vinegar
1 small sweet onion, peeled and diced
1 stalk celery, thinly chopped
8 medium tomatoes, deseeded and quartered
1 (12-ounce / 340-g) jar roasted red peppers, drained and diced
4 cups chicken broth
1 tablespoon cooking sherry
½ cup julienned fresh basil leaves, divided
1 teaspoon salt
1 teaspoon ground black pepper
1 cup whole milk

1. Set the Instant Pot to the Sauté mode and heat the olive oil and balsamic vinegar for 30 seconds. Add the onion and celery to the pot and sauté for 5 minutes, or until the onion is translucent. Add the tomatoes and sauté for 3 minutes, or until the tomatoes break down.
2. Stir in the roasted red peppers, chicken broth, sherry, ¼ cup of the basil, salt and pepper.
3. Close and secure the lid. Select the Manual mode and set the cooking time for 7 minutes on High Pressure. Once cooking is complete, use a quick pressure release. Carefully open the lid.
4. Pour in the milk. Use an immersion blender to purée the mixture in the pot.
5. Divide the dish among 4 bowls and serve topped with the remaining ¼ cup of the basil.

## Tomato and Chicken Chili

**Prep time: 10 minutes | Cook time: 21 minutes | Serves 4**

1 tablespoon olive oil
1 pound (454 g) ground chicken
1 medium yellow onion, peeled and diced
1 stalk celery, diced
3 cloves garlic, peeled and minced
1 (28-ounce / 794-g) can diced tomatoes, undrained
1 (14.5-ounce / 411-g) can great northern beans, rinsed and drained
2 (4-ounce / 113-g) cans diced green chiles, undrained
1 cup chicken broth
1 tablespoon fresh thyme leaves
1 tablespoon chili powder
1 teaspoon salt
1 cup sour cream

1. Set the Instant Pot to the Sauté mode and heat the oil. Add the ground chicken, onion and celery to the pot and sauté for 5 minutes, or until the chicken is no longer pink. Add the garlic to the pot and cook for 1 minute.
2. Stir in the remaining ingredients, except for sour cream.
3. Set the lid in place. Select the Manual setting and set the cooking time for 15 minutes on High Pressure. When the timer goes off, perform a natural pressure release for 10 minutes, then release any remaining pressure. Open the lid.
4. Stir in the sour cream. Ladle the chili into 4 bowls and serve warm.

## Veggie Corn Chowder

**Prep time: 20 minutes | Cook time: 25 to 28 minutes | Serves 8**

6 slices bacon, divided
1 large carrot, peeled and diced
1 large sweet onion, peeled and diced
½ cup diced celery
2 large Yukon Gold potatoes, peeled and diced
6 cups chicken broth
3 cups fresh corn kernels
2 tablespoons fresh thyme leaves, divided
1 teaspoon sea salt
1 teaspoon ground black pepper
½ teaspoon honey
1 bay leaf
1 cup heavy cream

1. Set the Instant Pot to the Sauté mode. Add the bacon to the pot and sear for 5 minutes, or until crispy. Transfer the bacon to a plate lined with paper towels and set aside.
2. Add the carrot, onion and celery to the pot and sauté for 3 to 5 minutes, or until the onion is translucent. Add the potatoes to the pot and continue to sauté for 2 to 3 minutes, or until the potatoes are lightly browned.
3. Stir in the chicken broth, corn, 1 tablespoon of the thyme, salt, pepper, honey and bay leaf. Crumble 2 pieces of the bacon and add to the soup.
4. Set the lid in place. Select the Manual mode and set the cooking time for 15 minutes on High Pressure. When the timer goes off, perform a quick pressure release. Carefully open the lid.
5. Remove and discard the bay leaf. Whisk int the heavy cream and use an immersion blender to purée the soup in the pot.
6. Divide the soup among bowls and garnish with the remaining 1 tablespoon of the thyme leaves. Crumble 4 pieces of the bacon and add to the soup.
7. Serve warm.

## Veggie Kidney Bean Chili

**Prep time: 20 minutes | Cook time: 39 minutes | Serves 8**

1 tablespoon olive oil
2 medium white onions, peeled and finely chopped
1 medium carrot, peeled and finely chopped
1 medium red bell pepper, deseeded and finely chopped
2 small jalapeño peppers, deseeded and finely chopped
2 cloves garlic, minced
1 (28-ounce / 794-g) can diced tomatoes
1 (15-ounce / 425-g) can tomato sauce
2 cups dried kidney beans, soaked overnight in water and drained
½ cup bulgur wheat
¼ cup chopped cilantro
¼ cup chili powder
1 tablespoon smoked paprika
1½ teaspoons ground cumin
1 teaspoon ground coriander
½ teaspoon salt
½ teaspoon black pepper
3 cups vegetable broth
1 cup water

1. Set the Instant Pot to the Sauté mode and heat the oil. Add the onions, carrot and bell pepper to the pot and sauté for 8 minutes, or until softened. Add the jalapeño peppers and garlic to the pot and sauté for 1 minute, or until fragrant. Stir in the remaining ingredients.
2. Close and secure the lid. Select the Bean/Chili setting and set the cooking time for 30 minutes at High Pressure. Once the timer goes off, do a quick pressure release. Carefully open the lid.
3. Serve warm.

## Authentic Pozole

**Prep time: 20 minutes | Cook time: 53 minutes | Serves 6**

2½ pounds (1.1 kg) boneless pork shoulder, cut into pieces
1 teaspoon salt, divided
1 teaspoon ground black pepper, divided
2 tablespoons vegetable oil
2 medium yellow onions, peeled and chopped
2 medium poblano peppers, deseeded and diced
1 chipotle pepper in adobo, minced
4 cloves garlic, peeled and minced
1 cinnamon stick
1 tablespoon smoked paprika
2 teaspoons chili powder
1 teaspoon dried oregano
1 teaspoon ground cumin
½ teaspoon ground coriander
1 (12-ounce / 340-g) can lager-style beer
4 cups chicken broth
2 (15-ounce / 425-g) cans hominy, drained and rinsed
1 tablespoon lime juice
½ cup chopped cilantro

1. Season the pork pieces with ½ teaspoon of the salt and ½ teaspoon of the pepper.
2. Press the Sauté button on the Instant Pot and heat the oil. Add half the pork to the pot in an even layer, making sure there is space between pieces to prevent steam from forming. Sear the pork for 3 minutes on each side, or until lightly browned. Remove the pork to a plate. Repeat with the remaining pork.
3. Add the onions and poblano peppers to the pot and sauté for 5 minutes, or until just softened. Add the chipotle pepper, garlic, cinnamon, paprika, chili powder, oregano, cumin and coriander to the pot. Sauté for 1 minute, or until fragrant.
4. Return the pork to the pot and turn to coat with the spices. Pour in the beer and chicken broth.
5. Lock the lid. Select the Manual mode and set the cooking time for 35 minutes on High Pressure. When the timer beeps, perform a natural pressure release for 20 minutes, then release any remaining pressure. Carefully open the lid.
6. Season with the remaining ½ teaspoon of the salt and ½ teaspoon of the pepper. Stir in the hominy, lime juice and cilantro. Serve hot.

# Chapter 14 Appetizers and Snacks

## Hearty Red Pepper Hummus

**Prep time: 10 minutes | Cook time: 30 minutes | Makes 1½ cups**

½ cup dried chickpeas
2 cups water
1 cup jarred roasted red peppers with liquid, chopped and divided
1 tablespoon tahini paste
1 tablespoon lemon juice
1 teaspoon lemon zest
¼ teaspoon ground cumin
2 cloves garlic, minced
¼ teaspoon smoked paprika
⅛ teaspoon cayenne pepper
¼ teaspoon salt
1 teaspoon sesame oil
1 tablespoon olive oil

1. Add chickpeas and water to the Instant Pot. Drain liquid from the roasted peppers into the pot. Set aside the drained peppers.
2. Lock the lid. Press the Beans / Chili button and set the time to 30 minutes on High Pressure. When the timer beeps, let pressure release naturally for 5 minutes, then release any remaining pressure. Unlock the lid.
3. Drain pot, reserving the liquid in a small bowl.
4. Make the hummus: Transfer the chickpeas into a food processor. Add ¼ cup of chopped red peppers, tahini paste, lemon juice and zest, cumin, garlic, smoked paprika, cayenne pepper, salt, sesame oil, and olive oil. If consistency is too thick, slowly add reserved liquid, 1 tablespoon at a time until it has a loose paste consistency.
5. Transfer the hummus to a serving dish. Garnish with remaining chopped roasted red peppers and serve.

## Beery Shrimp with Thai Sauce

**Prep time: 10 minutes | Cook time: 10 minutes | Serves 10**

**Thai Sauce:**

¼ cup Thai sweet chili sauce
1 tablespoon Sriracha sauce

¼ cup sour cream
2 teaspoons lime juice
½ cup mayonnaise

**Shrimp:**

1 (12-ounce / 340-g) bottle beer
4 pounds (1.8 kg)

large shrimp, shelled and deveined

1. Combine ingredients for the Thai sauce in a small bowl. Cover the bowl in plastic and refrigerate until ready to serve.
2. Pour the beer into the Instant Pot and insert the steamer basket. Place shrimp in basket.
3. Lock the lid. Press the Steam button and set the cook time for 10 minutes on Low Pressure.
4. When timer beeps, quick release the pressure and then unlock the lid.
5. Transfer shrimp to a serving dish and serve with the Thai sauce.

## Bacon Stuffed Mini Peppers

**Prep time: 15 minutes | Cook time: 16 minutes | Serves 4**

1 ounce (28 g) bacon, chopped
1 garlic clove, minced
2 tablespoons chopped onion
½ teaspoon Worcestershire sauce
2 ounces (57 g) Mexican cheese

blend, crumbled
½ teaspoon Taco seasoning
4 mini sweet bell peppers, deseeded and membranes removed
1 cup water
1 tablespoon fresh cilantro, chopped

1. Press the Sauté button of the Instant Pot. Add and cook the bacon for 8 minutes or until it is crisp. Flip the bacon halfway through and crumble with a spatula. Set aside.
2. Add and cook the garlic and onion for 3 minutes or until tender and fragrant.
3. Add the Worcestershire sauce, cheese, and Taco seasoning. Stir in the reserved bacon.
4. Divide the mixture among the peppers on a clean work surface.
5. Pour the water in the Instant Pot. Arrange a trivet over the water. Place the stuffed peppers onto the trivet.
6. Secure the lid. Choose the Manual mode and set the cooking time for 5 minutes at High pressure.
7. Once cooking is complete, perform a natural pressure release for 5 minutes, then release any remaining pressure. Carefully open the lid.
8. Serve the bacon stuffed pepper on a platter garnished with fresh cilantro.

## Chicken and Vegetable Salad Skewers

**Prep time: 15 minutes | Cook time: 5 minutes | Serves 4**

1 cup water
1 pound (454 g) chicken breast halves, boneless and skinless
Celery salt and ground black pepper, to taste
½ teaspoon Sriracha sauce
1 zucchini, cut into

thick slices
1 cup cherry tomatoes, halved
1 red onion, cut into wedges
¼ cup olives, pitted
1 tablespoon fresh lemon juice
2 tablespoons olive oil

**Special Equipment:**
4 bamboo skewers

1. Pour the water in the Instant Pot. Arrange a trivet in the pot. Place the chicken on the trivet.
2. Secure the lid. Choose Poultry mode and set the cooking time for 5 minutes at High Pressure.
3. Once cooking is complete, perform a natural pressure release for 5 minutes, then release any remaining pressure. Carefully open the lid.
4. Slice the chicken into cubes. Sprinkle chicken cubes with salt, pepper, and drizzle with Sriracha.
5. Thread the chicken cubes, zucchini, cherry tomatoes, onion, and olives onto bamboo skewers. Drizzle the lemon juice and olive oil over and serve.

## Bacon Wrapped Wieners

**Prep time: 15 minutes | Cook time: 3 minutes | Serves 10**

1 pound (454 g) cocktail wieners
½ pound (227 g) bacon, cut into slices
2 tablespoons apple cider vinegar
¼ cup ketchup
1 tablespoon ground

mustard
1 tablespoon onion powder
½ cup chicken broth
Salt and ground black pepper, to taste
½ cup water

1. Wrap each cocktail wiener with a slice of bacon and secure with a toothpick.
2. Lay the bacon-wrapped cocktail wieners in the bottom of the Instant Pot. Repeat with the remaining cocktail wieners.
3. In a bowl, combine the remaining ingredients. Stir to mix well. Pour the mixture over the bacon-wrapped cocktail wieners.
4. Secure the lid. Choose the Manual mode and set the cooking time for 3 minutes on Low Pressure.
5. Once cooking is complete, perform a natural pressure release for 5 minutes, then release any remaining pressure. Carefully open the lid.
6. Serve immediately.

## Chili and Meat Nachos

**Prep time: 25 minutes | Cook time: 45 minutes | Serves 8**

1 tablespoon olive oil
1 medium green bell pepper, seeded and diced
1 small red onion, peeled and diced
4 ounces (113 g) ground pork
½ pound (227 g) ground beef
1 (4-ounce / 113-g) can chopped green chiles, with juice
1 (14.5-ounce / 411-g) can diced tomatoes, with juice

1 teaspoon garlic powder
1 tablespoon chili powder
1 teaspoon ground cumin
1 teaspoon salt
4 ounces (113 g) cream cheese
2 Roma tomatoes, deseeded and diced
½ cup shredded Cheddar cheese
4 scallions, sliced
1 bag corn tortilla chips

1. Press the Sauté button on the Instant Pot. Heat the olive oil until shimmering.
2. Add the bell pepper and onion to pot. Sauté for 5 minutes or until onions are translucent. Add the pork and beef and sauté for 5 more minutes.
3. Add the chiles with juice, tomatoes with juice, garlic powder, chili powder, cumin, and salt to pot and stir to combine.
4. Lock the lid. Press the Meat / Stew button and set the time for 35 minutes on High Pressure. When the timer beeps, let pressure release naturally for 10 minutes, then release any remaining pressure.
5. Unlock the lid. Stir in cream cheese until melted and evenly distributed.
6. Transfer chili mixture to a serving dish. Garnish with Roma tomatoes, Cheddar, and scallions. Serve warm with chips.

## Cauliflower Tots

**Prep time: 15 minutes | Cook time: 23 minutes | Serves 6**

1 cup water
1 head cauliflower, broken into florets
2 eggs, beaten
½ cup grated Parmesan cheese
½ cup grated Swiss

cheese
2 tablespoons fresh coriander, chopped
1 shallot, chopped
Sea salt and ground black pepper, to taste

1. Add the water to the Instant Pot. Set a steamer basket in the pot.
2. Arrange the cauliflower florets in the steamer basket.
3. Secure the lid. Choose the Manual mode and set the cooking time for 3 minutes at High Pressure.
4. Once cooking is complete, perform a quick pressure release. Carefully open the lid.
5. Mash the cauliflower in a food processor and add the remaining ingredients. Pulse to combine well.
6. Form the mixture into a tater-tot shape with oiled hands.
7. Place cauliflower tots on a lightly greased baking sheet. Bake in the preheated oven at 400ºF (205ºC) for about 20 minutes. Flip halfway through the cooking time.
8. Serve immediately.

## Italian Seafood Appetizer

**Prep time: 20 minutes | Cook time: 10 minutes | Serves 4**

¼ cup olive oil
28 ounces (794 g) canned tomatoes, chopped
2 jalapeño peppers, chopped
½ cup chopped white onion
¼ cup balsamic vinegar

¼ cup veggie stock
2 garlic cloves, minced
2 tablespoons crushed red pepper flakes
2 pounds (907 g) mussels, scrubbed
½ cup chopped basil
Salt, to taste

1. Press the Sauté button on the Instant Pot and heat the olive oil.
2. Add the tomatoes, jalapeño, onion, vinegar, veggie stock, garlic, and red pepper flakes and stir well. Cook for 5 minutes. Stir in the mussels.
3. Secure the lid. Select the Manual mode and set the cooking time for 4 minutes at Low Pressure.
4. Once cooking is complete, do a quick pressure release. Carefully open the lid.
5. Sprinkle with the basil and salt and stir well. Divide the mussels among four bowls and serve.

## Mushroom Stuffed Tomatoes

**Prep time: 20 minutes | Cook time: 10 minutes | Serves 4**

4 tomatoes
1 tablespoon ghee
2 tablespoons celery, chopped
1 yellow onion, chopped
½ cup mushrooms, chopped

1 tablespoon parsley, chopped
1 cup cottage cheese
Salt and black pepper, to taste
¼ teaspoon caraway seeds
½ cup water

1. On a clean work surface, remove the tops of each tomato about 1 inch, then scoop the tomato pulp out and reserve in a small bowl. Set aside.
2. Set the Instant Pot on Sauté mode. Add the ghee and heat until melted.
3. Add the celery and onion. Sauté for 3 minutes or until softened.

4. Add the mushrooms, tomato pulp, parsley, cheese, salt, pepper, and caraway seeds, then stir well. Sauté for 3 minutes more. Stuff the hollowed tomatoes with the mixture.
5. Pour the water in the Instant Pot, then arrange the steamer basket in the pot. Place the stuffed tomatoes inside.
6. Seal the Instant Pot lid and set to the Manual mode. Set the cooking time for 4 minutes on High Pressure.
7. Once cooking is complete, perform a quick pressure release. Carefully open the lid.
8. Arrange the stuffed tomatoes on a platter and serve immediately.

## Crab, Bacon, and Cheese Dip

**Prep time: 30 minutes | Cook time: 14 minutes | Serves 8**

8 bacon strips, sliced
½ cup coconut cream
1 cup grated Parmesan cheese, divided
2 poblano pepper, chopped
½ cup mayonnaise
2 tablespoons lemon juice

8 ounces (227 g) cream cheese
4 garlic cloves, minced
4 green onions, minced
Salt and black pepper, to taste
12 ounces (340 g) crab meat

1. Set the Instant Pot on sauté mode. Add the bacon and cook for 8 minutes or until crispy. Transfer onto a plate and pat dry with paper towels. Set aside.
2. In a bowl, mix the coconut cream with half of the Parmesan, poblano peppers, mayo, lemon juice, cream cheese, garlic, green onions, salt, pepper, crab meat and bacon and stir well.
3. Add the mixture to the Instant Pot. Spread the remaining Parmesan on top. Seal the Instant Pot lid and select the Manual mode. Set the cooking time 14 minutes on High Pressure.
4. Once cooking is complete, perform a quick pressure release. Carefully open the lid.
5. Divide into 8 bowls and serve immediately.

## Eggplant and Olive Spread

**Prep time: 20 minutes | Cook time: 8 minutes | Serves 6**

¼ cup olive oil
2 pounds (907 g) eggplant, peeled and cut into medium chunks
4 garlic cloves, minced
½ cup water
Salt and black

pepper, to taste
1 tablespoon sesame seed paste
¼ cup lemon juice
1 bunch thyme, chopped
3 olives, pitted and sliced

1. Set the Instant Pot on Sauté mode. Add the olive oil and heat until shimmering.
2. Add eggplant pieces and Sauté for 5 minutes. Add the garlic, water, salt and pepper, then stir well.
3. Close the lid, set to the Manual mode and set the cooking time for 3 minutes on High Pressure.
4. Once cooking is complete, perform a quick pressure release. Carefully open the lid.
5. Transfer to a blender, then add sesame seed paste, lemon juice and thyme, pulse to combine well.
6. Transfer to bowls, sprinkle olive slices on top and serve.

## Herbed Polenta Squares

**Prep time: 1 hour 15 minutes | Cook time: 15 minutes | Serves 4**

½ cup cornmeal
½ cup milk
1½ cups water
½ teaspoon kosher salt
½ tablespoon butter
$1/_3$ cup cream cheese
1 tablespoon chives, finely chopped

1 tablespoon cilantro, finely chopped
½ teaspoon basil
½ tablespoon thyme
½ teaspoon rosemary
$1/_3$ cup bread crumbs
1 tablespoon olive oil

1. Make the polenta: Add the cornmeal, milk, water, and salt to the Instant Pot. Stir to mix well.
2. Press the Sauté button and bring the mixture to a simmer.

3. Secure the lid. Choose the Manual mode and set the cooking time for 8 minutes at High pressure.
4. Once cooking is complete, perform a quick pressure release. Carefully open the lid.
5. Grease a baking pan with butter. Add the cream cheese and herbs to the polenta.
6. Scoop the polenta into the prepared baking pan and refrigerate for an hour or until firm. Cut into small squares. Spread the breadcrumbs on a large plate, coat the polenta squares with breadcrumbs.
7. Heat the olive oil in a skillet over medium heat.
8. Cook the polenta squares in the skillet for about 3 minutes per side or until golden brown. Serve immediately.

## Roasted Nuts, Chickpeas, and Seeds

**Prep time: 10 minutes | Cook time: 11 minutes | Serves 2 to 4**

2 tablespoons pecans halves
¼ cup canned chickpeas
2 tablespoons almonds
1 tablespoon pumpkin seeds
1 tablespoon sunflower seeds

¼ teaspoon grated nutmeg
¼ teaspoon ground ginger
2 tablespoons maple syrup
1 tablespoon butter
¼ teaspoon kosher salt
¼ cup Sultanas

1. Place all ingredients, except for the Sultanas, in the Instant Pot. Stir to combine well.
2. Press the Sauté button and sauté for 1 minute until the butter melts and the nuts are well coated.
3. Secure the lid. Choose the Manual mode and set the cooking time for 10 minutes at High pressure.
4. Once cooking is complete, perform a quick pressure release. Carefully open the lid.
5. Transfer them on a baking pan and bake in the preheated oven at 375ºF (190ºC) for about 8 minutes.
6. Remove the pan from the oven. Add the Sultanas and stir to combine. Serve immediately.

## Herbed Button Mushrooms

**Prep time: 10 minutes | Cook time: 4 minutes | Serves 4**

6 ounces (170 g) button mushrooms, rinsed and drained
1 clove garlic, minced
½ cup vegetable broth
½ teaspoon dried basil
½ teaspoon onion powder
½ teaspoon dried oregano
1/3 teaspoon dried rosemary
½ teaspoon smoked paprika
Coarse sea salt and ground black pepper, to taste
1 tablespoon tomato paste
1 tablespoon butter

1. Put all the ingredients, except for the tomato paste and butter, in the Instant Pot. Stir to mix well.
2. Secure the lid. Choose the Manual mode and set the cooking time for 4 minutes at High pressure.
3. Once cooking is complete, perform a quick pressure release. Carefully open the lid.
4. Stir in the tomato paste and butter. Serve immediately.

## Chinese Wings

**Prep time: 10 minutes | Cook time: 16 minutes | Serves 6**

1 teaspoon Sriracha sauce
2 teaspoons Chinese five-spice powder
¼ cup tamari
¼ cup apple cider vinegar
3 cloves garlic, minced
1 tablespoon light brown sugar
2 tablespoons sesame oil
5 scallions, sliced and separated into whites and greens
3 pounds (1.4 kg) chicken wings, separated at the joint
1 cup water
¼ cup toasted sesame seeds

1. In a large bowl, combine the Sriracha, Chinese five-spice powder, tamari, apple cider vinegar, garlic, brown sugar, sesame oil, and whites of scallions. Stir to mix well. Transfer 2 tablespoons of the sauce mixture to a small bowl and reserve until ready to use.

2. Add wings to the remaining sauce and toss to coat well. Wrap the bowl in plastic and refrigerate for at least 1 hour or up to overnight.
3. Add the water to the Instant Pot and insert a steamer basket. Place the chicken wings in the single layer in the steamer basket. Lock the lid.
4. Press the Manual button and set the cook time for 10 minutes on High Pressure. When the timer beeps, let pressure release naturally for 5 minutes, then release any additional pressure and unlock the lid.
5. Using a slotted spoon, transfer the wings to a baking sheet. Brush with 2 tablespoons of reserved sauce. Broil the wings in the oven for 3 minutes on each side to crisp the chicken.
6. Transfer the wings to a serving dish and garnish with sesame seeds and greens of scallions. Serve immediately.

## Hungarian Cornmeal Squares

**Prep time: 15 minutes | Cook time: 55 minutes | Serves 4**

1¼ cup water, divided
1 cup yellow cornmeal
1 cup yogurt
1 egg, beaten
½ cups sour cream
1 teaspoon baking soda
2 tablespoons safflower oil
¼ teaspoon salt
4 tablespoons plum jam

1. Pour 1 cup of water in the Instant Pot. Set a trivet in the pot. Spritz a baking pan with cooking spray.
2. Combine the cornmeal, yogurt, egg, sour cream, baking soda, ¼ cup of water, safflower oil, and salt in a large bowl. Stir to mix well.
3. Pour the mixture into the prepared baking pan. Spread the plum jam over. Cover with aluminum foil. Lower the pan onto the trivet.
4. Secure the lid. Choose the Manual mode and set the cooking time for 55 minutes at High pressure. Once cooking is complete, perform a quick pressure release, carefully open the lid.
5. Transfer the corn meal chunk onto a cooling rack and allow to cool for 10 minutes. Slice into squares and serve.

## Lentil and Beef Slider Patties

**Prep time: 25 minutes | Cook time: 25 minutes | Makes 15 patties**

1 cup dried yellow lentils
2 cups beef broth
½ pound (227 g) 80/20 ground beef
½ cup chopped old-fashioned oats
2 large eggs, beaten
2 teaspoons Sriracha sauce
2 tablespoons diced yellow onion
½ teaspoon salt

1. Add the lentils and broth to the Instant Pot. Lock the lid.
2. Press the Manual button and set the cook time for 15 minutes on High Pressure. When the timer beeps, let pressure release naturally for 10 minutes, then release any remaining pressure. Unlock the lid.
3. Transfer the lentils to a medium bowl with a slotted spoon. Smash most of the lentils with the back of a spoon until chunky.
4. Add beef, oats, eggs, Sriracha, onion, and salt. Whisk to combine them well. Form the mixture into 15 patties.
5. Cook in a skillet on stovetop over medium-high heat in batches for 10 minutes. Flip the patties halfway through.
6. Transfer patties to serving dish and serve warm.

## Port Wined Short Ribs

**Prep time: 20 minutes | Cook time: 1 hour 45 minutes | Serves 4**

½ tablespoon lard
1 pound (454 g) short ribs
¼ cup port wine
1 tablespoon rice vinegar
1 tablespoon molasses
1 thyme sprig
1 rosemary sprig
1 garlic clove
½ cup beef bone broth
½ teaspoon cayenne pepper
Sea salt and ground black pepper, to season

1. Press the Sauté button and melt the lard in the Instant Pot.
2. Add the short ribs and cook for 4 to 5 minutes, flipping periodically to ensure even cooking.

3. Add the remaining ingredients and stir to mix well.
4. Secure the lid. Choose the Manual mode and set the cooking time for 90 minutes at High pressure.
5. Once cooking is complete, perform a natural pressure release for 30 minutes, then release any remaining pressure. Carefully open the lid.
6. Transfer the short ribs into the broiler and broil for 10 minutes or until crispy. Transfer the ribs to a platter and serve immediately.

## Sausage Stuffed Bella Mushrooms

**Prep time: 10 minutes | Cook time: 7 minutes | Makes 10 mushrooms**

1 tablespoon olive oil
4 ounces (113 g) ground pork sausage
1 tablespoon diced yellow onion
1 tablespoon horseradish
1 tablespoon bread crumbs
1 teaspoon yellow mustard
2 tablespoons cream
cheese, at room temperature
¼ teaspoon garlic salt
1 cup water
8 ounces (227 g) whole baby bella mushrooms, stem removed
2 tablespoons chopped fresh Italian flat-leaf parsley

1. Press the Sauté button on the Instant Pot and heat the olive oil until shimmering.
2. Add the sausage and onion to the pot. Sauté for 5 minutes until the sausage is lightly browned.
3. Transfer the sausage and onion to a small bowl and use paper towels to pat dry. Add the horseradish, bread crumbs, yellow mustard, cream cheese, and garlic salt.
4. Pour the water into the Instant Pot. Stuff the sausage mixture into each mushroom cap and place in a steamer basket. Insert the steamer basket in the pot and lock the lid.
5. Press the Manual button and set the cook time for 2 minutes on Low Pressure. When timer beeps, quick release the pressure. Unlock lid.
6. Transfer the stuffed mushrooms to a serving dish. Garnish with chopped parsley. Serve warm.

## Honey Carrots with Raisins

**Prep time: 5 minutes | Cook time: 5 minutes | Serves 3**

1 pound (454 g) carrots, peeled and cut into chunks
2 tablespoons golden raisins
½ cup water
½ tablespoon honey
²/₃ teaspoon crushed red pepper flakes
½ tablespoon melted butter
Salt, to taste

1. Add the carrots, raisins, and water to the Instant Pot
2. Secure the lid and select the Manual function. Set the cooking time for 5 minutes on Low Pressure.
3. When the timer beeps, do a quick release, then open the lid.
4. Strain the carrots and transfer them to a large bowl.
5. Put the remaining ingredients into the bowl and toss well.
6. Serve warm.

## Easy Chicken in Lettuce

**Prep time: 15 minutes | Cook time: 13 to 15 minutes | Serves 4**

6 ounces (170 g) chicken breasts
1 cup water
1 teaspoon sesame oil
½ small onion, finely diced
1 garlic clove, minced
½ teaspoon ginger, minced
Kosher salt and
ground black pepper, to taste
1 tablespoon hoisin sauce
½ tablespoon soy sauce
1 tablespoon rice vinegar
½ head butter lettuce, leaves separated

1. Add the chicken breasts and water to the Instant Pot.
2. Secure the lid. Choose the Manual mode and set the cooking time for 8 minutes at High pressure.
3. Once cooking is complete, perform a quick pressure release. Carefully open the lid. Shred the chicken with forks.
4. Press the Sauté button and heat the sesame oil.

5. Add and cook the garlic and onion for 3 to 4 minutes or until softened.
6. Add the chicken and cook for 2 to 3 minutes more.
7. Stir in the hoisin sauce, rice vinegar, soy sauce, ginger, salt, and black pepper. Cook for another minute.
8. Spoon the chicken mixture over the lettuce leaves on a large plate, wrap and serve immediately.

## Shrimp and Blue Cheese on Sticks

**Prep time: 10 minutes | Cook time: 1 minute | Serves 6**

1 pound (454 g) shrimp, shelled and deveined
¼ cup rice wine vinegar
¾ cup water
4 ounces (113 g) blue cheese, cubed
1 celery stalk, diced
½ cup olives, pitted
2 bell peppers, sliced
1 cup cherry tomatoes
1 tablespoon olive oil
½ teaspoon cayenne pepper
Sea salt and ground black pepper, to taste
½ teaspoon paprika

**Special Equipment:**
6 cocktail sticks

1. Place the shrimp, rice wine vinegar, and water in the Instant Pot.
2. Secure the lid. Choose the Manual mode and set the cooking time for 1 minute at Low Pressure.
3. Once cooking is complete, perform a quick pressure release. Carefully open the lid.
4. Thread the shrimp, blue cheese, celery, olives, peppers, and cherry tomatoes onto the cocktail sticks.
5. Drizzle olive oil over and sprinkle with cayenne pepper, salt, black pepper, and paprika. Arrange the skewers on a serving platter and serve.

## Jalapeño Peanuts

**Prep time: 3 hours 20 minutes | Cook time: 45 minutes | Serves 4**

4 ounces (113 g) raw peanuts in the shell
1 jalapeño, sliced
1 tablespoon Creole seasoning
½ tablespoon cayenne pepper
½ tablespoon garlic powder
1 tablespoon salt

1. Add all ingredients to the Instant Pot. Pour in enough water to cover. Stir to mix well. Use a steamer to gently press down the peanuts.
2. Secure the lid. Choose the Manual mode and set the cooking time for 45 minutes at High pressure.
3. Once cooking is complete, perform a natural pressure release for 15 minutes, then release any remaining pressure. Carefully open the lid.
4. Transfer the peanut and the liquid in a bowl, then refrigerate for 3 hours before serving.

## Lemony Potato Cubes

**Prep time: 5 minutes | Cook time: 10 minutes | Serves 2**

2½ medium potatoes, scrubbed and cubed
1 tablespoon chopped fresh rosemary
½ tablespoon olive
oil
Freshly ground black pepper, to taste
1 tablespoon fresh lemon juice
½ cup vegetable broth

1. Put the potatoes, rosemary, oil, and pepper to the Instant Pot. Stir to mix well.
2. Set to the Sauté mode and sauté for 4 minutes.
3. Fold in the remaining ingredients.
4. Secure the lid and select the Manual function. Set the cooking time for 6 minutes at High Pressure.
5. Once cooking is complete, do a quick release, then open the lid.
6. Serve warm.

## Little Smokies with Grape Jelly

**Prep time: 10 minutes | Cook time: 2 minutes | Serves 4**

3 ounces (85 g) little smokies
2 ounces (57 g) grape jelly
¼ teaspoon jalapeño, minced
¼ cup light beer
¼ cup chili sauce
1 tablespoon white vinegar
½ cup roasted vegetable broth
2 tablespoons brown sugar

1. Place all ingredients in the Instant Pot. Stir to mix.
2. Secure the lid. Choose the Manual mode and set the cooking time for 2 minutes at High pressure.
3. Once cooking is complete, perform a quick pressure release. Carefully open the lid.
4. Serve hot.

## Queso Fundido

**Prep time: 15 minutes | Cook time: 6 minutes | Serves 4 to 6**

1 pound (454 g) chorizo sausage, chopped
½ cup tomato salsa
1 red onion, chopped
1 cup cream cheese
1 teaspoon Mexican oregano
½ teaspoon cayenne pepper
½ cup water
¼ teaspoon ground black pepper
1 teaspoon coriander
1 cup Cotija cheese

1. Combine the sausage, tomato salsa, red onion, cream cheese, oregano, cayenne pepper, water, black pepper, and coriander in the Instant Pot.
2. Secure the lid. Choose the Manual mode and set the cooking time for 6 minutes at High Pressure.
3. Once cooking is complete, perform a natural pressure release for 5 minutes, then release any remaining pressure. Carefully open the lid.
4. Add the Cotija cheese and press the Sauté button. Sauté until heated through. Serve warm.

## Super Pickles Deviled Eggs

**Prep time: 15 minutes | Cook time: 4 minutes | Makes 12 deviled eggs**

1 cup water
6 large eggs
1 teaspoon finely diced dill pickles
½ teaspoon dill pickle juice
1 teaspoon yellow mustard
3 tablespoons

mayonnaise
⅛ teaspoon smoked paprika
⅛ teaspoon salt
⅛ teaspoon ground black pepper
½ cup crushed dill pickle flavored potato chips

1. Add water to the Instant Pot and insert a steamer basket. Place the eggs in the basket. Lock the lid.
2. Press the Manual button and set the cook time for 4 minutes on High Pressure. When timer beeps, quick release pressure, and then unlock the lid.
3. Transfer the eggs in a large bowl of ice water. Peel the eggs under the water. Slice each egg in half lengthwise and place yolks in a small bowl. Place egg white halves on a serving tray.
4. Add the diced pickles, pickle juice, mustard, mayonnaise, smoked paprika, salt, and pepper to the small bowl with yolks. Stir until smooth.
5. Spoon the yolk mixture into egg white halves. Sprinkle with crushed chips. Serve immediately.

## Simple Broiled Baby Carrots

**Prep time: 10 minutes | Cook time: 2 minutes | Serves 4**

½ pound (227 g) baby carrots, trimmed and scrubbed
1 tablespoon raisins
¼ cup orange juice
1 tablespoon red wine vinegar
½ tablespoon soy sauce
½ teaspoon mustard powder

¼ teaspoon cumin seeds
½ teaspoon shallot powder
½ teaspoon garlic powder
1 teaspoon butter, at room temperature
½ cup water
1 tablespoon sesame seeds, toasted

1. Place all ingredients, except for the sesame seeds, in the Instant Pot. Stir to mix well.

2. Secure the lid. Choose the Manual mode and set the cooking time for 2 minutes at High pressure.
3. Once cooking is complete, perform a quick pressure release. Carefully open the lid.
4. Transfer them into a large bowl, sprinkle the sesame seeds over and serve.

## Simple Cinnamon Popcorn

**Prep time: 5 minutes | Cook time: 1 minute | Serves 2**

1 tablespoon coconut oil
¼ cup popcorn kernels

½ tablespoon ground cinnamon
3 tablespoons icing sugar

1. Press the Sauté button and melt the coconut oil in the Instant Pot.
2. Stir in the popcorn kernels and stir to cover. Cook for about a minute or until the popping slows down.
3. Transfer the popped corn to a large bowl and toss with cinnamon and icing sugar to coat well. Serve immediately.

## Simple Prosciutto Wrapped Asparagus

**Prep time: 10 minutes | Cook time: 4 minutes | Serves 4**

8 asparagus spears
8 ounces (227 g) prosciutto slices

2 cups water
Salt, to taste

1. Wrap the asparagus spears into prosciutto slices and arrange them on a cutting board.
2. Pour the water to the Instant Pot and sprinkle with a pinch of salt.
3. Set a steamer basket in the Instant Pot and place the asparagus inside.
4. Seal the Instant Pot lid and set to the Manual mode. Set the cooking time for 4 minutes on High Pressure.
5. Once cooking is complete, perform a quick pressure release. Carefully open the lid.
6. Arrange the asparagus on a platter and serve.

## Cajun Shrimp and Asparagus

**Prep time: 7 minutes | Cook time: 3 minutes | Serves 4**

1 cup water
1 pound (454 g) shrimp, peeled and deveined
1 bunch asparagus, trimmed
½ tablespoon Cajun seasoning
1 teaspoon extra virgin olive oil

1. Pour the water into the the Instant Pot and insert a steamer basket. Put the shrimp and asparagus in the basket. Sprinkle with the Cajun seasoning and drizzle with the olive oil. Toss a bit.
2. Secure the lid. Select the Manual mode and set the cooking time for 3 minutes at High Pressure.
3. Once cooking is complete, do a quick pressure release. Carefully open the lid.
4. Remove from the basket to a plate and serve.

## Crispy Brussels Sprouts with Aioli Sauce

**Prep time: 10 minutes | Cook time: 10 minutes | Serves 4**

1 tablespoon butter
½ cup chopped scallions
¾ pound (340 g) Brussels sprouts
Aioli Sauce:
¼ cup mayonnaise
1 tablespoon fresh lemon juice
½ teaspoon Dijon mustard
1 garlic clove, minced

1. Set your Instant Pot to Sauté and melt the butter.
2. Add the scallions and sauté for about 5 minutes until softened. Stir in the Brussels sprouts and cook for an additional 1 minute.
3. Lock the lid. Select the Manual mode and set the cooking time for 4 minutes at High Pressure.
4. Meanwhile, stir together all the ingredients for the aioli sauce in a small bowl.
5. When the timer beeps, perform a quick pressure release. Carefully remove the lid.
6. Remove the Brussels sprouts from the Instant Pot and serve alongside the aioli sauce.

## Turkey and Pork Meatballs in Tomato

**Prep time: 15 minutes | Cook time: 8 minutes | Serves 6**

½ pound (227 g) ground turkey
½ pound (227 g) ground pork
$1/3$ cup almond flour
2 eggs
1 cup Romano cheese, grated
¼ cup minced fresh mint, plus more for garnish
1 teaspoon dried basil
2 garlic cloves, minced
½ teaspoon dried thyme
Sea salt and ground black pepper, to taste
½ cup puréed tomatoes
½ cup beef bone broth
2 tablespoons scallions

1. Combine all ingredients, except for tomatoes, broth, and scallions in a large bowl.
2. Shape the mixture into 2-inch meatballs. Set aside.
3. Add the tomatoes, beef bone broth, and scallions to the Instant Pot. Arrange the meatballs in this liquid.
4. Secure the lid. Choose the Manual mode. Set the cooking time for 8 minutes at High Pressure.
5. Once cooking is complete, perform a quick pressure release. Carefully open the lid. Serve immediately.

## Mexican Broccoli and Cheese Balls

**Prep time: 20 minutes | Cook time: 20 minutes | Serves 8**

1 cup water
1 head broccoli, broken into florets
3 ounces (85 g) Ricotta cheese, cut into small chunks
1½ cups crumbled Cotija cheese
½ cup shredded Añejo cheese
1 teaspoon chili pepper flakes

1. Pour the water into the Instant Pot and insert a steamer basket, then put the broccoli florets in the basket.
2. Lock the lid. Select the Manual mode and set the cooking time for 5 minutes at Low Pressure.
3. When the timer beeps, perform a quick pressure release. Carefully open the lid.
4. Transfer the broccoli florets to a food processor, along with the remaining ingredients. Pulse until everything is completely mixed. Form the mixture into balls with your hands.
5. Arrange the balls on a baking sheet lined with parchment paper and bake in the preheated oven at 390ºF (199ºC) for 15 minutes until cooked through.
6. Let the broccoli balls cool for 5 to 10 minutes before serving.

## Cheesy Rutabaga and Bacon Bites

**Prep time: 10 minutes | Cook time: 5 minutes | Serves 8**

1 cup water
½ pound (227 g) rutabaga, grated
7 ounces (198 g) Gruyère cheese, shredded
4 slices meaty bacon, chopped
3 eggs, lightly beaten
3 tablespoons almond flour
1 teaspoon shallot powder
1 teaspoon granulated garlic
Sea salt and ground black pepper, to taste

1. Pour the water into the Instant Pot and insert a trivet.
2. Stir together the remaining ingredients in a bowl until well combined. Pour the mixture into a greased silicone pod tray and cover with a sheet of aluminum foil. Place it on top of the trivet.

3. Lock the lid. Select the Manual mode and set the cooking time for 5 minutes at Low Pressure.
4. When the timer beeps, perform a quick pressure release. Carefully remove the lid.
5. Allow to cool for 5 minutes before serving.

## Spiced Chicken Wings

**Prep time: 15 minutes | Cook time: 10 minutes | Serves 6**

1½ pounds (680 g) chicken wings
½ cup barbecue sauce
½ cup chicken broth
¼ cup rice vinegar
1 tablespoon fish sauce
2 teaspoons butter, melted
1 teaspoon grated fresh ginger
Sea salt ground black
pepper, to taste
½ teaspoon crushed red pepper
½ teaspoon garlic powder
½ teaspoon cumin
½ teaspoon celery seeds
½ teaspoon caraway seeds
2 tablespoons Thai basil

1. Combine all the ingredients except the Thai basil in the Instant Pot.
2. Lock the lid. Select the Poultry mode and set the cooking time for 10 minutes at High Pressure.
3. When the timer beeps, perform a natural pressure release for 10 minutes, then release any remaining pressure. Carefully remove the lid.
4. Sprinkle the Thai basil on top for garnish before serving.

# Chapter 15 Desserts

## Jasmine Rice and Mango Pudding

**Prep time: 15 minutes | Cook time: 5 minutes | Serves 4**

1 cup jasmine rice
1 mango, chopped into small bits
1 cup whole milk
1 teaspoon vanilla extract
½ teaspoon nutmeg
powder
1 tablespoon unsalted butter
¼ cup granulated sugar
Salt, to taste
1 cup water

1. In the Instant Pot, combine all the ingredients. Stir to mix well.
2. Seal the lid, set to the Manual mode and set the cooking time for 5 minutes on High Pressure.
3. When cooking is complete, perform a natural pressure release for 10 minutes, then release any remaining pressure.
4. Unlock the lid. Spoon the pudding into serving bowls. Serve warm.

## Apricots Dulce de Leche

**Prep time: 15 minutes | Cook time: 25 minutes | Serves 6**

5 cups water
2 cups sweetened condensed milk
4 apricots, halved, cored, and sliced

1. Pour the water in the Instant Pot and fit in a trivet. Divide condensed milk into 6 medium jars and close with lids. Place jars on trivet.
2. Seal the lid, set to the Manual mode and set the timer for 25 minutes at High Pressure.
3. When cooking is complete, use a natural pressure release for 10 minutes, then release any remaining pressure. Unlock the lid.
4. Use a fork to whisk until creamy. Serve with sliced apricots.

## Chocolate Oreo Cookie Cake

**Prep time: 8 hours 35 minutes | Cook time: 35 minutes | Serves 6**

12 Oreo cookies, smoothly crushed
2 tablespoons salted butter, melted
16 ounces (454 g) cream cheese, softened
½ cup granulated sugar
2 large eggs
1 tablespoon all-purpose flour
¼ cup heavy cream
2 teaspoons vanilla extract
16 whole Oreo cookies, coarsely crushed
1½ cups water
1 cup whipped cream
2 tablespoons chocolate sauce, for topping

1. Line a springform pan with foil, then spritz with cooking spray.
2. Make the crust: In a bowl, combine smoothly crushed Oreo cookies with butter, then press into bottom of pan. Freeze for 15 minutes.
3. In another bowl, add cream cheese, and beat until smooth. Add sugar to whisk until satiny. Beat in the eggs one by one until mixed. Whisk in flour, heavy cream, and vanilla.
4. Fold in 8 coarsely crushed cookies and pour the mixture onto the crust in the springform pan. Cover pan tightly with foil.
5. Pour the water in the Instant Pot and fit in a trivet. Place the pan on trivet.
6. Seal the lid, set to the Manual mode and set the cooking time for 35 minutes at High Pressure.
7. When cooking is complete, allow a natural pressure release for 10 minutes, then release any remaining pressure. Carefully open the lid.
8. Remove the trivet with cake pan from the pot. Remove foil and transfer to a cooling rack to chill. Refrigerate for 8 hours. Top with whipped cream, remaining cookies, and chocolate sauce. Slice and serve.

## Apple and Oatmeal Crisps

**Prep time: 15 minutes | Cook time: 5 minutes | Serves 4**

5 apples, cored and chopped
1 tablespoon honey
2 teaspoons cinnamon powder
½ teaspoon nutmeg powder
1 cup water
¾ cup old fashioned rolled oats

¼ cup all-purpose flour
4 tablespoons unsalted butter, melted
½ teaspoon salt
¼ cup brown sugar
1 cup vanilla ice cream, for topping

1. In the Instant Pot, mix the apples, honey, cinnamon, nutmeg, and water.
2. In a medium bowl, combine the rolled oats, flour, butter, salt, and brown sugar. Drizzle the mixture over the apples.
3. Seal the lid, set to the Manual mode and set the cooking time for 5 minutes on High Pressure.
4. When cooking is complete, allow a natural pressure release for 10 minutes, then release any remaining pressure. Carefully open the lid.
5. Spoon the apple into serving bowls, top with vanilla ice cream and serve immediately.

## Brown Rice and Coconut Milk Pudding

**Prep time: 15 minutes | Cook time: 22 minutes | Serves 6**

1 cup long-grain brown rice, rinsed
2 cups water
1 (15-ounce / 425-g) can full-fat coconut milk

½ teaspoon pure vanilla extract
½ teaspoon ground cinnamon
⅓ cup maple syrup
Pinch fine sea salt

1. Combine the rice and water in the Instant Pot and secure the lid. Select the Manual mode and set the cooking time for 22 minutes on Low Pressure.
2. When timer beeps, allow the pressure to naturally release for 10 minutes, then release any remaining pressure. Carefully open the lid.

3. Add the coconut milk, vanilla, cinnamon, maple syrup, and salt. Stir well to combine.
4. Use an immersion blender to pulse the pudding until creamy. Serve warm or you can refrigerate the pudding for an hour before serving.

## Bourbon and Date Pudding Cake

**Prep time: 15 minutes | Cook time: 25 minutes | Serves 4**

¾ cup all-purpose flour
¼ teaspoon allspice
½ teaspoon baking soda
¼ teaspoon cloves powder
½ teaspoon cinnamon powder
¼ teaspoon salt
1 teaspoon baking powder
2 tablespoons

bourbon
3 tablespoons unsalted butter, melted
6 tablespoons hot water
2 tablespoons whole milk
1 egg, beaten
½ cup chopped dates
1 cup water
½ cup caramel sauce

1. In a bowl, combine the flour, allspice, baking soda, cloves, cinnamon, salt, and baking powder.
2. In another bowl, mix the bourbon, butter, hot water, and milk. Pour the bourbon mixture into the flour mixture and mix until well mixed. Whisk in egg and fold in dates.
3. Spritz 4 medium ramekins with cooking spray. Divide the mixture among them, and cover with foil.
4. Pour the water in the Instant Pot, then fit in a trivet and place ramekins on top.
5. Seal the lid, select the Manual mode and set the cooking time for 25 minutes at High Pressure.
6. When cooking is complete, perform a natural pressure release for 10 minutes, then release any remaining pressure.
7. Unlock the lid and carefully remove ramekins, invert onto plates, and drizzle caramel sauce on top. Serve warm.

## Creamy Raspberry Cheesecake

**Prep time: 3 hours 30 minutes | Cook time: 40 minutes | Serves 4**

12 graham crackers, crushed
2 tablespoons melted butter
1 pound (454 g) cream cheese, softened
1 cup granulated sugar
12 large raspberries,
plus more for garnish
2 eggs
1 teaspoon vanilla extract
3 tablespoons maple syrup
2 teaspoons cinnamon powder
½ cup heavy cream
1 cup water

1. Make the crust: Mix the crushed graham crackers with butter. Pour the mixture into a springform pan and press to fit with a spoon. Refrigerate for 15 minutes or until firm.
2. In a bowl, whisk the cream cheese and sugar until smooth. Add the raspberries, eggs, vanilla, maple syrup, cinnamon, and heavy cream, and mix until well combined.
3. Remove the cake pan from refrigerator and pour cream cheese mixture on top. Spread evenly and cover pan with foil.
4. Pour the water in Instant Pot, then fit in a trivet, and place cake pan on top.
5. Seal the lid, select the Manual mode and set to 40 minutes on High Pressure.
6. When cooking is complete, allow a natural pressure release for 10 minutes, then release any remaining pressure.
7. Unlock the lid and carefully remove the pan. Allow cooling for 10 minutes and chill in the fridge for 3 hours. Invert the cake on a plate and garnish with more raspberries. Slice and serve.

## Cardamom Yogurt Pudding

**Prep time: 20 minutes | Cook time: 15 minutes | Serves 4**

1½ cups Greek yogurt
1 teaspoon cocoa powder
2 cups sweetened condensed milk
1 teaspoon cardamom powder
1 cup water
¼ cup mixed nuts, chopped

1. Spritz 4 medium ramekins with cooking spray. Set aside.
2. In a bowl, combine the Greek yogurt, cocoa powder, condensed milk, and cardamom powder. Pour mixture into ramekins and cover with foil.
3. Pour the water into the Instant Pot, then fit in a trivet, and place ramekins on top.
4. Seal the lid, select the Manual mode and set the cooking time for 15 minutes at High Pressure.
5. When cooking is complete, perform a natural pressure release for 15 minutes, then release any remaining pressure. Unlock the lid.
6. Remove the ramekins from the pot, then take off the foil. Top with mixed nuts and serve immediately.

## Caramel Apple Cobbler

**Prep time: 30 minutes | Cook time: 2 minutes | Serves 4**

5 apples, cored, peeled, and cut into 1-inch cubes, at room temperature
2 tablespoons caramel syrup
½ teaspoon ground nutmeg
2 teaspoons ground cinnamon
2 tablespoons maple syrup
½ cup water
¾ cup old-fashioned oats
¼ cup all-purpose flour
1/3 cup brown sugar
4 tablespoons salted butter, softened
½ teaspoon sea salt
Vanilla ice cream, for serving

1. Place the apples in the Instant Pot and top with the caramel syrup, nutmeg, cinnamon, maple syrup, and water. Stir to coat well.
2. Combine the oats, flour, brown sugar, butter and salt in a large bowl. Mix well and pour over the apple mixture in the pot.
3. Secure the lid, then select the Manual mode and set the cooking time for 2 minutes on High Pressure.
4. When cooking is complete, perform a natural pressure release for 20minutes, then release any remaining pressure. Carefully open the lid.
5. Transfer the cobbler to a plate, then topped with vanilla ice cream and serve.

## Classic Cheesecake

**Prep time: 3 hours 40 minutes | Cook time: 40 minutes | Serves 4**

2 cups graham crackers, crushed
3 tablespoons brown sugar
¼ cup butter, melted
2 (8 ounce / 227-g) cream cheese, softened
½ cup granulated sugar
2 tablespoons all-purpose flour
1 teaspoon vanilla extract
3 eggs
1 cup water
1 cup caramel sauce

1. Make the crust: Mix the crushed crackers with brown sugar and butter. Spread the mixture at the bottom of a springform pan and use a spoon to press to fit. Freeze in refrigerator for 10 minutes.
2. In a bowl, whisk the cream cheese and sugar until smooth. Mix in the flour and vanilla. Whisk in the eggs. Remove the pan from refrigerator and pour mixture over crust. Cover the pan with foil.
3. Pour the water in Instant Pot, then fit in a trivet and place the pan on top.
4. Seal the lid, select the Manual mode and set the timer for 40 minutes on High Pressure.
5. When cooking is complete, allow a natural pressure release for 10 minutes, then release any remaining pressure. Open the lid.
6. Carefully remove the cake pan and take off the foil. Let cool for 10 minutes. Pour the caramel sauce over and refrigerate for 3 hours.
7. Remove the pan from the refrigerator and invert the cheesecake on a plate. Slice and serve.

## Coconut-Potato Pudding

**Prep time: 5 minutes | Cook time: 10 minutes | Serves 4**

1 cup water
1 large sweet potato (about 1 pound / 454 g), peeled and cut into 1-inch pieces
½ cup canned coconut milk
6 tablespoons pure maple syrup
1 teaspoon grated fresh ginger (about ½-inch knob)

1. Pour the water into the Instant Pot and fit in a steamer basket.
2. Place the sweet potato pieces in the steamer basket and secure the lid. Select the Manual mode and set the cooking time for 10 minutes at High Pressure.
3. When timer beeps, use a quick pressure release. Unlock the lid.
4. Transfer the cooked potatoes to a large bowl. Add the coconut milk, maple syrup, and ginger. Use an immersion blender to purée the potatoes into a smooth pudding.
5. Serve the pudding immediately or chill in the refrigerator for an hour before serving.

## Flourless Chocolate Brownies

**Prep time: 15 minutes | Cook time: 15 minutes | Makes 16 brownies**

1 egg
¾ cup almond butter
1/3 cup raw cacao powder
¾ cup coconut sugar
½ teaspoon baking soda
¼ teaspoon fine sea salt
½ teaspoon pure vanilla extract
½ cup dark chocolate chips
1 cup water

1. Line a springform pan with parchment paper. In a large bowl, whisk together the egg, almond butter, cacao powder, coconut sugar, baking soda, salt, and vanilla and stir well until it has a thick consistency.
2. Transfer the batter to the prepared pan and level the batter with a spatula. Sprinkle with the chocolate chips.
3. Pour 1 cup water into the Instant Pot and fit in a trivet. Place the pan on top of the trivet and cover it with an upside-down plate.
4. Secure the lid. Select the Manual mode and set the cooking time for 15 minutes at High Pressure.
5. When timer beeps, let the pressure naturally release for 10 minutes, then release any remaining pressure. Unlock the lid.
6. Slice into 16 brownies and serve.

## Classic New York Cheesecake

**Prep time: 3 hours 45 minutes | Cook time: 40 minutes | Serves 4**

12 graham crackers, crushed
2 tablespoons melted salted butter
1½ tablespoons brown sugar
16 ounces (454 g) cream cheese, softened
1 cup granulated sugar
2 eggs
½ cup sour cream
2 tablespoons cornstarch
1 teaspoon vanilla extract
¼ teaspoon salt
1 cup water

1. Mix the crushed graham crackers with butter and brown sugar. Pour mixture into a springform pan and use a spoon to press to fit. Freeze for 15 minutes until firm.
2. In a bowl, beat cream cheese and sugar until smooth. Whisk in the eggs, sour cream, cornstarch, vanilla, and salt.
3. Remove the pan from refrigerator and pour cream cheese mixture on top. Spread evenly using a spatula and cover the pan with foil.
4. Pour the water in Instant Pot, then fit in a trivet, and place cake pan on top.
5. Seal the lid, select the Manual mode and set the cooking time for 40 minutes on High Pressure.
6. When cooking is complete, do a natural pressure release for 10 minutes, then release any remaining pressure.
7. Unlock the lid and carefully remove cake pan. Allow cooling for 10 minutes and chill in refrigerator for 3 hours. Remove from refrigerator, then slice and serve.

## Chocolate Pudding

**Prep time: 15 minutes | Cook time: 5 minutes | Serves 4**

4 tablespoons cocoa powder
3 medium eggs, cracked
3¼ cups whole milk
¼ cup collagen
1¼ teaspoons gelatin
1½ tablespoons vanilla extract
¼ cup maple syrup
1 tablespoon coconut oil
1 cup water

1. In a blender, combine all the ingredients, except for the water. Process until smooth.
2. Pour the mixture into 4 ramekins and cover with aluminum foil. Pour the water in Instant Pot, fit in a trivet, and place the ramekins on top.
3. Seal the lid, select the Manual mode and set cooking time to 5 minutes on High Pressure.
4. When cooking is complete, allow a natural pressure release for 10 minutes, then release any remaining pressure. Unlock the lid.
5. Refrigerate overnight and serve.

## Easy Pecan Monkey Bread

**Prep time: 15 minutes | Cook time: 25 minutes | Serves 6**

1½ cinnamon powder
¼ cup brown sugar
¼ cup toasted pecans, chopped
1 pound (454 g) dinner rolls, cut in half lengthwise
½ cup butter, melted
1 cup water
2 teaspoons whole milk
½ cup powdered sugar

1. Spritz a bundt pan with cooking spray.
2. In a shallow plate, mix the cinnamon, brown sugar, and pecans. Coat the dinner rolls in the mixture, then in butter, and then place in bundt pan, making sure to build layers. Cover pan with foil and allow rising overnight.
3. Pour the water into Instant Pot, then fit in a trivet and place bundt pan on top.
4. Seal the lid, select the Manual mode and set the cooking time for 25 minutes at High Pressure.
5. When cooking is complete, allow a natural release for 10 minutes, then release any remaining pressure.
6. Unlock the lid, remove the pan from the pot, take off the foil, and allow to cool completely.
7. In a bowl, whisk milk with sugar until smooth.
8. Invert the bread on a serving platter and drizzle with sweetened milk.
9. Slice and serve.

## Caramel Glazed Popcorns

**Prep time: 5 minutes | Cook time: 7 minutes | Serves 4**

| | |
|---|---|
| 4 tablespoons butter | 3 tablespoons brown sugar |
| 1 cup sweet corn kernels | ¼ cup whole milk |

1. Set the Instant Pot to Sauté mode, melt butter and mix in the corn kernels, heat for 1 minute or until the corn is popping.
2. Cover the lid, and keep cooking for 3 more minutes or until the corn stops popping. Open the lid and transfer the popcorns to a bowl.
3. Combine brown sugar and milk in the pot and cook for 3 minutes or until sugar dissolves. Stir constantly.
4. Drizzle caramel sauce over corns and toss to coat thoroughly. Serve warm.

## Peanut Butter and Chocolate Tart

**Prep time: 20 minutes | Cook time: 25 minutes | Serves 4 to 6**

| | |
|---|---|
| 5 tablespoons unsalted butter | 2 large eggs |
| 1 cup granulated sugar | 1 cup all-purpose flour |
| 2 tablespoons peanut butter | 1 teaspoon baking powder |
| 1 tablespoon vegetable oil | 2 teaspoons vanilla extract |
| ¼ cup chocolate chips | ½ teaspoon salt |
| ½ cup peanut butter chips | 2 tablespoons water |
| $1/_3$ cup cocoa powder | 5 ounces (142 g) chocolate chip cookie dough, rolled into teaspoon-size balls |

1. Combine the butter, sugar, and peanut butter in a microwave-safe bowl and microwave for a minute to melt and mix well.
2. Add the vegetable oil to the bowl of butter mixture and whisk to combine.
3. Whisk in the remaining ingredients, except for the cookie dough balls.
4. Spritz a springform pan with cooking spray. Line the with parchment paper, then spritz with another layer of cooking spray.

5. Pour the mixture into the pan and use a spatula to level the top. Arrange the cookie-dough balls and slightly push them into the mixture and they're still visible on the surface.
6. Pour 2 cups of water in the Instant Pot, then fit in a trivet. Place the pan on the trivet.
7. Secure the lid, and select the Manual mode and set the cooking time for 25 minutes.
8. When cooking is complete, do a natural pressure release for 10 minutes, then release any remaining pressure. Open the lid.
9. Carefully remove the pan and trivet from the Instant Pot and let cool for 30 minutes before slicing and serving.

## Oat and Raisin Cookie

**Prep time: 10 minutes | Cook time: 25 minutes | Serves 8**

| | |
|---|---|
| ½ cup all-purpose flour | cinnamon |
| ¼ teaspoon baking soda | 1 egg |
| ½ cup sugar | ¼ cup melted butter |
| ¼ teaspoon fine sea salt | ½ teaspoon pure vanilla extract |
| 1 teaspoon ground | ½ cup oats |
| | ½ cup raisins |
| | 1 cup water |

1. Spritz a springform pan with cooking spray and line with parchment paper.
2. In a large bowl, stir together the flour, baking soda, sugar, salt, and cinnamon. Whisk in the egg, butter, and vanilla and stir until smooth.
3. Fold in the oats and raisins to make the batter thick and sticky. Transfer the batter to the prepared pan and use a spatula to smooth the top.
4. Pour the water into the Instant Pot and fit in a trivet on the bottom. Place the pan on top of the trivet and cover it with an upside-down plate.
5. Secure the lid. Select the Manual mode and set the cooking time for 25 minutes at High Pressure.
6. When timer beeps, let the pressure naturally release for 10 minutes, then release any remaining pressure. Unlock the lid.
7. Cut and serve.

## Creamy Banana Pudding

**Prep time: 5 minutes | Cook time: 5 minutes | Serves 4**

| | |
|---|---|
| 1 cup whole milk | 2 tablespoons cold |
| 2 cups half-and-half | butter, cut into 4 |
| ¾ cup plus | pieces |
| 1 tablespoon | 1 teaspoon vanilla |
| granulated sugar, | extract |
| divided | 2 medium banana, |
| 4 egg yolks | peeled and sliced |
| 3 tablespoon | 1 cup heavy cream |
| cornstarch | |

1. Set the Instant Pot to Sauté mode. Mix the milk, half-and-half, and ½ cup of sugar in the pot.
2. Heat for 3 minutes or until sugar dissolves. Stir constantly.
3. Meanwhile, beat the egg yolks with ¼ cup of sugar in a medium bowl. Add cornstarch and mix well.
4. Scoop ½ cup of milk mixture into egg mixture and whisk until smooth. Pour mixture into Instant Pot.
5. Seal the lid, select the Manual mode and set the cooking time for 2 minutes on High Pressure.
6. When cooking is complete, do a quick pressure release and unlock the lid.
7. Stir in butter and vanilla. Lay banana pieces into 4 bowls and top with pudding.
8. In a bowl, whisk heavy cream with remaining sugar; spoon mixture on top of pudding. Refrigerate for 1 hour before serving.

## Easy Bread Pudding

**Prep time: 15 minutes | Cook time: 25 minutes | Serves 8**

| | |
|---|---|
| 2 cups milk | 5 cups (about ½ |
| 5 large eggs | loaf) bread, slice into |
| 1/3 cup granulated | 2-inch cubes |
| sugar | 2 tablespoons |
| 1 teaspoon vanilla | unsalted butter, cut |
| extract | into small pieces |

1. In a medium bowl, whisk together the eggs, milk, sugar, and vanilla. Add the bread cubes and stir to coat well. Refrigerate for 1 hour.

2. Spritz the Instant Pot with cooking spray. Pour in the bread mixture. Scatter with the butter pieces.
3. Lock the lid. Select the Manual mode. Set the timer for 25 minutes on High Pressure.
4. When timer beeps, let the pressure release naturally for 10 minutes, then release the remaining pressure. Unlock the lid.
5. Serve the pudding immediately or chill in the refrigerator for an hour before serving.

## Classic Pumpkin Pie

**Prep time: 4 hours 20 minutes | Cook time: 35 minutes | Serves 6**

| | |
|---|---|
| ½ cup crushed | 1½ cups canned |
| graham crackers | pumpkin purée |
| (about 7 graham | 1½ teaspoons |
| crackers) | pumpkin pie spice |
| 2 tablespoons | ½ teaspoon sea salt |
| unsalted butter, | ½ cup evaporated |
| melted | milk |
| ½ cup brown sugar | 1 cup water |
| 1 large egg | |

1. Make the crust: In a small bowl, combine the graham cracker crumbs and butter and mix until well combined. Press the mixture into the bottom and 1 inch up the sides of a springform pan. Set aside.
2. In a large mixing bowl, whisk together the egg, pumpkin purée, pumpkin pie spice, sugar, salt, and milk. Pour the filling into the prepared crust. Cover the pan with aluminum foil.
3. Place a trivet in the Instant Pot and pour in the water. Lower the pan onto the trivet.
4. Lock the lid. Select the Manual mode. Set the time for 35 minutes on High Pressure.
5. When timer beeps, let the pressure release naturally for 10 minutes, then release the remaining pressure.
6. Unlock the lid. Remove the pan from the pot and then remove the foil. Allow the pie to cool. Cover with plastic wrap and refrigerate for at least 4 hours before serving.

## Easy Orange Cake

**Prep time: 5 minutes | Cook time: 30 minutes | Serves 6**

1½ cups orange soda
1 (15.25-ounce / 432-g) box orange cake mix

1 cup water
1 tablespoon caster sugar, for garnish

1. Spritz a bundt pan with cooking spray.
2. In a bowl, mix orange soda and orange cake mix until well combined. Pour into bundt pan, cover with a foil.
3. Pour the water in the Instant Pot, then fit in a trivet, and place the pan on top.
4. Seal the lid, select the Manual mode and set the cooking time for 30 minutes at High Pressure.
5. When cooking is complete, do a quick pressure release. Open the lid.
6. Remove the pan from the pot and allow cooling. Turn over onto a platter, sprinkle with caster sugar. Slice and serve.

## Hearty Apricot Cobbler

**Prep time: 20 minutes | Cook time: 25 minutes | Serves 4**

4 cups sliced apricots
2 tablespoons plus ¾ cup all-purpose flour, divided
½ teaspoon cinnamon powder
¼ teaspoon nutmeg powder
1 teaspoon vanilla extract
½ cup plus ¼ cup

brown sugar, divided
1½ teaspoons salt, divided
1¼ cup water, divided
½ teaspoon baking powder
½ teaspoon baking soda
3 tablespoons butter, melted

1. In a baking pan, mix the apricots, 2 tablespoons of flour, cinnamon, nutmeg, vanilla, ½ cup of brown sugar, ½ teaspoon of salt, and ¼ cup of water; set aside.
2. In another bowl, mix the remaining flour, salt and brown sugar, baking powder and soda, and butter. Spoon mixture over apricot mixture and spread to cover.
3. Pour 1 cup of water in the pot, then fit in a trivet and place the pan on top.

4. Seal the lid, select the Manual mode and set the timer for 25 minutes at High Pressure.
5. When cooking is complete, perform a natural pressure release for 10 minutes, then release any remaining pressure.
6. Carefully open the lid. Remove the pan and serve.

## Hearty Crème Brulee

**Prep time: 2 hours 40 minutes | Cook time: 10 minutes | Serves 4**

2 cups graham crackers, crushed
3 tablespoons brown sugar
¼ cup butter, melted
Salt, to taste
2 (8-ounce / 227-g) cream cheese, softened
½ cup granulated

sugar
2 large eggs
2 teaspoons vanilla extract
½ cup sour cream
2 tablespoons cornstarch
1 cup water
4 teaspoons white sugar

1. Make the crust: Mix the crushed graham crackers with brown sugar, butter, and salt in a medium bowl. Spoon the mixture into 4 medium ramekins. Place in refrigerator for 15 minutes to harden.
2. In a bowl, stir the cream cheese and sugar until smooth. Whisk in eggs and vanilla until smooth. Fold in sour cream and cornstarch.
3. Remove ramekins from the refrigerator, then pour in the cream cheese mixture, and cover with foil.
4. Pour the water in the Instant Pot, then fit in a trivet, and place ramekins on top.
5. Seal the lid, select the Manual mode and set the timer for 10 minutes at High Pressure.
6. When cooking is complete, allow a natural pressure release for 10 minutes, then release any remaining pressure.
7. Unlock the lid, carefully remove the ramekins and take off the foil. Allow to cool for 10 minutes and then chill further for 2 hours in the refrigerator.
8. Remove the ramekins from the refrigerator and sprinkle 1 teaspoon of sugar on each ramekin. Use a torch to caramelize the sugar until browned in color. Serve immediately.

## Super Easy Chocolate Cookie Fudge

**Prep time: 2 hours 5 minutes | Cook time: 10 minutes | Serves 6**

1½ cups white chocolate chips
1 teaspoon almond extract
2 cups condensed
milk
1¼ cups sugar cookie mix
2 tablespoons butter

1. Set the Instant Pot to Sauté mode. Put in white chocolate chips, almond extract, condensed milk, sugar cookie mix, and butter.
2. Cook for 10 minutes or until the chocolate is melted. Stir constantly.
3. Pour mixture into cake pan and refrigerate for 2 hours. Remove from the refrigerator and slice to serve.

## Yellow Pineapple Cake

**Prep time: 25 minutes | Cook time: 18 minutes | Serves 4**

1 (18.5-ounce / 524-g) box yellow cake mix
2 tablespoons butter, melted
¼ cup brown sugar
1 cup pineapple slices
1 cup water

1. In a medium bowl, prepare the cake mix according to the instructions on box. Set aside.
2. Grease a springform pan with butter, sprinkle the brown sugar at the bottom of the pan and place the pineapple slices on top.
3. Pour the cake batter all over and cover the pan with foil. Pour the water in the Instant Pot, then fit in a trivet, and place the pan on top.
4. Seal the lid, select the Manual mode and set the timer for 18 minutes at High Pressure.
5. When cooking is complete, do a natural pressure release for 10 minutes, then release any remaining pressure.
6. Carefully remove cake pan, take off foil and let cool for 10 minutes. Turn cake over onto a plate. Slice and serve.

## Pecan, Date, Sultana Stuffed Apples

**Prep time: 10 minutes | Cook time: 3 minutes | Serves 6**

¼ cup toasted pecans, chopped
½ cup dates, chopped
¼ cup sultanas
1 tablespoon cinnamon powder
2 tablespoons brown
sugar
4 tablespoons butter
6 red apples, whole and cored
4 tablespoons chocolate sauce, for topping

1. In a bowl, mix the pecans, dates, sultanas, cinnamon, brown sugar, and butter. Stuff apples with mixture.
2. Pour 1 cup of water in Instant Pot and place stuffed apples in water. Seal the lid, select the Manual mode and set the timer for 3 minutes on Low Pressure.
3. When cooking is complete, do a natural pressure release for 5 minutes, then release any remaining pressure. Open the lid.
4. Carefully remove apples onto plates and drizzle with chocolate sauce.

## Simple Arrounce Con Leche

**Prep time: 15 minutes | Cook time: 20 minutes | Serves 6**

1 cup long-grain white rice, rinsed and drained
2 cups milk
1¼ cups water
2 tablespoons sugar
⅛ teaspoon sea salt
1 (10-ounce / 284-g) can condensed milk
1 teaspoon vanilla extract

1. Combine the rice, milk, water, sugar, and salt in the Instant Pot. Stir to mix well.
2. Lock the lid. Select the Porridge mode and set the cooking time for 20 minutes on High Pressure.
3. When timer beeps, let the pressure release naturally for 10 minutes, then release the remaining pressure. Carefully open the lid.
4. Stir in the sweetened condensed milk and vanilla. Serve warm.

## Instant Pot Bananas Foster

**Prep time: 15 minutes | Cook time: 2 minutes | Serves 4**

¼ cup light rum
1 teaspoon cinnamon
1 cup brown sugar
8 tablespoons salted butter, cubed
¼ cup water
1 teaspoon vanilla

extract
6 bananas, firm, peeled and sliced into 1-inch pieces
Vanilla ice cream, for serving

1. In the Instant Pot, combine the rum, cinnamon, brown sugar, butter, water, and vanilla. Stir to mix well until chunky.
2. Add the bananas and stir gently to avoid breaking the bananas and coat them with the sauce.
3. Secure the lid, and select the Manual mode and set the cooking time for 2 minutes.
4. When cooking is complete, use a natural pressure release for 5 minutes, then release any remaining pressure. Carefully open the lid.
5. Let cool for a few moments before serving over bowls of vanilla ice cream.

## Simple Lemon Pudding

**Prep time: 1 hour 10 minutes | Cook time: 7 minutes | Serves 4**

2½ cups whole milk
¼ cup cornstarch
Zest of 2 lemons
¼ teaspoon salt
1 cup granulated sugar
2 eggs

2 egg yolks
1 tablespoon butter, melted
¼ cup lemon juice
1 cup water

1. In a pot, combine the milk, cornstarch, lemon zest, salt, and sugar. Bring to a boil in a saucepan over medium heat for 2 minutes. Stir constantly.
2. Turn off the heat. In a medium bowl, beat the eggs and egg yolks. Slowly whisk in the milk mixture until well combined. Mix in butter and lemon juice.
3. Pour the mixture into 4 medium ramekins and cover with foil. Pour the water into Instant Pot, then fit in trivet and place ramekins on top.
4. Seal the lid, select the Manual mode and set cooking time to 5 minutes on High Pressure.

5. When cooking is complete, perform a quick pressure release.
6. Unlock the lid, transfer the ramekin onto a flat surface, take off foil, and allow to cool. Chill in refrigerator for an hour before serving.

## Apple Wontons

**Prep time: 10 minutes | Cook time: 12 minutes | Serves 8**

1 (8-ounce / 227-g) can refrigerated crescent rolls
1 large apple, peeled, cored, and cut into 8 wedges
4 tablespoons unsalted butter

2 teaspoons ground cinnamon
¼ teaspoon ground nutmeg
½ cup brown sugar
1 teaspoon vanilla extract
¾ cup orange juice

1. Make the dumplings: Unfold the crescent rolls on a clean work surface, then separate into the 8 triangles. Place 1 apple wedge on each crescent roll triangle and fold the dough around the apple to enclose it. Set aside.
2. Select the Sauté mode of the Instant Pot. Add the butter and heat for 2 minutes until melted.
3. Add the cinnamon, nutmeg, sugar, and vanilla, heating and stirring until melted.
4. Place the dumplings in the Instant Pot and mix in the orange juice.
5. Lock the lid. Select the Manual mode. Set the time for 10 minutes at High Pressure.
6. When cooking is complete, let the pressure release naturally for 5 minutes, then release any remaining pressure. Unlock the lid.
7. Serve immediately.

## Orange Toast

**Prep time: 10 minutes | Cook time: 15 minutes | Serves 4**

2 large eggs
1 cup milk
2 teaspoons vanilla extract
1 teaspoon ground cinnamon

Zest of 1 orange
6 bread slices, cubed
1 cup water
Maple syrup, for topping

1. Beat the eggs with the milk, vanilla extract, cinnamon and orange zest in a mixing bowl.
2. Add the bread cubes and mix to coat. Pour the mixture into a greased baking pan and cover with aluminium foil.
3. Pour the water into the Instant Pot and fit in a trivet. Place the covered pan on top.
4. Seal the lid, select the Manual mode and set the cooking time for 15 minutes on High Pressure.
5. When cooking is complete, perform a quick pressure release. Unlock the lid, remove the pan, and take off the foil.
6. Let cool for 5 minutes. Drizzle with maple syrup to serve.

## Simple Strawberry Pancake Bites

**Prep time: 15 minutes | Cook time: 10 minutes | Serves 4**

½ cup fresh strawberries, chopped
2 large eggs

1 cup pancake mix
1¾ cup water, divided
¼ cup olive oil

1. In a medium bowl, combine strawberries, eggs, pancake mix, ¾ cup of water, and olive oil. Spoon the mixture into 4 muffin cups and cover with foil.
2. Pour 1 cup of water in Instant Pot, fit in a trivet, and place muffin cups on top.
3. Seal the lid, select the Manual mode and set the timer to 10 minutes on High Pressure.
4. When cooking is complete, allow a natural release for 10 minutes, then release any remaining pressure.
5. Unlock the lid, carefully remove cups, and take off the foil. Transfer the pancake bites onto plates and serve.

## Hearty Blackberry Yogurt

**Prep time: 2 hours 15 minutes | Cook time: 8 hours 5 minutes | Serves 4**

8 cups whole milk
½ cup plain Greek yogurt

2 tablespoons vanilla bean paste
1 cup blackberries

1. Pour milk into the Instant Pot. Seal the lid, select the Yogurt mode, and adjust to Boil.
2. When cooking is complete, unlock the lid. Remove the milk from the Instant Pot and allow cooling up to 100ºF (38ºC).
3. Whisk in yogurt and vanilla bean paste. Return the mixture to the Instant Pot.
4. Seal the lid, select the Yogurt mode and set cooking time for 8 hours.
5. When cooking is complete, transfer the yogurt in a bowl and refrigerate for 2 hours.
6. Meanwhile, mash the blackberries in a bowl using a fork. Pour the blackberries into the bowl of yogurt and serve.

## Tapioca Pearl Pudding

**Prep time: 1 hour 25 minutes | Cook time: 25 minutes | Serves 4**

1 cup tapioca pearls
3 cups whole milk
¼ teaspoon salt
2 eggs, beaten

½ cup granulated sugar
1 teaspoon vanilla extract

1. In Instant Pot, add tapioca, milk, and salt. Seal the lid, select the Manual mode and set cooking time to 15 minutes on High Pressure.
2. When cooking is complete, perform a natural pressure release for 20 minutes, then release any remaining pressure. Unlock lid and select the Sauté mode.
3. Stir the beaten eggs into the tapioca mixture along with sugar and vanilla. Cook in the pot for 10 minutes.
4. Dish out and refrigerate for an hour. Serve chilled.

## Super Key Lime Pie

**Prep time: 3 hours 40 minutes | Cook time: 40 minutes | Serves 4**

1 cup graham crackers, crushed
4 tablespoons unsalted butter, melted
3 large egg yolks
2 tablespoons granulated sugar
Juice of 9 key limes
1 tablespoon lime zest

1 (14-ounce / 397-g) can condensed milk
1 cup water
½ cup heavy cream
¼ cup granulated sugar
1 teaspoon key lime zest

1. Make the crust: Mix the crushed crackers with butter. Spread the mixture at the bottom of a springform pan and use a spoon to press to fit. Freeze in refrigerator for 10 minutes.
2. In a large bowl, whisk the egg yolks and sugar until yolk is pale yellow and thickened. Fold in the lime juice, lime zest, and condensed milk.
3. Remove the pan from refrigerator and pour in lime juice mixture. Cover pan with foil. Pour the water in Instant Pot, then fit in a trivet, and place the pan on top.
4. Seal the lid, select the Manual mode and set the cooking time for 40 minutes at High Pressure.
5. When cooking is complete, allow a natural release for 10 minutes, then release any remaining pressure.
6. Unlock the lid and carefully remove the pan. Allow to cool for 10 minutes.
7. Meanwhile, whisk the heavy cream in a bowl, fold in the sugar at the same time until stiff. Spoon mixture into a piping bag and press decorative mounds on the pie.
8. Sprinkle the pie with lime zest and chill the pie in refrigerator for 3 hours. Slice and serve.

# Appendix 1: Measurement Conversion Charts

## VOLUME EQUIVALENTS(DRY)

| US STANDARD | METRIC (APPROXIMATE) |
|---|---|
| 1/8 teaspoon | 0.5 mL |
| 1/4 teaspoon | 1 mL |
| 1/2 teaspoon | 2 mL |
| 3/4 teaspoon | 4 mL |
| 1 teaspoon | 5 mL |
| 1 tablespoon | 15 mL |
| 1/4 cup | 59 mL |
| 1/2 cup | 118 mL |
| 3/4 cup | 177 mL |
| 1 cup | 235 mL |
| 2 cups | 475 mL |
| 3 cups | 700 mL |
| 4 cups | 1 L |

## VOLUME EQUIVALENTS(LIQUID)

| US STANDARD | US STANDARD (OUNCES) | METRIC (APPROXIMATE) |
|---|---|---|
| 2 tablespoons | 1 fl.oz. | 30 mL |
| 1/4 cup | 2 fl.oz. | 60 mL |
| 1/2 cup | 4 fl.oz. | 120 mL |
| 1 cup | 8 fl.oz. | 240 mL |
| 1 1/2 cup | 12 fl.oz. | 355 mL |
| 2 cups or 1 pint | 16 fl.oz. | 475 mL |
| 4 cups or 1 quart | 32 fl.oz. | 1 L |
| 1 gallon | 128 fl.oz. | 4 L |

## TEMPERATURES EQUIVALENTS

| FAHRENHEIT(F) | CELSIUS(C) (APPROXIMATE) |
|---|---|
| 225 °F | 107 °C |
| 250 °F | 120 °C |
| 275 °F | 135 °C |
| 300 °F | 150 °C |
| 325 °F | 160 °C |
| 350 °F | 180 °C |
| 375 °F | 190 °C |
| 400 °F | 205 °C |
| 425 °F | 220 °C |
| 450 °F | 235 °C |
| 475 °F | 245 °C |
| 500 °F | 260 °C |

## WEIGHT EQUIVALENTS

| US STANDARD | METRIC (APPROXIMATE) |
|---|---|
| 1 ounce | 28 g |
| 2 ounces | 57 g |
| 5 ounces | 142 g |
| 10 ounces | 284 g |
| 15 ounces | 425 g |
| 16 ounces (1 pound) | 455 g |
| 1.5 pounds | 680 g |
| 2 pounds | 907 g |

# Appendix 2: Instant Pot Cooking Timetable

## Dried Beans, Legumes and Lentils

| Dried Beans and Legume | Dry (Minutes) | Soaked (Minutes) |
|---|---|---|
| Soy beans | 25 – 30 | 20 – 25 |
| Scarlet runner | 20 – 25 | 10 – 15 |
| Pinto beans | 25 – 30 | 20 – 25 |
| Peas | 15 – 20 | 10 – 15 |
| Navy beans | 25 – 30 | 20 – 25 |
| Lima beans | 20 – 25 | 10 – 15 |
| Lentils, split, yellow (moong dal) | 15 – 18 | N/A |
| Lentils, split, red | 15 – 18 | N/A |
| Lentils, mini, green (brown) | 15 – 20 | N/A |
| Lentils, French green | 15 – 20 | N/A |
| Kidney white beans | 35 – 40 | 20 – 25 |
| Kidney red beans | 25 – 30 | 20 – 25 |
| Great Northern beans | 25 – 30 | 20 – 25 |
| Pigeon peas | 20 – 25 | 15 – 20 |
| Chickpeas (garbanzo bean chickpeas) | 35 – 40 | 20 – 25 |
| Cannellini beans | 35 – 40 | 20 – 25 |
| Black-eyed peas | 20 – 25 | 10 – 15 |
| Black beans | 20 – 25 | 10 – 15 |

## Fish and Seafood

| Fish and Seafood | Fresh (minutes) | Frozen (minutes) |
|---|---|---|
| Shrimp or Prawn | 1 to 2 | 2 to 3 |
| Seafood soup or stock | 6 to 7 | 7 to 9 |
| Mussels | 2 to 3 | 4 to 6 |
| Lobster | 3 to 4 | 4 to 6 |
| Fish, whole (snapper, trout, etc.) | 5 to 6 | 7 to 10 |
| Fish steak | 3 to 4 | 4 to 6 |
| Fish fillet, | 2 to 3 | 3 to 4 |
| Crab | 3 to 4 | 5 to 6 |

## Fruits

| Fruits | Fresh (in Minutes) | Dried (in Minutes) |
|---|---|---|
| Raisins | N/A | 4 to 5 |
| Prunes | 2 to 3 | 4 to 5 |
| Pears, whole | 3 to 4 | 4 to 6 |
| Pears, slices or halves | 2 to 3 | 4 to 5 |
| Peaches | 2 to 3 | 4 to 5 |
| Apricots, whole or halves | 2 to 3 | 3 to 4 |
| Apples, whole | 3 to 4 | 4 to 6 |
| Apples, in slices or pieces | 2 to 3 | 3 to 4 |

## Meat

| Meat and Cuts | Cooking Time (minutes) | Meat and Cuts | Cooking Time (minutes) |
|---|---|---|---|
| Veal, roast | 35 to 45 | Duck, with bones, cut up | 10 to 12 |
| Veal, chops | 5 to 8 | Cornish Hen, whole | 10 to 15 |
| Turkey, drumsticks (leg) | 15 to 20 | Chicken, whole | 20 to 25 |
| Turkey, breast, whole, with bones | 25 to 30 | Chicken, legs, drumsticks, or thighs | 10 to 15 |
| Turkey, breast, boneless | 15 to 20 | Chicken, with bones, cut up | 10 to 15 |
| Quail, whole | 8 to 10 | Chicken, breasts | 8 to 10 |
| Pork, ribs | 20 to 25 | Beef, stew | 15 to 20 |
| Pork, loin roast | 55 to 60 | Beef, shanks | 25 to 30 |
| Pork, butt roast | 45 to 50 | Beef, ribs | 25 to 30 |
| Pheasant | 20 to 25 | Beef, steak, pot roast, round, rump, brisket or blade, small chunks, chuck, | 25 to 30 |
| Lamb, stew meat | 10 to 15 | | |
| Lamb, leg | 35 to 45 | Beef, pot roast, steak, rump, round, chuck, blade or brisket, large | 35 to 40 |
| Lamb, cubes, | 10 t0 15 | | |
| Ham slice | 9 to 12 | Beef, ox-tail | 40 to 50 |
| Ham picnic shoulder | 25 to 30 | Beef, meatball | 10 to 15 |
| Duck, whole | 25 to 30 | Beef, dressed | 20 to 25 |

## Vegetables (fresh/frozen)

| Vegetable | Fresh (minutes) | Frozen (minutes) | Vegetable | Fresh (minutes) | Frozen (minutes) |
|---|---|---|---|---|---|
| Zucchini, slices or chunks | 2 to 3 | 3 to 4 | Mixed vegetables | 2 to 3 | 3 to 4 |
| Yam, whole, small | 10 to 12 | 12 to 14 | Leeks | 2 to 4 | 3 to 5 |
| Yam, whole, large | 12 to 15 | 15 to 19 | Greens (collards, beet greens, spinach, kale, turnip greens, swiss chard) chopped | 3 to 6 | 4 to 7 |
| Yam, in cubes | 7 to 9 | 9 to 11 | | | |
| Turnip, chunks | 2 to 4 | 4 to 6 | Green beans, whole | 2 to 3 | 3 to 4 |
| Tomatoes, whole | 3 to 5 | 5 to 7 | Escarole, chopped | 1 to 2 | 2 to 3 |
| Tomatoes, in quarters | 2 to 3 | 4 to 5 | Endive | 1 to 2 | 2 to 3 |
| Sweet potato, whole, small | 10 to 12 | 12 to 14 | Eggplant, chunks or slices | 2 to 3 | 3 to 4 |
| Sweet potato, whole, large | 12 to 15 | 15 to 19 | Corn, on the cob | 3 to 4 | 4 to 5 |
| Sweet potato, in cubes | 7 to 9 | 9 to 11 | Corn, kernels | 1 to 2 | 2 to 3 |
| Sweet pepper, slices or chunks | 1 to 3 | 2 to 4 | Collard | 4 to 5 | 5 to 6 |
| Squash, butternut, slices or chunks | 8 to 10 | 10 to 12 | Celery, chunks | 2 to 3 | 3 to 4 |
| Squash, acorn, slices or chunks | 6 to 7 | 8 to 9 | Cauliflower flowerets | 2 to 3 | 3 to 4 |
| Spinach | 1 to 2 | 3 to 4 | Carrots, whole or chunked | 2 to 3 | 3 to 4 |
| Rutabaga, slices | 3 to 5 | 4 to 6 | Carrots, sliced or shredded | 1 to 2 | 2 to 3 |
| Rutabaga, chunks | 4 to 6 | 6 to 8 | Cabbage, red, purple or green, wedges | 3 to 4 | 4 to 5 |
| Pumpkin, small slices or chunks | 4 to 5 | 6 to 7 | Cabbage, red, purple or green, shredded | 2 to 3 | 3 to 4 |
| Pumpkin, large slices or chunks | 8 to 10 | 10 to 14 | Brussel sprouts, whole | 3 to 4 | 4 to 5 |
| Potatoes, whole, large | 12 to 15 | 15 to 19 | Broccoli, stalks | 3 to 4 | 4 to 5 |
| Potatoes, whole, baby | 10 to 12 | 12 to 14 | Broccoli, flowerets | 2 to 3 | 3 to 4 |
| Potatoes, in cubes | 7 to 9 | 9 to 11 | Beets, small roots, whole | 11 to 13 | 13 to 15 |
| Peas, in the pod | 1 to 2 | 2 to 3 | Beets, large roots, whole | 20 to 25 | 25 to 30 |
| Peas, green | 1 to 2 | 2 to 3 | Beans, green/yellow or wax, whole, trim ends and strings | 1 to 2 | 2 to 3 |
| Parsnips, sliced | 1 to 2 | 2 to 3 | | | |
| Parsnips, chunks | 2 to 4 | 4 to 6 | Asparagus, whole or cut | 1 to 2 | 2 to 3 |
| Onions, sliced | 2 to 3 | 3 to 4 | Artichoke, whole, trimmed without leaves | 9 to 11 | 11 to 13 |
| Okra | 2 to 3 | 3 to 4 | Artichoke, hearts | 4 to 5 | 5 to 6 |

## Rice and Grains

| Rice & Grain | Water Quantity (Grain: Water ratios) | Cooking Time (in Minutes) | Rice & Grain | Water Quantity (Grain: Water ratios) | Cooking Time (in Minutes) |
|---|---|---|---|---|---|
| Wheat berries | 1:3 | 25 to 30 | Oats, steel-cut | 1:1 | 10 |
| Spelt berries | 1:3 | 15 to 20 | Oats, quick cooking | 1:1 | 6 |
| Sorghum | 1:3 | 20 to 25 | Millet | 1:1 | 10 to 12 |
| Rice, wild | 1:3 | 25 to 30 | Kamut, whole | 1:3 | 10 to 12 |
| Rice, white | 1:1.5 | 8 | Couscous | 1:2 | 5 to 8 |
| Rice, Jasmine | 1:1 | 4 to 10 | Corn, dried, half | 1:3 | 25 to 30 |
| Rice, Brown | 1:1.3 | 22 to 28 | Congee, thin | 1:6 ~ 1:7 | 15 to 20 |
| Rice, Basmati | 1:1.5 | 4 to 8 | Congee, thick | 1:4 ~ 1:5 | 15 to 20 |
| Quinoa, quick cooking | 1:2 | 8 | Barley, pot | 1:3 ~ 1:4 | 25 to 30 |
| Porridge, thin | 1:6 ~ 1:7 | 15 to 20 | Barley, pearl | 1:4 | 25 to 30 |

# Appendix 3: References

How to Use Instant Pot Ultimate Beginners Guide: Amy + Jacky. (2020, June 19). https://www.pressurecookrecipes.com/how-to-use-instant-pot/

Instant Pot Eats. (2019, November 20). 7 Ways To Use The Instant Pot Trivet. https://instantpoteats.com/7-ways-to-use-the-instant-pot-trivet/

Lacoma, T. (2020, April 12). Most Instant Pot problems are easy to fix. We'll show you how to handle them. https://www.digitaltrends.com/home/common-instant-pot-problems-and-how-to-fix-them/

Licata, E. (2019, October 18). The Smart Feature on Your Instant Pot You're Probably Not Using. https://www.thekitchn.com/your-instant-pot-has-a-built-in-lid-holder-256492

Rawes, E., & Liu, G. (2020, April 21). Thinking of buying an Instant Pot? Here's what you need to know. https://www.digitaltrends.com/home/what-is-an-instant-pot/

Schieving, B. (2020, March 24). Instant Pot Quick Release vs. Natural Release - Pressure Cooking Today. https://www.pressurecookingtoday.com/quick-pressure-release-or-natural-pressure-release/

Manufactured by Amazon.ca
Bolton, ON

29763255R00103